INTENDING DEATH

The Ethics of Assisted Suicide and Euthanasia

Edited By

TOM L. BEAUCHAMP

Georgetown University

Prentice Hall
Upper Saddle River, New Jersey 07458

Library of Congress Cataloging–in–Publication Data

Intending death: the ethics of assisted suicide and euthanasia/
    edited by Tom L. Beauchamp.
            p. cm.
        Includes bibliographical references
        ISBN 0–13–199555–3
        1. Assisted suicide. 2. Euthanasia. I. Beauchamp, Tom L.
    R726.I58 1996
    179'.7—dc20

95–4250
CIP

Acquisitions editor: *Ted Bolen*
Editorial assistant: *Meg McGuane*
Production editor: *Jean Lapidus*
Copy editor: *Maria Caruso*
Cover designer: *Bruce Kenselaar*
Cover credit: *Suisan Marsh*
            Copyright Barrie Rokeach 1995
Manufacturing buyer: *Lynn Pearlman*

©1996 by Prentice–Hall, Inc.
Simon & Schuster/A Viacom Company
Upper Saddle River, New Jersey 07458

Printed in the United States of America
10 9 8 7 6 5 4 3 2

ISBN 0-13-199555-3

PRENTICE–HALL INTERNATIONAL (UK) LIMITED, LONDON
PRENTICE–HALL OF AUSTRALIA PTY. LIMITED, SYDNEY
PRENTICE–HALL CANADA INC., TORONTO
PRENTICE–HALL HISPANOAMERICANA, S.A., MEXICO
PRENTICE–HALL OF INDIA PRIVATE LIMITED, NEW DELHI
PRENTICE–HALL OF JAPAN, INC., TOKYO
SIMON & SCHUSTER ASIA PTE. LTD., SINGAPORE
EDITORA PRENTICE–HALL DO BRASIL, LTDA. RIO DE JANEIRO

For Joel Feinberg
Just for Being a Friend

Contents

Part II. Clinical Perspectives   150

Part III. Political, Legal, and Economic Perspectives   188

Preface

This volume contains previously unpublished manuscripts that were developed before and after a three–day conference in Annapolis, Maryland. The Conference was sponsored by selected faculty from the Kennedy Institute of Ethics at Georgetown University and the Schools of Medicine and Public Health at The Johns Hopkins University. During the conference each paper was criticized by authors of the other papers and by a few invited guests who attended the conference. All papers were subsequently revised over a two–year period and made suitable for publication.

The title of this volume belies some uncertainty that surrounds the issues examined. The phrase "Intending Death" avoids some implications of more widely used terminology, such as "physician–assisted suicide," which is here incorporated only in the subtitle. A major purpose of these essays is to explore issues that law and public policy have often skirted or wished away by the choice of a neutral terminology. The most important topic running through all the essays is *intentionally causing death by either an active or a passive means.*

I owe a substantial debt of gratitude to Mark Rogers, Vice President of the Duke University Medical Center. He arranged the original conference in Annapolis and gave constant encouragement and guidance. I am also grateful to John Freeman, Ruth Faden, and Peter Terry of the Johns Hopkins Medical Institutions and Madison Powers and Bob Veatch of Georgetown, all of whom helped in planning the conference and in creating this volume's structure. Alan Meisel helped me frame parts of the Introduction, and I have relied also at a few points on work previously written with Jim Childress.

A select but comprehensive bibliography is found at the end of the manuscript. It was compiled with the help of professional librarians at the Kennedy Institute Library. I acknowledge with appreciation the assistance provided by the information retrieval project at the library, which kept me in touch with the most important literature and reduced the burdens of research. Mary Coutts deserves a special thanks for her many computer searches. A talented research staff also assisted me in preparing the manuscripts for publication. Wendy Madigosky and Clint McCulloch provided invaluable service in checking the final manuscripts, and Moheba Hanif saw the full manuscript through to completion. I also wish to thank Ted Bolen of Prentice Hall for helpful and supportive editorial advice.

Tom L. Beauchamp

Introduction

TOM L. BEAUCHAMP
Georgetown University, Washington, D.C.

No stronger or more enduring prohibition exists in medicine than the rule against killing patients. Nonetheless, in recent years we have seen a trend toward more flexibility in allowing persons who are seriously or terminally ill to die and even helping them to die. Efforts to legalize assisted suicide and euthanasia have been launched in several states in the United States, and many arguments in the literature on medical ethics suggest a need to reform law and medical practice to enable physicians to help more patients die, and perhaps to cause their deaths by an active means.

Questions presently under discussion include the following: Is forgoing life-sustaining treatment sometimes a form of killing and, if so, is it suicide or euthanasia? What, if anything, distinguishes killing from intentionally letting a person die? Are there morally relevant differences between killing and letting die? Under what conditions, if any, is it permissible for health professionals to engage in assisted suicide or active euthanasia? This introduction provides a map of the territory of these and other questions addressed by the contributors to this volume. (For another map of parts of this territory, see the essay by Allen Buchanan, pp. 23–41.) This introduction does not outline or discuss their articles. Instead, it serves to identify the main issues, to offer definitions of terms such as "euthanasia" and "assisted suicide," and to explain some leading positions that have been taken on the issues.

Some of these issues have been treated by philosophers and theologians for much of recorded history. Many have reflected, in particular, on ethical issues surrounding suicide.[1] Plato, Aristotle, and the Stoics in the ancient world, Augustine and Thomas Aquinas in the medieval period, and John Donne, Michel de Montaigne, David Hume, and Immanuel Kant in the early modern period have left an important legacy of argument and set of issues about suicide. In the ancient and medieval worlds suicide was, with a few exceptions, rigidly condemned. (See the essay by Albert R. Jonsen, pp. 42–53.) During the sixteenth century a few philosophers began to view suicide more as a matter of personal choice than a morally unacceptable act. Eventually suicide was decriminalized in almost all countries. However, few countries have decriminalized either assisted suicide or active euthanasia.

In the United States, an important forum for the recent debate has occurred in courts and state legislatures. A general consensus has evolved in the courts and in public policy about legitimate conduct.[2] This consensus is built around a distinction between *forgoing* medical interventions and *assisting* in an act of suicide or euthanasia. Decisions to forgo treatments by both physicians and patients are considered unavoidable and legitimate in contemporary medicine, whereas assisted suicide and euthanasia are considered illegal and a dangerous threat to vulnerable patients.[3]

One might suppose, given this legal and public policy agreement, that a consensus has evolved concerning the morality of ending life. Here, however, far less agreement exists, and any consensus is narrowly focused. For example, there is general agreement that *intentionally allowing death* in medicine is morally permissible under some circumstances. The clearest and simplest case is the competent person with a terminal illness who chooses not to undergo therapy although he or she understands the options and their consequences. But on close examination, any consensus surrounding even this relatively simple case will vanish when underlying or related issues are considered. For example, even those who agree about the acceptability of death in this simple case will not always agree on how to describe the person's conduct and will enter into controversy about the nature of the act performed. Specifically, some call it suicide, whereas others deny that it qualifies as suicide.

Among those who agree that it is morally acceptable for a person with a terminal condition to choose not to undergo treatment, many would dissent if the person sought to hasten death by throwing himself before an oncoming train or even by taking an overdose of a prescribed medication. And another split arises among those who find it morally acceptable for the dying person to hasten death by the self-administration of a lethal overdose when it is proposed that a physician be allowed to provide the patient with the fatal medication. Among those who do not condemn such behavior by the physician, there is yet another split between persons who do or do not prohibit the physician's administration of such a medication to a person too weak from terminal illness to self-administer it.

We can now turn to the philosophical disputes that cause these splits of opinion, beginning with some conceptual issues about the nature of assisted suicide and euthanasia.

THE DISTINCTION BETWEEN ASSISTED SUICIDE AND EUTHANASIA

The term *euthanasia* is derived from two Greek roots meaning "good death," but this simple definition has been filled out in several competing ways. If used *narrowly*, it means the act or practice of intentionally, mercifully, and painlessly causing the death of persons suffering from serious injuries, system failures, or fatal diseases. Here the emphasis is on acting rather than omitting to act, suggesting killing rather than allowing a death to occur. By contrast, a 1975 reference work, the *New Columbia Encyclopedia*, defines euthanasia *broadly* as "either painlessly putting to death or failing to prevent death from natural causes in cases of terminal illness," thus including forms of omission of action. The entry continues as follows:

> The term formerly referred only to the act of painlessly putting incurably ill patients to death. However, technological advances in medicine, which have made it possible to prolong the lives of patients who have no hope of recovery, have led to the use of the term *negative [or passive] euthanasia*, i.e., the withdrawing of extraordinary means used to preserve life.[4]

Before the 1970s, euthanasia was primarily understood as the active termination of the life of a terminally ill patient by a second party, but if one accepts the definition proposed by the *New Columbia Encyclopedia*, two main subtypes of euthanasia are distinguishable: active (or positive) euthanasia and passive (or negative) euthanasia. Further, if the patient requests the action, it is classified as *voluntary* euthanasia (and, when the patient causes death, *assisted suicide*). In cases in which the patient is not mentally competent to make an informed choice, the action is called *nonvoluntary* euthanasia. The combination of these several categories yields four subtypes of euthanasia, represented schematically in Fig. 1.

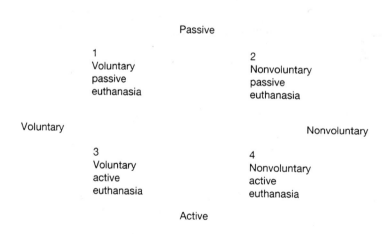

Passive

1
Voluntary
passive
euthanasia

2
Nonvoluntary
passive
euthanasia

Voluntary

Nonvoluntary

3
Voluntary
active
euthanasia

4
Nonvoluntary
active
euthanasia

Active

Figure 1

(We can also distinguish involuntary euthanasia, which involves a person capable of making an informed request but who has not done so. However, involuntary euthanasia is rarely discussed or defended by anyone.)

These four categories exhibit the main types of euthanasia, but conceptual con-

fusion still often surrounds the meaning of the parent term *euthanasia*. In this introduction, a death will be considered euthanasia of any type if and only if the following conditions are satisfied: (1) The death is intended by at least one other person
whose action is a contributing cause of death; (2) the person who dies is either acutely suffering or irreversibly comatose (or soon will be), and this condition alone is the
primary reason for intending the person's death; and (3) the means chosen to produce
the death must be as painless as possible, or a sufficient moral justification must exist
for a more painful method.[5]

Physician-assisted suicide is often considered a form of voluntary active
euthanasia, because in the latter the death often seems to be both a suicide and physician-assisted. Some courts and many commentators have even viewed acts of authorizing the withdrawal or withholding of treatment for patients as involving either suicide or assisted suicide. However, others see no specific suicidal intent in these cases,
and some courts evade the question altogether by confining their discussion to the
right to privacy, the right to choose death, and the right to refuse medical treatment.
(On the distinction between withdrawal of treatment and killing, see the essays by
Baruch Brody and Judith Jarvis Thomson, pp. 90–108.)

In the Cruzan case, U.S. Supreme Court Justice Antonin Scalia argued that the
withdrawing or withholding of treatment does sometimes constitute suicide.[6] He
maintained that any means productive of death can be arranged to the end of killing
oneself. This is so even if the death of a terminally ill person is imminent and even if
the causes of death are natural. Stopping a respirator is not relevantly different from
shooting oneself with a pistol if the intention to end life and the reason for putting an
end to life are relevantly similar. From this perspective, suicidal intent could be present in any circumstance of intentional refusal of lifesaving treatment. Exactly like
typical suicides, these patients intend to end their lives because of the future's grim
prospects. Death is self-inflicted, whether by a lethal poison or by disconnecting a
respirator. Yet, the majority of judicial decisions maintain that refusals of treatment
are not suicides; judges therefore allow various forms of assistance that physicians
provide in helping patients die by withholding treatment.

The phrase "assisted death," particularly "physician-assisted death," though
now widely used, incorporates several forms of assistance under a single general
heading. Both assisted suicide and voluntary active euthanasia involve some form of
assistance in bringing about another's death. In "assisted suicide," as this term will be
used here, the person whose death is brought about must be the final cause of death
(the final link in a causal chain leading to death), whereas in "voluntary active
euthanasia" the final cause of one person's death must be another person's action. In
cases of assisted suicide there is no conceptual requirement that the person who dies
be acutely suffering or that such a condition forms the reason for the act of suicide or
for assisting in the act. There is also no conceptual requirement that the means chosen be as painless as possible. In these respects, assisted suicide is broader in scope
than euthanasia.

As we will see, when physicians assist in or administer death to their patients, both the physicians' *intentions* and the *causes* involved can make a considerable difference to the classification and evaluation of their acts. But what are the *relevant causes* of death and the *proper intentions* when assisting a person in dying?

CAUSATION: WHAT CAUSES DEATH?

When physicians at the request of their patients withhold or withdraw respirator support, withhold or remove feeding tubes, terminate nutrition and hydration, and the like, they often play a role in bringing about the patient's death at the time it occurs. Do they therefore cause the patient's death? Physicians and nurses have long been concerned that when they withhold or withdraw treatment and a patient dies, they might be killing the patient and might be held criminally liable. Patients have a parallel concern that when they withdraw or withhold treatment they are committing suicide; if so, health professionals assist in suicide by cooperating in the refusal. Typical cases involve persons suffering from a terminal illness or mortal injury who refuse a therapy without which they will die, but with which their life can be extended for several months or years.

In the past, physicians, lawyers, and moral philosophers have characteristically construed acts of forgoing treatment as letting die, not as acts of either causing death or killing. When an individual forgoes life-sustaining treatment, courts have offered interesting reasons why the death should not be categorized as either suicide or homicide. Arguments that rest on the following account of (legal) causation have been relied on heavily: In acts of forgoing treatment, an underlying disease, system failure, or injury is the cause of death. Medical technology, for example, a respirator, merely delays the natural course of the underlying condition. When the technology is removed, a natural death occurs, because natural conditions continue to do what they would have done if the technology had never been initiated. The patient's affliction becomes the nearest and only fundamental cause of death, not the physician's, surrogate's, or patient's action. Therefore, neither homicide nor assisted suicide occurs.

This legal approach to causation helps to alleviate fears of health professionals concerning legal liability, but it may not be a comprehensive or fully adequate account for medical ethics and also may not be the best account of legal causation and liability. In many cases the patient's death is intended and occurs not merely by natural causes (sometimes not by natural causes at all), but by the intentional action of a physician, a patient, or both. The patient's decision and the physician's intentional action play an important causal role in the outcome in the circumstance in which death occurs. Their actions are in many (not all) cases necessary, and perhaps sufficient, conditions of death at the time and in the way it occurs. For example, to withhold nutrition and hydration so that a patient starves to death is both a necessary and a sufficient condition of death by starvation at the time the death occurs. If the patient is suffering from a condition such as severe brain damage, pneumonia, cancer, or quadriplegia, these conditions (the reason for refusing treatment) are neither a neces-sary nor a sufficient cause of death by starvation. They are not the cause of death as it occurs and when it occurs.

To see this point, consider an unintentional and unjustified action. Suppose a physician mistakenly removes a respirator from a quadriplegic patient who wanted to continue living and could easily have continued living. We could not reasonably say, "the physician did not cause the patient's death; he only allowed the patient to die." By "letting" the patient die, he killed the patient. It would be preposterous in this case for the physician to protest a legal indictment by saying, "I did not kill him; the dis-ease killed him. I merely allowed him to die." We would also consider the physician's act to be unjustified. Yet this physician's act seems to be the same act that the physi-cian performs (usually at a patient's or a family's request) in a standard case of "allowing to die." What the physician does is causally no different than what a stranger would do if he or she walked into the hospital and removed a patient's life-line.

Why, then, does a physician's justifiable act not also cause death? Can physi-cians rightly say, "We do not cause the death of our patients; only the underlying dis-eases, system failures, or injuries do"? According to some contemporary writers,[7] the intentional withdrawal or withholding of life-sustaining treatment can cause death, and thereby can constitute killing. Generally, the motives of patients and physicians are proper and both moral and legal justification exist for the action. But whether the motive is evil or noble, the act remains an intentionally caused death. For example, the Superior Court of New Jersey, Appellate Division, held in the *Conroy* case that removing the NG-tube (nasogastric tube) from 84-year-old Claire Conroy would not be merely forgoing treatment. The court thought that because her physicians would dehydrate and starve Conroy, they would kill her. This court said the patient "would have been actively killed by independent means," which the court held to be euthana-sia.[8]

However, the Supreme Court of New Jersey later overturned this lower court opinion. It followed the dominant view in law and medicine that natural causes account for the patient's death under these circumstances.[9] But was the Superior Court entirely wrong? Are the natural causes the only morally relevant type of caus-es? Are not both natural causes and human causes at work in these cases? In some dif-ficult and controversial circumstances, physician intervention (whether at the patient's request or not) and a relevant causal condition of disease, system failure, or injury are present. In some cases, multiple causal conditions may be relevant, each forming an independent causal sequence powerful enough to bring about death. That is, any one of several causal sequences (distinct sequences of causally linked events) may itself be sufficient to cause death. To isolate a single event that causes death may not be possible, because our concepts of causation both in law and elsewhere are not sufficiently precise to allow us to isolate "the cause."

THE LANGUAGE OF "KILLING"

We can now address the question, "Are killing and letting die conceptually distinct?" Unfortunately, ordinary language provides an unstable basis for the needed distinctions. In ordinary language, *killing* is any form of deprivation or destruction of something, including animal and plant life. It can mean nothing more than "bringing an end to something," as in the expression "killing a legislative bill." Neither in ordinary language nor in law does the word "killing" entail a wrongful act or a crime, even if human persons are killed. Ordinary language also does not require that a killing be intentional. It permits us to say that persons are killed in accidental shootings and automobile collisions.

In ordinary language, killing represents a related set of ideas whose central condition is causation of another's death, whereas allowing to die represents another family of ideas whose central condition is intentional avoidance of causal intervention so that disease, system failure, or injury causes death. This distinction is fuzzy, not sharp. It is easy to see why from the fact that one can kill a person by intentionally allowing that person to die (as when a physician intentionally allows a patient to die who should have been treated). Many now believe that forgoing treatment to allow death cannot be meaningfully distinguished from taking active steps to end life when the motives, intentions, and projected consequences are identical in the two types of case. In either case, the patient's death is intended and the central actors may be moved by compassion, mercy, and the like.

Therefore, if we are to retain the distinction between killing and letting die, we need to provide clearer, more precise meanings that are useful for medical ethics. For example, killing could be reserved for circumstances in which one person *intentionally and unjustifiably* causes the death of another human being, a usage that clearly moves beyond the ordinary-language meaning. Many persons now use the term killing—even mercy killing—exclusively as a normative term meaning *unjustified homicide*. From their perspective, justified acts of arranging for death in medicine cannot be instances of killing; they must be cases of allowing to die: Physicians do not kill when they remove a life-sustaining treatment in accordance with a patient's request or interest, and patients do not kill themselves when they forgo treatment. However, if a physician unjustifiably omits care by withdrawing medical treatment, then the physician kills the patient.

Killing has here been given an intrinsically moral meaning in an attempt to protect health-care professionals from homicide charges; it is no longer merely a causal or factual category concerning the conditions that brought about death. Thus, moral judgments about justified and unjustified actions underlie judgments about what should be classified as killing and what as allowing to die from preexisting conditions.

Imagine that a patient's father detached the patient's respirator against medical, moral, and legal advice and that the patient died as a consequence (which has happened in actual cases[10]). Few would say, "preexisting conditions killed the patient, not the father." However, if the father had sound moral motives and weighty medical, legal, and moral support for the same action, many would come to identify with and justify or excuse it. As a result, they would consider the act to be letting die, not causing death or killing. Using this logic we can say that by not categorizing the withholding and withdrawing of medical treatment as killing (which we could have done without seriously distorting the ordinary meaning of the word), we have signalled our acceptance of the conduct. Had we found withholding and withdrawing treatment morally unacceptable, we likely would have referred to such conduct as killing (perhaps mercy killing), just as we currently apply such terms to the administration of a lethal dosage of morphine. Had we wished not to legitimate the refusal by a competent person to initiate or continue life-sustaining treatment, we could have chosen not to incorporate that conduct under the umbrella of forgoing life-sustaining treatment, and instead have referred to it as suicide, as we would do if the same competent person were to self-administer a lethal dose of barbiturates.

Part of the reason for moralizing the cause can be traced to the legal doctrine of *proximate cause*, which drives many judgments about causal responsibility. To be a proximate cause is to become legally liable for an outcome. These legal judgments about causation and liability often are decided by a person's preexisting obligations. If a physician has a role obligation to treat, then omission of treatment breaches that obligation and causes death (an unjustified homicide); but, if no obligation to treat exists, then preexisting disease, system failure, or injury is the proximate cause, and the physician escapes liability.

Conceptually, this invocation of proximate causation in the law can obscure issues about killing, and even from a legal perspective there may be a better account than "the preexisting disease caused the death." An alternative account is that legal liability should not be imposed on physicians or surrogates unless they have an obligation to provide or to continue the treatment. If no obligation to treat exists, then questions of legal causation and liability would not arise. On this account, there is a reason for avoiding discussions about killing and letting die altogether and instead focusing on health-care professionals' obligations.

But does this conclusion suggest that we can altogether dispense with the language of killing and letting die without suffering serious moral and conceptual confusion? Could we discuss these issues exclusively in the language of optional and obligatory treatments, without any reference to killing and letting die?

THE MORAL RELEVANCE OF THE DISTINCTION BETWEEN KILLING AND LETTING DIE

Even if a distinction between killing and allowing to die can be drawn and should be retained in our moral discourse, a problem remains about the moral relevance of this distinction. Some writers hold that if it is morally permissible to intend that a patient die, then terminating a patient's life by an active means is justified when it causes less suffering to the patient than would be caused by allowing him or her to die.[11] But others argue that active killing is not justified even if suffering is thereby reduced for the patient, on grounds either that killing is always morally wrong or that seriously harmful consequences might occur if the killing/letting-die distinction were accepted in society as morally irrelevant.[12]

Here we must ask, "Is killing in itself no different morally than allowing to die?" Assume for a moment, based on our earlier discussion (pp. 7–8), that killing is not a morally loaded term, but simply terminology that identifies certain ways of causing death. Under this assumption, to assert that killing is no different morally than allowing to die is to say that correct labeling of an act as killing or as letting die does not determine whether one type of action is better or worse than the other, or whether either is acceptable. Some particular instance of killing (a callous murder, say) may clearly be morally worse than some particular instance of allowing to die (forgoing treatment for a dying and comatose patient, say); but some particular instance of letting die (not resuscitating a patient who could easily be saved, say) also may clearly be morally worse than some particular instance of killing (mercy killing at the patient's request, say).

In this account, nothing about either killing or allowing to die, understood as morally neutral terms, entails judgments about the wrongness or rightness of either type of action, or about the beneficence or nonmaleficence of the actor in performing the act. Rightness and wrongness depend on the merit of the justification underlying the action, not on the type of action it is. Neither killing nor letting die, in this account, is per se wrongful, and in this regard they are to be distinguished from murder, which is per se wrongful.

It would be absurd to consider all cases of letting die morally justified, and, from this perspective, it is no less absurd to view all forms of killing (for example, killing in self-defense) as unjustified. A judgment that an act of either killing or letting die is justified or unjustified entails that something else be known about the act besides its being a case of killing or a case of allowing to die. The actor's motive (whether benevolent or malicious, for example), the patient's request, and the consequences of the act are all relevant to questions of justification. These additional factors give us a moral compass and allow us to make a normative judgment. All instances of both killing and letting die must, on this account, satisfy independent criteria, such as the balance of benefits over burdens to the patient, in order to determine their acceptability.

If one denies that killing and letting die are morally neutral categories, then one will reject this entire line of argument. If killing is used to mean unjustified homicide, it is not controversial whether a direct connection exists between killing and moral wrongness. Thus, as we have seen throughout this section, the meanings we give to killing can be very important. However, as we will now see, issues about killing and letting die are far from merely problems about the meanings of words.

INTENTION: ARE MERELY FORESEEN EFFECTS INTENDED?

Many controversies about causing death, killing, and letting die raise the question of what a person, often a physician, intends in performing a particular action. For example, if a physician intends to let a patient die, does the physician intend that patient's death? or does a physician intend death only in an act of killing? In assisting the suicide of another, must one intend the person's death, or could one intend only to help the other do what is in the other's best interest? Is it morally important what one intends, as long as one does not act immorally?

Those who emphasize the category of intention need an account of intentional actions and of the intended effects of action that properly distinguishes them from nonintentional actions and unintended (though perhaps foreseen) effects. The literature on intention analyzes it in terms of concepts as diverse as volition, deliberateness, willing, reasoning, and planning. Among the few shared views in this literature is that intentional actions require an agent's plan—a map or representation of the means and ends projected for an action—and a disposition to execute the plan. For the action to be intentional, it must correspond to the agent's conception of how it was planned to be performed; an intended effect also must be part of the plan.

Many philosophers and theologians believe that merely foreseen effects are not intentional.[13] This account relies on a narrow conception of what is intended, but it has the apparent advantage of avoiding the conclusion that an agent intentionally brings about all the consequences of an action that the agent foresees. On this analysis, we should distinguish between acts and effects, and then between effects that are desired or wanted and effects that are foreseen but not desired or wanted. The latter effects are foreseen only, not intended. To see the force of this claim, imagine that a hospital patient is incontinent and has an accident while no health professional is in the room. The patient decides to clean up his mess with a good towel, although he knows it will ruin the towel. On the analysis that makes merely foreseen effects unintentional, cleaning up the bed is intentional but ruining the towel is an unintended effect or byproduct.

On a different, competitor analysis of intention, the language of desiring and wanting is discarded, and undesired or unwanted effects are viewed as a part of the larger plan of an intentional action. If one uses a model of intentionality based on what is willed (in the plan), rather than what is wanted, intentional actions and intended effects include any action or effect willed in accordance with the plan, including unwanted but tolerated effects. The latter are viewed as not so undesirable that the actor would choose not to perform the act that produces them. On this conception, a physician can desire not to do what she intends to do, just as we often find ourselves willing to do something, but wishing that we could nonetheless avoid doing it. Even if we detest doing it, we may be willing to do it. Undesirable effects and significant risks that attend particular procedures usually fall into this category. Under this conception of intentional acts and intended effects, a sharp distinction cannot be made between what is intended and what is merely foreseen.

On this second analysis, a person who knowingly and voluntarily acts to bring about an effect does it intentionally. The effect is intended even if the person did not desire it, did not will it for its own sake, or did not intend it as the goal of the action. For example, if a surgeon during an operation must seriously damage an organ in order to remove a cancerous tumor from it, the surgeon cannot say that there was no intention to damage the organ or that it was done unintentionally. Although the surgical cut created damage that the surgeon would under other circumstances avoid, it would be conceptually mistaken to say that the surgeon unintentionally brought about the damage by removing the tumor.

These philosophical distinctions have a direct and practical bearing on contemporary issues of physician-assisted suicide. Consider some judicial reasoning in the important Canadian case of *Rodriguez v. British Columbia*, a case that eventually reached the Supreme Court of Canada. A 42-year-old woman suffering from A.L.S. or Lou Gehrig's disease sought a declaration that she was entitled to have assistance from a physician in ending her life. The court dismissed her application, reasoning as follows:[14] Clear distinctions *based on intent* can be drawn between palliative care and physician-assisted suicide and between withdrawing treatment and active euthanasia. Alleviating pain by administering drugs knowing that death will be hastened is an act done only with the intention of lessening pain. In physician-assisted suicide, by contrast, the intention in administering drugs is to cause death. Similarly, to intend to lessen suffering by withdrawing treatment is not the same as the intent in active euthanasia, which is to cause death.

What is the moral basis of such reasoning, and how should it be evaluated?

THE DOCTRINE OF DOUBLE EFFECT

A venerable attempt to come to terms with these problems about intending death is the doctrine of double effect (DDE), often called the *principle of double effect*. This doctrine relies heavily on the pivotal distinction between intended effects and foreseen effects. The DDE has the objective of justifying the claim that a single act having two foreseen effects (consequences), one good (such as saving a life) and one harmful (such as death), is not always morally prohibited. The key premise is that if the harmful effect is not intended, then the action can, under certain circumstances, be justified.

A well-known example of the use of the DDE is the seriously suffering patient who requests a physician's help in ending her life. If the physician directly kills her in order to end the suffering, her death is caused intentionally. Do matters change if the physician provides medication to relieve the patient's pain and suffering, knowing that a substantial risk exists that the patient's death will be hastened as a result of the medication? If the physician refuses to administer the toxic analgesia, the patient will suffer continuing pain; but if the physician provides the medication, the patient's death may be hastened. Under the DDE, in providing the medication, the physician must intend to relieve the suffering and must not intend to hasten death. If a lethal effect is not intended, then the act may not be prohibited.

According to mainstream formulations of the DDE,[15] four conditions or elements must be satisfied for an act with good and bad effects to be permissible. Each is a necessary condition and together they form jointly sufficient conditions of morally permissible action, despite the bad effect.

1. *Good or neutral act.* The act must be morally good or morally neutral, independent of its effects.

2. *Intention.* The agent must intend the good effect only. The bad effect can be foreseen and permitted, but not intended.

3. *Direct means.* The bad effect must not be a means to the good effect (because then the agent would intend the bad effect in pursuit of the good effect).

4. *Proportionality.* The good effect must proportionally outweigh the bad effect. This outweighing compensates for permitting the foreseen bad effect.

All four conditions have been criticized by opponents of DDE, and occasionally even by proponents of DDE, but the second condition has been the focus of particularly intense scrutiny.[16] Critics of the DDE contend that it is difficult and perhaps impossible through DDE conditions to establish a morally relevant difference between many cases, such as giving a patient additional pain-killing medication and giving a life-ending overdose. In neither case does the agent want or desire the death of the person, and the descriptions of the acts do not introduce any morally relevant differences. It is not clear, say critics, why an overdose intentionally given to a patient is killing rather than medicating for pain with the unintended result that the patient dies. It is also not clear why in the case of administering additional pain-killing medication, the death is only foreseen and not intended. A proponent of the DDE must have a way to distinguish the intended from the merely foreseen, but it has proved difficult to draw defensible moral lines between the many possible cases.

Is it plausible, then, to distinguish morally between intentionally causing the death of a patient by an overdose and intentionally using an unusually large dose of pain-killing medication that has the side effect of causing the death of a patient? In both actions, the intention is to relieve the patient's suffering, with knowledge that the life of the patient likely will be lost. No person seeks a bad result (the patient's death) for its own sake, and no agent would have tolerated the bad result if its avoidance were morally preferable. Each accepts the bad effect only because it cannot be deleted without loss of the good effect.

It is a matter of ongoing controversy whether defenders of the DDE can resolve such problems, but they are not the only problems the DDE faces. Critics who accept a consequentialist ethical theory argue that some clearly unacceptable consequences must be deemed acceptable in DDE. (See the essays by Raymond G. Frey and Alisa L. Carse, pp. 68–89.) For example, slowly causing death by administering medication to reduce pain can involve painful days or weeks of a life that a patient wishes not to live, whereas a larger and lethal dose of the same painkiller would end life quickly and with less pain and suffering. Critics therefore charge that the DDE unjustifiably requires acceptance of less humane methods of ending human life than could be provided, whereas defenders view this criticism as a misunderstanding of the nature and moral importance of the account.

Even if one accepts the DDE, it may not be capable of resolving many pressing problems about harm, letting die, and killing currently being debated in biomedical ethics, including the issues surrounding assisted suicide and voluntary active euthanasia. The DDE is directed exclusively at circumstances in which both a bad and a good effect occur, but often the key issue is whether an effect such as death is bad or good. Nothing in the DDE decides this issue, despite the first of its four conditions. But if one, therefore, cannot decide from the DDE whether various forms of euthanasia produce a bad or a good effect, this question must be answered on grounds independent of the DDE.

VOLUNTARY ACTIVE EUTHANASIA

Almost all arguments favoring voluntary active euthanasia appeal to the importance of respecting competent persons' decisions about whether their pain, physical discomfort, and psychological suffering warrant an end to their lives. The overarching moral problem about voluntary active euthanasia is often presented by its proponents in terms of the *autonomy rights* of patients: If competent patients have a legal and moral right to refuse treatment that brings about their deaths, is there not a similar moral right to enlist the assistance of physicians to help patients cause their deaths by an active means? And is it not morally acceptable for physicians to assist these patients? (For some answers to these questions, see the essays by N. Ann Davis and Dan W. Brock, pp. 111–149.) In 1989, twelve prominent American physicians published a statement in *The New England Journal of Medicine* in which they placed the latter question before American medicine, themselves defending the moral permissibility of assistance.[17]

Many proponents (but far from all) also support a legal right, that is, they favor legalizing voluntary active euthanasia and physician-assisted suicide.[18] They reason that if treatment refusal is justified by respect for autonomy and we are able to live with the consequences of this rule (as we have been), then this same right might be reinterpreted so that physicians are free to prescribe barbiturates and to administer lethal injections to aid patients in killing themselves. This argument proposes reform in ethics and in law, because of the apparent inconsistency between (1) the autonomy rights in law that allow persons in grim circumstances to refuse treatment and thereby bring about their deaths, and (2) the denial of similar autonomy rights to arrange for a directly caused death under similarly grim circumstances.

One prominent view advanced by defenders of voluntary active euthanasia holds that physician assistance is justified if a condition is overwhelmingly burden-some for a patient, pain management is inadequate, and only a physician is likely to be able to bring relief. Medicine and law seem now to say to such patients, "If you were on life-sustaining treatment, you could withdraw the treatment and we could let you die. But since you are not, we can only give you palliative care until you die a natural death." This position seems to its critics to condemn the patient to live out a life he or she does not want. Many patients and physicians now view the denial of assistance in dying for these patients as a form of cruelty that violates the patient's rights and prevents discharging the fiduciary obligations of the physician.

Those who use this argument do not claim that physicians face large numbers of desperately ill patients. Pain management has made circumstances at least bearable for most of today's patients, but some patients still cannot be satisfactorily relieved, and, even if they could, questions would remain about the autonomy rights of patients: If there is a right to stop a medical treatment that sustains life, why is there not a right to stop one's life by arrangement with a physician?

Whatever the merit of these arguments, the right to voluntary active euthanasia has never been recognized in the laws of nations or in codes of medical ethics (possibly excepting the Netherlands).[19] The traditional and still dominant view is that killing should be altogether prohibited in medicine, and letting die authorized in only a limited range of cases. Codes of medical ethics from the Hippocratic corpus to today prohibit killing or assisting in the killing of patients, even under the most favorable circumstances of mercy. Although courts in the United States have often defended the autonomy of patients in cases of passive euthanasia, the courts have never allowed active euthanasia. In their opposition to active euthanasia, moralists and judges often cite a principle of respect for life, according to which human life has a value in itself that deserves respect, and a "state interest" in the protection or the preservation of life. However, judicial opinions differ regarding how to interpret and implement such standards. Increasingly, courts have examined the quality of life and the possibilities a patient has for recovery, not merely a general principle requiring respect for life.

Those who support these medical and legal traditions often appeal to either (1) professional role obligations that prohibit bringing about death, or (2) the devastating consequences for society that would result from changing its moral traditions. The first argument is straightforward: Killing patients is inconsistent with traditionally assigned roles of nursing, caregiving, and healing—and voluntary active euthanasia is a form of killing. The second argument—regarding social consequences—is more complex and has come to be a centerpiece of discussion because of its prediction of grave dangers to society that would occur as a result of the legalization of voluntary active euthanasia.

The main argument of this type is referred to as the *wedge argument* or the *slippery slope argument*. It proceeds as follows: Even if particular acts of killing are sometimes morally justified with particularly pain-ridden patients, sanctioning practices of killing would run serious social risks of abuse, misuse, and neglect. The argument is not that negative consequences will occur immediately on legalization, but that they will grow incrementally over time as the practices become routine ways of handling the seriously ill and injured. Society might start by carefully restricting the number of patients who qualify for euthanasia or assistance in suicide, but these restrictions would be revised and expanded over time, with an ever increasing risk of unjustified killing or allowing to die. Unscrupulous persons would learn how to abuse the system, just as they do through tax evasion. In short, society's value system would be deeply affected, and there would always be a lingering problem of erroneous diagnoses, abuse and neglect, and undue risks for society's most vulnerable members.

These arguments are rendered plausible by well-known features of our current social support system for vulnerable patients. Many families, and sometimes communities, abandon patients when they become seriously ill or injured. Patients and physicians alike may be unaware of the options available in the medical system, including advances in pain control that could help patients but are not routinely provided. To allow assistance in ending life could, under these conditions, lead patients to end their lives unnecessarily or prematurely. Patients might also be encouraged to choose one way or the other in a system that requires a choice of either treatment or death, and there might be powerful forces shifting the burden of proof onto the patient for the needed medical resources. (For two essays that address this and related problems, see Raanan Gillon and Norman Daniels, pp. 203–220.) Patients who choose "incorrectly" may wind up even more abandoned than they were previously, by both families and the health-care system. The argument is that neither the plight of these patients nor our compassion toward them justifies a fundamental modification in society's moral traditions.

The success or failure of these arguments about the negative consequences of legalization depends on speculative predictions of a progressive erosion of society's moral sensibility and forms of protection for the vulnerable. If these projected consequences will in fact result from the legalization of assisted suicide or voluntary active euthanasia, then the argument is sound and such practices should not be legalized. But how accurate is the evidence that the projected dire consequences will occur? Is there any solid basis for thinking that we cannot maintain adequate monitoring systems through carefully fashioned public policies? Could we not require physician consultation and hospital committee review whenever intolerable suffering motivates patients to end their lives? These are major questions in the current discussion about active euthanasia, especially the debate over its legalization.

The legalization of voluntary active euthanasia and assisted suicide gained a momentum in 1994 that it previously lacked. During this year courts in three states in the United States upheld the possibility of granting legal rights to competent, terminally ill patients to end their lives with professional assistance from physicians. First, in April 1994, the Oregon Supreme Court approved a ballot measure in the state to authorize standards for physician-assisted suicide, and the measure was then placed on the ballot in the Fall. The ballot permitted terminally ill patients to obtain a physician's prescription for lethal drugs with the intent to end life. Second, one month later a federal district court judge in the state of Washington ruled that the 140-year-old legal prohibition of assisted suicide in that state is unconstitutional because its laws violate the Fourteenth Amendment of the U.S. Constitution against state encroachment on individual liberties. The judge in this case could not see the logic of a law that permits withholdings of treatment that knowingly lead to death, while prohibiting physician-assisted suicide. Third, in the same month of the ruling in Washington, a court in Michigan acquitted Jack Kevorkian of charges that he violated the state's newly enacted law on physician-assisted suicide by administering carbon monoxide to a patient. A jury decision in this case found that Kevorkian did not have the relevant intention to be in violation of the Michigan law. This law exempted physicians whose intent is to relieve pain or discomfort rather than to cause death. The jury found, as Kevorkian's lawyer had argued, that Kevorkian had only intended to relieve the suffering of his patients, not to cause their deaths. Shortly thereafter, a state panel in Michigan began to draft guidelines for assisted suicide.[20]

Several commentators in biomedical ethics believe that sufficient moral reasons exist to justify some acts of assisting in death, but they also hold that these reasons are not sufficient to support revisions in either laws, professional codes, or public policies. In addressing whether we should retain or modify current prohibitions, therefore, we need to be clear about whether the topic of discussion is the moral justification of individual acts or the justification of institutional rules and public laws that permit or prohibit practices or policies. This distinction is especially important for discussions of physician-assisted suicide.

PHYSICIAN-ASSISTED SUICIDE

A central question about physician-assisted suicide concerns why some actions by physicians of causing death are morally condemnable, though others are not. What makes the act of assistance wrong when it is wrong, and what makes it acceptable when it is acceptable?

The Wrongness in Causing or Assisting in Death. Most people believe that it is not always morally wrong to cause someone's death. For example, one can justifiably kill another in an act of self-defense. Causing a person's death is wrong not because it ends the person's life, but because an unjustified harm or loss to the person is produced. If the act does not cause unjustifiable harm, the case becomes very different from the typical circumstance. Thus, what makes killing or "assisting" in causing a death wrong, when it is wrong, is that a person is unjustifiably harmed, that is, unjustifiably suffers a setback to interests that the person otherwise would not have experienced. In particular, the person is caused the loss of goods and the capacity to plan and choose a future. But if a person chooses death, rather than life's typical goods and projects, then helping that person bring about death may neither harm nor wrong the person. (This helping might still harm society by setting back its interests, and this consequence might be a reason against allowing the practice, but it would not alter one's perspective on the justification of the act.) Not helping persons of this description in their dying may interrupt or frustrate their plans and, from their perspective, cause them harm, indignity, or despair.

Those who take this view also reason as follows: If passive letting die does not harm or wrong a patient because it does not violate the patient's rights, then assisted suicide and voluntary active euthanasia also do not harm or wrong the person who dies. If this account is right, then those who believe it is sometimes morally acceptable to let people die, but not to take active steps to help them die, must give a different account of the wrongfulness of killing persons. From this perspective, the burden of justification rests on persons who would refuse assistance to those who have an enduring and rational wish to die, rather than on those who would help them. This is the core of the argument in favor of the moral justifiability of acts of assisted suicide, though it may offer little in the way of support for legalization of a practice or policy. But does the argument, if valid, also support physician-assisted suicide?

The Quill Case. The most widely discussed of the recent cases about physician-assisted suicide involves physician Timothy Quill, who publicly reported his relationship in helping a leukemia patient die.[21] Quill prescribed the barbiturates desired by this 45-year-old woman, who had been his patient for many years. Many believe that Quill's actions were justified for the following reasons: The patient was competent and acting voluntarily; there was an ongoing patient-physician relationship; there was mutual and informed decisionmaking by patient and physician; there was a probing discussion before the decision; there had been a considered rejection of alternatives; there was a durable death wish by the patient; there was, or at least would be, unbearable suffering and indignity (from the patient's perspective); and a means was used that was as painless as possible in ending the patient's life. In 1994 Quill defended his views with the argument that such acts are justified not so much by the rights of patients as by the physician's compassionate response "to an exceptional circumstance where suffering is overwhelming and there are no good choices."[22]

Nonetheless, some critics have found the action by Quill unjustified. He violated a New York State law against assisted suicide, exposing himself to criminal liability and leading to the possibility of misconduct charges from the New York State Health Department. Quill was intentionally acting against state law and against established canons of physician ethics. Furthermore, in order to protect himself and the patient's family, and to avoid a police investigation and an ambulance at the scene, he lied to the medical examiner by reporting that a hospice patient had died of acute leukemia. (A grand jury in Rochester, New York, where the events occurred, declined to indict him.)

Can society legally permit forms of assisted suicide such as Quill's and, at the same time, protect the lives of the vulnerable? This takes us to the subject of particularly troublesome acts and policies involving physician-assisted suicide. (For an attempt to address some of these problems, see the essay by Alexander Morgan Capron, pp. 192–202.)

Kevorkian's Cases. Jack Kevorkian's now famous suicide machines offer examples of unregulated physician activities that many fear would be widespread if physician-assisted suicide were legalized. In his first and most famous case, Janet Adkins, an Oregon grandmother with Alzheimer's disease, had reached a decision that she wanted to take her life rather than lose her cognitive capacities, which she was convinced were slowly deteriorating. After Adkins read about Kevorkian's machine in the news media, she flew from Oregon to Michigan to meet with him. Following brief discussions over a weekend, she and Kevorkian drove to a park. He inserted a tube in her arm and started a saline flow. His machine was constructed so that Adkins could then press a button to inject other drugs, eventuating in potassium chloride, which would physically cause her death. She then pressed the button.[23]

This case raises several concerns about physician involvement and about the absence of social monitoring. Adkins was in the fairly early stages of the crippling effects of Alzheimer's. At 54 years of age, she still enjoyed nearly a full schedule of activities with her husband and played tennis with her son. She might have been able to live a meaningful life for several years. There was a slight possibility that the Alzheimer's diagnosis was incorrect, and she might have been more psychologically depressed than Kevorkian appreciated. More important, she had limited contact with him before they collaborated in her death, and he had not administered examinations to confirm either her diagnosis or her level of competence to commit suicide. Being a pathologist rather than a clinician, he lacked the professional expertise to evaluate her specific condition.

Kevorkian's actions have been almost universally condemned by lawyers, physicians, and writers in ethics. His actions raise many fears about killing in medicine: abuse, lack of social control, physicians acting without accountability, and unverifiable circumstances of a patient's death. Kevorkian has had no longstanding relationship with his patients, who receive no careful clinical evaluation. Although his approach to assisted suicide has been criticized for these reasons, Kevorkian's "patients" raise profound questions about the lack of a support system in medicine or elsewhere for handling their problems. Having thought for over a year about her future, Adkins decided that her suffering would exceed the benefits of continuing to live. She apparently had firm views about what she wanted, and she carefully calculated both the costs and the benefits. She faced a bleak future from her perspective as a person who had lived an unusually vigorous life. She believed that her brain would be slowly destroyed, with progressive and devastating cognitive loss and confusion, fading memory, immense frustration, and lack of all capacity to take care of herself.

She also believed that her family would have to assume the full burden of responsibility for her care. From her perspective, what Kevorkian offered was better than other physicians offered, which, to her, was no help at all.

Current social institutions, including the medical system, have not proved adequate for patients like Adkins. Dying persons often face inadequate counseling, emotional support, pain information, or pain control. Their condition is intolerable from their perspective, and without any avenue of hope. To maintain that these persons act immorally by arranging for death is a harsh judgment that needs to be backed by persuasive argument. But even if their decisions and acts can be justified, is it also justifiable for physicians to assist in their suicides? Should we judge the physician's decision differently than the patient's? Or is the only real problem that physicians too often lack the clinical knowledge and counseling skills needed to reassure, comfort, and give care to these patients, who are in pain and fearful for their futures? (For various ways of addressing these questions, see the essays by Ronald E. Cranford, Edmund D. Pellegrino, and John M. Freeman, pp. 152–191.)

PRACTICE AND POLICY IN THE NETHERLANDS

As the controversy over voluntary active euthanasia and physician-assisted suicide has heightened, increasing attention has been devoted to policies and practices in the Netherlands, where approximately 2 percent of deaths are acts of voluntary euthanasia involving the assistance of physicians. Many persons inside and outside the medical profession in the Netherlands believe that physician-killing in cases of seriously ill and dying patients can be morally and legally justified. Voluntary active euthanasia has been endorsed by the Dutch medical establishment and at least permitted by the legal system. However, not all requests are acceded to by physicians. In one study, investigators found that Dutch physicians complied with fewer than one of every three requests for euthanasia.[24]

Under Holland's national legislation and somewhat loose-knit system of supervision, killing at the patient's informed request must be authorized by state and medical authorities. The conditions of justified euthanasia consist of an informed request by a patient who is suffering unbearably, physician consultation with a second physician, and careful review of the patient's condition by the physician performing the euthanasia procedure. By policy, all cases must be reported to the Ministry of Justice, although there appear to be many unreported cases. Among the most troubling discoveries by those who have studied the situation in the Netherlands have been data indicating that in 0.8 percent of all deaths, physicians performed active euthanasia without a clear prior request from a patient, thus violating accepted guidelines.[25]

The Dutch experience is now being used by proponents of voluntary active euthanasia in many countries to defend their local proposals to ease rules against mercy killing and assisted suicide. The results in the Netherlands are being used by opponents, who believe events in that country amount to a tragic social experiment.

Significant differences have emerged in this debate between certain North American attitudes toward euthanasia and certain Dutch attitudes. Whereas North American critics of practices in the Netherlands often see that country as dangerously sliding down a slippery slope, many Dutch citizens see it the other way around. They believe that American approval of nonvoluntary passive euthanasia in which persons are allowed to die who have never explicitly requested to die is a steeper slippery slope than voluntary active euthanasia, where the patient always initiates the request. It could be, of course, that both countries find themselves on slippery slopes and that both will see massive changes in their practices and policies in upcoming years. But should those practices and policies change, and, if so, how?

NOTES

1. An outstanding survey of the historical sources is found in Baruch Brody, ed. *Suicide and Euthanasia: Historical and Contemporary Themes*. Dordrecht, Holland: Kluwer Academic Publishers, 1989.

2. See Alan Meisel, "The Legal Consensus about Forgoing Life-Sustaining Treatment: Its Status and Its Prospects," *Kennedy Institute of Ethics Journal* 2; 1992: 309–345.

3. For a comprehensive view of the legal developments, see Alan Meisel, *The Right to Die*. New York: John Wiley and Sons, 1989, with Cumulative Supplements published in 1992 and 1993, New York: Wiley.

4. William H. Harris and Judith S. Levey, eds., *The New Columbia Encyclopedia*. New York: Columbia University Press, 1975, p. 904.

5. This account is developed in detail in Tom L. Beauchamp and Arnold Davidson, "The Definition of Euthanasia," *Journal of Medicine and Philosophy* 4; 1979, and reprinted in Samuel Gorovitz, et al., eds., *Moral Problems in Medicine*, 2nd ed. Englewood Cliffs, NJ: Prentice-Hall, 1983.

6. Justice Antonin Scalia, concurring in *Cruzan v. Director, Missouri Department of Health*, 110 S.Ct. 2841 (1990): 2859–2863.

7. For two examples, see Dan Brock, "Forgoing Life-Sustaining Food and Water: Is it Killing?" in Joanne Lynn, ed., *By No Extraordinary Means*. Bloomington, Indiana University Press, 1986, pp. 118–129; and Kenneth F. Schaffner, "Recognizing the Tragic Choice: Food, Water, and the Right to Assisted Suicide," *Critical Care Medicine*, October, 1988: 1063–1068.

8. *In re Conroy*, 190 N.J. Sup. 453, 464 A.2d 303 (App. Div. 1983).

9. *In the Matter of Claire C. Conroy*, 485 A. 2d 1209 (1985), 1224–1225.

10. See *Law, Medicine, and Health Care* 17; 1989. Special issue on the "Linares Case," the best known case of this description.

11. The most widely discussed argument to this effect is James Rachels, "Active and Passive Euthanasia," *New England Journal of Medicine* 292, No. 2; January 9, 1975: 78–80. See also his *The End of Life: Euthanasia and Morality*. Oxford: Oxford University Press, 1986.

12. See the essay by Edmund Pellegrino in the present volume, and also his "Doctors Must Not Kill," *The Journal of Clinical Ethics* 3; 1992: 95–102.

13. See Anthony Kenny, "The History of Intention in Ethics," *Anatomy of the Soul*. Oxford: Basil Blackwell, 1973, Appendix; and Thomas Nagel, *The View from Nowhere*. New York: Oxford University Press, 1986.

14. British Columbia Court of Appeal, *Rodriguez v. British Columbia (Attorney General)* [1993], B.C.J. No. 641 (Q.L.) (B.C.C.A.). Chief Justice McEachern dissented, citing liberty rights and security of the person. This court's opinion was later upheld in the Supreme Court of Canada by a one-vote margin: Supreme Court of Canada, *Sue Rodriguez v. Attorney General of Canada*, September 30, 1993, File No. 23476.

15. See Joseph T. Mangan, S.J., "An Historical Analysis of the Principle of Double

Effect," *Theological Studies* 10; 1949: 41–61; Joseph Boyle, "Who Is Entitled to Double Effect?" *Journal of Medicine and Philosophy* 16; 1991: 475–494; and "Toward Understanding the Principle of Double Effect," Ethics 90; 1980: 527–538; David Granfield, The Abortion Decision. Garden City, NY: Image Books, 1971; Donald Marquis, "Four Versions of Double Effect," *Journal of Medicine and Philosophy* 16; 1991: 515–544.

16. See Philippa Foot, "The Problem of Abortion and the Doctrine of Double Effect," *The Oxford Review* 5; 1967: 59–70; H. L. A. Hart, "Intention and Punishment," *Punishment and Responsibility.* Oxford: Clarendon Press, 1968, for influential analyses in recent philosophy.

17. Sidney H. Wanzer, Daniel D. Federaman, S. James Adelstein, et al. "The Physician's Responsibility Toward Hopelessly Ill Patients: A Second Look," *New England Journal of Medicine* 320; March 30, 1989: 844–849.

18. For an instructive example, see Franklin G. Miller, Timothy Quill, Howard Brody, John C. Fletcher, Lawrence O. Gostin, D. E. Meier, "Regulating Physician-Assisted Death," *New England Journal of Medicine* 331; 1994: 119–123.

19. See, for example, American Medical Association, Council on Ethical and Judicial Affairs, *Euthanasia: Report C, in Proceedings of the House of Delegates.* Chicago: American Medical Association, June 1988: 258–260; *Current Opinions,* § 2.20, 1989; "Decisions Near the End of Life," Report B. Adopted by the House of Delegates, 1991: 11–15; and "Decisions Near the End of Life," *Journal of the American Medical Association* 267; April 22/29, 1992: 2229–2233; American Geriatrics Society, Public Policy Committee, "Voluntary Active Euthanasia," *Journal of the American Geriatrics Society* 39; August 1991.

20. See John Warden, "Decisions in U.S. Say that Doctors Can Assist Suicides," *British Medical Journal* 308; May 14, 1994: 1255–1256; *Hastings Center Report* 24(2); 1994: 3; Michael McCarthy, "U.S. Court Ruling on Physician-Assisted Suicide," Lancet 343; 1994: 1215–1216.

21. Timothy Quill, "Death and Dignity: A Case of Individualized Decision Making," *New England Journal of Medicine* 324; March 7, 1991: 691–694. Reprinted with additional analysis in Quill, *Death and Dignity.* New York: W. W. Norton, 1993.

22. Timothy Quill, "Incurable Suffering," *Hastings Center Report* 24; March/April, 1994: 45.

23. Based on Kevorkian's description of the events in his *Prescription: Medicide.* Buffalo: Prometheus Books, 1991; pp. 221–231, and on news reports in: *New York Times,* June 6, pp. A1, B6; June 7, 1990, pp. A1, D22; June 9, p. A6; June 12, p. C3; *Newsweek,* June 18, 1990, p. 46.

24. P. J. van der Maas, J. J. M. van Delden, L. Pijnenborg, *Euthanasia and other Medical Decisions Concerning the End of Life: An Investigation Performed Upon Request of the Commission of Inquiry into the Medical Practice Concerning Euthanasia.* Amsterdam: Elsevier Science Publishers, 1992. See also their report (with Caspart W. N. Looman), "Euthanasia and other Medical Decisions concerning the End of Life," *Lancet* 338; September 14, 1991: 669–674.

25. L. Pijnenborg, P. J. van der Maas, J. J. M. van Delden, C. W. N. Looman, "Life Terminating Acts without Explicit Request of Patient," *Lancet* 341; 1993: 1196–1199.

PART I. PHILOSOPHICAL PERSPECTIVES

Intending Death: The Structure of the Problem and Proposed Solutions

ALLEN BUCHANAN

University of Wisconsin, Madison, Wisconsin

THE PROBLEM OF INTENDING DEATH

Intending death may be a special problem in medicine, but controversies over the moral status of intentional killing reach far beyond medicine. The prohibition against intentionally taking human life is so deeply ingrained–so morally primal–that the killing of heinous criminals and aggressors in wars is rejected by some persons of undoubted moral integrity. Indeed, even those who find capital punishment and the killing of aggressors acceptable usually do so with a sense of profound moral loss and feel obliged to articulate and refine moral justifications for such exceptions to the general prohibition. To take intentionally an innocent person's life may seem like the very paradigm of an immoral act. One is tempted to say: if anything is wrong, *that* is wrong.

Virtually every moral code and ethical theory, religious or secular, includes the general prohibition against intentionally taking innocent human life.[1] This prohibition lies at the heart of the criminal law as well: not only is murder the most serious offense,[2] but the consent of the victim himself is not recognized as a defense in homicide. Even more strikingly, the criminal law's requirement of *mens rea* (guilty state of mind) is interpreted so as to be compatible with the life-taker acting from a good motive. The fact that a person kills another with the intent to benefit this person–say by ending this person's misery–neither excuses nor justifies.[3] It is the intention to kill, not the motive in killing, that constitutes the *mens rea* required for the crime of homicide.[4]

The legal prohibition against intentional killing is not limited to the killing of another. Until this century suicide was a crime, and to this day assisted suicide is a felony in almost half the jurisdictions of this country.[5] The legal definition of *suicide* is simply the intentional bringing about of one's own death.[6] Neither the means of achieving death nor the motive in seeking it are part of the definition. And as with homicide generally, the former crime of suicide and the present crime of assisted suicide admit of no defense on grounds of good motive.

The criminalization of suicide is the most extreme legal expression of the prohibition against the intentional taking of life. While the law's refusal to recognize consent as a defense in the killing of another implies that the right to life cannot be waived so that others are released from their obligation not to kill an individual, the prohibitions against suicide and assisted suicide go further still in the direction of absolutism, amounting to a denial that the person has the authority to take his or her own life.

A series of landmark "right to die" cases, from *Quinlan* to *Conroy*, provide still more evidence of the depth of the law's commitment to the prohibition. In each instance the courts found it necessary to declare an important state interest in preventing suicide–and then to argue, quite unconvincingly, that refusal of life-support was not suicide.[7]

Codes of medical ethics, from the Hippocratic Oath to resolutions adopted by the American Medical Association, usually forbid physicians from killing patients, even from the best of motives and with the patient's consent or direction.[8] Especially for those who identify themselves as healers and savers of lives, the idea that it is permissible for them to kill patients–let alone the claim that respect for patient autonomy may require them to do so–may seem utterly unacceptable, even repugnant.

Yet there is an equally firm conviction, one that seems to be growing in this country, that in some instances intentionally taking the life of an innocent person is morally permissible, at least in certain medical contexts. It is true that those who hold this conviction sometimes disagree among themselves either as to which cases of intending death are permissible or as to which cases are instances in which the death that occurs was intended. Nevertheless, there are some cases that clearly are instances of intending death and which many find justifiable. The following are two of the most compelling types of cases.

Case 1: Active Voluntary Euthanasia. The competent, well-informed, terminally ill patient is in severe pain. Adequate pain relief is either unattainable or would so impair the patient's cognitive abilities and his capacity for interacting with others that he finds this option incompatible with his conception of personal dignity and of a fitting end to his life. He rejects the proposal that he be allowed to die of dehydration or to succumb to an infection, saying that this would be too hard on his family, both emotionally and financially. Merely withdrawing other forms of life-support would result in prolonged suffering. His physician finally agrees to give him a lethal injection.

Case 2: Assisted Suicide. Jones is a competent, well-informed patient suffering from a terminal, incurable, degenerative disease that will soon rob him of his cognitive capacities, then his ability to act, and finally his life. He is living at home, where he can freely interact with family and friends, and is adamant that he not be rehospitalized. After much reflection and discussion with those he loves and respects, he decides to end his life quickly and painlessly, before further loss of capacities occurs. Because he finds some methods distasteful and fears that he may be unable to achieve his goal with certainty if he acts alone, he asks a friend to help him administer a drug intravenously and to make sure it works. The friend agrees.

The problem about intending death, then, is the apparent contradiction between allegiance to the prohibition against intentionally taking innocent human life, on the one hand, and the conviction that, at least in cases such as these, intentionally killing is permissible. But since the prohibition against intentional killing is deeply entrenched in the fabric of our society, resolving the problem may require more than a mere change in belief. It may necessitate changes in our institutions and in social roles as well. There are two questions to answer. First, "How, if at all, can the apparent contradiction be resolved?" and second, "What changes, if any, will its resolution require in our institutions and in our conception of what it is to be a physician—or, if assisted suicide for the terminally ill becomes widely accepted, in our conception of what it is to be a friend?"

In this essay I begin the task of answering the first question by articulating the main strategies for resolving the apparent contradiction. Although I will not attempt to provide a conclusive evaluation of their respective merits, I will indicate which of them I think is most promising. In the end, an adequate response to the problem of intending death will require an act of moral self-consciousness so fundamental that it is rarely even contemplated, much less performed: we must make explicit the nature of the wrong we do, when we do wrong, in intentionally killing a human being.

THE STRATEGIES

Assuming, at least provisionally, that it is not an acceptable option to abandon entirely the prohibition against intentionally killing, there are five strategies for resolving the contradiction between the general prohibition and conflicting intuitions in particular cases.

Strategy 1. Acknowledge that intentionally ending the life of an innocent human being is always wrong, but then argue that what appear to be cases of justifiably intending death are not, because the individual is already dead. On this view, intentionally bringing about the death of an anencephalic infant or of an older patient who is permanently unconscious is only bringing about the death of a system of organs, not of a human being. Call this the "they're already dead strategy."

Strategy 2. Defend the general prohibition, but only on the condition that its application is restricted to human beings that have interests. Then argue that some living human beings lack the rudimentary capacities for pleasure and pain required for having interests and are, therefore, not covered by the general prohibition. Call this the "no interests, no right to life strategy."

Strategy 3. Affirm the general prohibition without exception, but argue that in all the cases in which bringing about the death of an innocent person is justifiable, the death was foreseen but not intended. Or argue that the doctrine of double effect adds so much support to the prohibition against intentional killing that we should revise those intuitions that conflict with it. Call this the "double effect strategy."

Strategy 4. Acknowledge that even though in principle intentionally bringing about the death of an innocent human being is sometimes permissible, there are a number of considerations which, taken together, show that morally sound public policy should not allow any exceptions to the prohibition, at least in medical contexts. These include the fallibility of human judgment, the dangers of abuse, the erosion of patient trust, and the tendency to descend a slippery slope toward morally unacceptable practices concerning death. Call this the "prudent public policy strategy."

Strategy 5. Show that the intuitively justifiable cases of intending death are principled exceptions to the general prohibition, supported by widely held and plausible moral values, including those that ground the general prohibition itself. Call this the "principled exception strategy." The principled exception strategy has two main variants: a moderate version which contends that only cases in which the one to be killed consents to being killed are justifiable exceptions to the general prohibition; and a radical version which allows the possibility of justifiable nonvoluntary intentional killing.

The first (they're already dead) and fourth (prudent public policy) strategies have this in common: both accept the prohibition and acknowledge no exceptions to it. The second (no interests, no right to life) and fifth (principled exception) strategies both seek to resolve the contradiction by acknowledging genuine exceptions to the prohibition.

The first and second strategies may be quickly dismissed if presented as complete solutions to the problem of intending death. Each does reconcile the prohibition against intended death with some intuitions about the justifiability of intending death, and in that sense both the first and second strategies offer partial solutions to the problem. But neither comes close to providing a reconciliation across the whole range of intuitively justifiable cases. If either of the two cases described above presents an apparent conflict with the general prohibition, then neither the first nor the second strategy solves the problem of intending death, since they say nothing about such cases. In neither Case 1 nor Case 2 is the patient dead according to any plausible conception of death and in both the patient clearly has substantial interests.[9]

FORESEEN BUT NOT INTENDED: THE DOUBLE EFFECT STRATEGY

The distinction is between what is intended, either as an end or as a means toward something else that is an end, and what is foreseen but intended neither as a means nor as an end. The doctrine of double effect holds that (1) it is sometimes permissible to bring about a death that one foresees without intending, when to bring that death about intentionally would be wrong.[10] There is some disagreement among those who endorse the doctrine as to what the conditions are which together make a case of killing in which death is merely foreseen a justifiable killing. There does seem to be agreement that a condition of proportionality must be satisfied: "the good effect must be sufficiently desirable to compensate for the allowing of the bad effect" or "there [must] be a proportionately grave reason for permitting the evil effect."[11] Thesis (1) must be distinguished from another, namely, that (2) it is never permissible to bring about an innocent person's death intentionally, but sometimes permissible to bring it about if one foresees but does not intend it. Thesis (1) does not entail thesis (2): (1) is compatible with there being some cases of intentionally bringing about death being permissible.[12]

Neither principle (1) nor (2), even when supplemented with appropriate conditions for justifiable foreseen killings, can provide a resolution to the problem of intending death unless at least those cases, such as 1 and 2, which seem to be the most compelling counter-examples to the prohibition against intentional killing, can be shown to be cases in which the death is merely foreseen but not intended. The difficulty is that there seems to be no good reason—aside from the desire to describe the cases so that the doctrine can be invoked–to characterize either cases of type 1 or type 2 as not being cases of intentional killing. In Case 1 it is quite natural to say that the physician intentionally kills the patient, at the patient's request. In Case 2 it is equally natural to say that the patient intentionally kills himself with the help of his friend.

A desperate dedication to the doctrine has led some to attempt to redescribe such cases as follows: The patient's intention–or as courts in the right to die cases cited above said, his "specific intention"–was not to die but only to avoid futile suffering. That this is so is shown by a counterfactual test: If he could have avoided the futile suffering without dying he would have done so.

This attempt at redescription is sheer sophistry. From the fact that one would prefer another means to an end if that other means were available, it does not follow that one isn't doing what one is doing, namely, intentionally performing the act in question as a means toward one's end. Analogously, from the fact that what a bank robber really wants is a large sum of money and that he wouldn't rob if it were given to him or if he won it in a lottery, it doesn't follow that when he robs a bank to get the money he didn't rob it intentionally.

Those who find the doctrine congenial point out that its invocation does resolve or avoid some painful moral dilemmas, by distinguishing cases of justifiable and unjustifiable killing. More specifically, the doctrine of double effect enables us to take consequences into account without falling into a purely consequentialist ethic. For example, the doctrine can explain why it would be permissible for an engineer to steer a runaway train down one track, where one will be killed, to avoid going down another, where five would be killed, while it would be wrong for a judge to have one innocent person executed to save five others. The explanation is that though the engineer kills a person, he does not intend that person's death, while the judge would be intentionally killing one to save five. We are told that the doctrine has another advantage: it frees us from the power of moral blackmailers. For example, if a ruthless tyrant or terrorist tells you to kill one innocent person or he will kill five, you can avoid feeling obliged to comply, if you console yourself with the fact that the deaths that result from your refusal are merely foreseen, but not intended by you.

For those who have more consequentialist intuitions these may be dubious benefits. But the main point is that there are other ways of avoiding pure consequentialism. Each of the examples just described can be accommodated by a distinction between positive and negative duties, along with a set of principles for resolving conflicts of duties.[13] For instance, the trolley case can be seen as a conflict of negative duties, with the governing principle being: when basic negative duties, that is, those of the same seriousness or moral importance, conflict, do the least harm. In the case of the judge, killing an innocent person to save others would be impermissible, according to the principle that when basic negative and positive duties conflict, negative duties override. And the same principle enables us to avoid moral blackmail: in the case of basic duties, the negative duty not to harm the one innocent person overrides the positive duty to save the lives of the five.[14]

A Kantian interpretation of the doctrine of double effect has been suggested by Warren Quinn.[15] According to this view, the doctrine is based on respect for persons as rational beings, which in turn requires not treating them as mere means. The idea is that at least in some instances, intending a person's death (either as one's end or as a means towards it) would be treating the person as a mere means, not as an end in oneself, while acting in such a way that his or her death is merely foreseen, but not intended, would not be treating him or her as a mere means.

For three reasons, a Kantian interpretation of the doctrine of double effect holds little promise as a solution to the problem of intending death. First, it limits the applicability of the doctrine to persons in the Kantian sense–rational beings capable of self-determination. Yet the general prohibition is against killing innocent human beings, including those who lack the capacity for rational self-determination.

Second, and more important, it makes good sense, on Kantian grounds, to say that when an autonomous agent freely consents to being killed (or freely requests that one kill him or her or help him or her do so) one is not treating this person as a mere means. But if this is so, then it will be the notion of consent, not the distinction between intended and merely foreseen consequences, that provides a resolution to the problem of intending death.

Third, one can fail to treat a person as an end by killing him or her, even though one only foresees and does not intend the death. For example, if my intention is to fire a round into the bull's eye of a target and I do so knowing that a person is resting against the other side of the target, I have in a very concrete sense not treated this person as an end. Instead, I have acted as if this person was a mere thing, like the target. What this suggests is that the distinction between treating persons as persons, or ends in themselves, and failing to treat them as such, is not congruent with the distinction between merely foreseeing and intending death.[16]

The appeal of the doctrine of double effect is that it allows us to hold fast to the absolute prohibition against intentional killing while still being able, at least in some cases, to take consequences into account, even if doing so requires killing—but without collapsing into pure consequentialism. In other words, at least for those who find pure consequentialism unacceptable, the doctrine *lowers the moral cost of adherence to the absolute prohibition* by allowing us to take consequences into account (as when we steer down the track with one person rather than five), yet without determining our conduct solely by what will produce the most good or avoid the most harm. And this brings us to the second, indirect, way in which the doctrine of double effect might be thought to resolve the conflict between our allegiance to the prohibition against intentional killing and our intuitions that it is permissible in cases such as 1 and 2. By lowering the moral cost of adherence to the prohibition against intentional killing, the doctrine might be though to lend independent support to the prohibition itself. And if this support made the prohibition sufficiently attractive, we might then even be led to revise our intuitions concerning cases of types 1 and 2–indeed to overrule them, as it were. We would then bring our responses to such cases in line with the prohibition rather than modifying or abandoning the prohibition.

However, as we have seen, there are other ways of taking consequences into account without collapsing into pure consequentialism that seem to do the job as well or better than the doctrine of double effect. So, reliance on the doctrine lends no significant independent support to the prohibition against intentional killing. But if that is so, and if cases like 1 and 2 are troubling apparent counter-examples to the prohibition, then the doctrine of double effect does not weaken their force significantly.

The inadequacy of the doctrine runs much deeper than this, however. What is most striking and disturbing is that the doctrine itself is utterly blind to the whole question of consent. Surely consent must at least be morally relevant in some cases of intentional killing, even if it should turn out not to be decisive as a justification. Any view, including the doctrine of double effect, which considers consent to be irrelevant to the question of whether intentional killing can be justified faces a painful dilemma. Either one must say that consent is relevant to the justifiability of withholding life-support, but not relevant to the justifiability of intentional killing; or one must say that consent is irrelevant in both cases.

The latter alternative is clearly untenable. Embracing it would amount to a denial of the competent patient's right to refuse life-sustaining treatment. The former alternative is scarcely more attractive: if consent is not only relevant, but morally decisive in cases of terminating life-support, how could it be the case that it is never of any moral consequence in any case of killing? It will not do, of course, to reply that in the latter case one is intentionally killing and that this is always wrong. This reply simply begs the question against those who argue, as I shall in the final section of this paper, that there are principled exceptions to the prohibition against intentional killing.

There is, however, an even more serious flaw in any attempt to escape the dilemma by admitting that consent can sometimes justify terminating life-support, while denying that consent can ever justify intentional killing: some cases of justified withdrawal of life-support are intentional killings. There are cases in which physicians kill patients by withdrawing life-support, and do so deliberately, with sound moral justification, and with increasing support from the law, ethical theory, and public opinion.

A familiar example will illustrate this important point. Suppose Smith, who is connected to a ventilator and will die without it, competently decides he does not wish to live in such a state of dependency, and convinces his physician to withdraw this means of life-support. However, before the physician can do so, Smith's wicked nephew, Brown, steals into Smith's room and shuts off the ventilator. When his foul deed is discovered, Brown lamely protests, with all the feigned indignation he can muster: "I didn't kill him, the disease did!"

The usual moral drawn from such examples is that killing is itself no worse than letting die.[17] But the hollowness of Brown's protest shows that we may draw a different conclusion. Withdrawing life-support can be killing in a straightforward sense: an act which results in death. And if the act is done with the intention of bringing about death—whether as a means of getting a fortune or as a means to relieving futile suffering—it is an act of intentional killing.

Those who use such examples to show that killing itself is not worse than letting die do us a great service by focusing on the real moral issues: whether a person is responsible for a death and whether, if responsible, he is culpable. But they concede too much. The proper conclusion to be drawn is that one can kill by withdrawing care, and that some cases of killing are justifiable and recognized as being justifiable, even if we do not always recognize them as cases of killing. And if some instances of withdrawing life-support are killings, then a defender of the doctrine of double effect cannot argue that consent is relevant for the justification of withdrawing life-support, but never relevant for killing because intentional killing is wrong even if there is consent. To argue in this way is both to beg the question against those who hold that there are principled exceptions against the prohibition on intentional killing and to assume, quite falsely, that no instances of withdrawing life-support are killings.

The next strategy for solving the problem of intentional killing fares better than the doctrine of double effect in this respect. It does answer the question, "Why is consent morally relevant in cases of terminating life-support, but not in cases of intentional killing?" The answer is that sound public policy should strictly prohibit intentional killing in medicine, while allowing that the competent patient's consent can justify withholding life-support.

THE PRUDENT PUBLIC POLICY ARGUMENT

This strategy acknowledges the validity of our intuitions in cases such as 1 and 2, without attempting to deny that these are cases of intending death. Instead, it is argued that even if there are cases, considered in isolation, in which intentional killing would be justified, the moral costs of a public policy that allowed intentional killing, including active voluntary euthanasia or assisted suicide, would be unacceptable. There are two versions of the prudent public policy argument. One contends that an exceptionless prohibition against voluntary active euthanasia and assisted suicide should extend to everyone, regardless of professional role. The other restricts the prohibition to members of the medical (and/or nursing) profession.

The first version, in its most plausible form, would begin by cataloguing the moral costs of a policy of permitting active voluntary euthanasia and assisted suicide, list the moral benefits of such a policy, and provide an assessment that shows the former to outweigh the latter. Unfortunately, most proponents of the argument, in either variant, at best execute the first step, while omitting an impartial consideration of the benefits of the policy they oppose–and leap to an ill-founded assessment that the costs are unacceptable.

The main possible moral costs of allowing voluntary active euthanasia and/or assisted suicide are these: (1) individuals who did not really wish to be killed would succumb to family or social pressure (because of the drive to contain costs); (2) in some cases outright murder might occur and be disguised as active voluntary euthanasia or assisted suicide; and (3) allowing even these limited instances of intentional killing would "weaken the reverence for life."[18]

The second version of the argument builds on the first, noting that there are additional special costs for a policy that allows physicians (or nurses) to kill patients. (4) If physicians (or nurses) were permitted to kill, then the fundamental trust on which so much that is good depends in the physician-patient (or nurse-patient) relationship would be damaged if not utterly destroyed.

Advocates of intentional killing in medicine are quick to emphasize the other side of the ledger. The chief moral values that would be served by allowing active voluntary euthanasia and/or assisted suicide are: (1) patient self-determination; and (2) patient well-being. It is these same two values that provide the foundation of the legal and moral doctrine that the competent patient has the right to accept or refuse care.[19] While not denying the possibility that serious moral costs may arise if physicians or others are allowed to kill, those who believe that intentional killing is sometimes justifiable contend that appropriate institutional safeguards would keep these costs within acceptable limits. To make their case they must also argue that the adoption and effective implementation of such safeguards is sufficiently likely to justify whatever moral risks would remain.

The difficulty in assessing the debate between the advocates of the prudent public policy argument and those who would permit some forms of intentional killing in medicine is the uncertainty of the predictions on both sides and the abstractness of the discussion about possible institutional safeguards. One great benefit of the current experiment with active euthanasia in the Netherlands is that it at least provides a concrete focus for debate.[20]

I will make no effort here to supply a conclusive assessment of the prudent public policy argument. Instead, I will only emphasize two considerations which significantly undercut its force. First, the stronger of the two versions of the argument, which appeals not only to general moral costs but also to those special costs that allowing physicians to kill might involve, mistakenly assumes that physicians *are not already killing patients* and that their doing so is not compatible with adequate patient trust. Second, those who assume that the moral costs of allowing active voluntary euthanasia or assisted suicide would be too great fail to appreciate that the case for allowing these forms of intentional killing rests on *the very values that support the general prohibition* against intentional killing, values that can both guide the development of appropriate safeguards and motivate us to implement them. Let us say that an account of exceptions to a general moral principle shows these exceptions to be deeply principled if it shows the exceptions to be justified by the same basic values that support the general principle itself.

When I say that physicians are already killing patients I do not mean simply that some physicians are already engaging in what is ordinarily considered to be active voluntary euthanasia and assisted suicide–as in Cases 1 and 2–in which the physician administers or helps the patient administer a lethal injection. Instead, what I have in mind is the point made in the preceding section of this paper, namely, that there are many more cases in which physicians *kill patients by withdrawing life-support*, and do so deliberately, with sound moral justification, and with increasing support from the law, ethical theory, and public opinion.

If withdrawing life-support can count as killing, and if, as is now widely agreed, the withdrawal of life-support is compatible with being a good physician, then it is hard to see why the same cannot be true for those other forms of killing, voluntary active euthanasia and assisted suicide. Including the permissibility of voluntary active euthanasia or assisted suicide within our conception of the role of physician does not require repudiating or even supplementing the basic values which underlie that role as it is now conceived, and which already support withdrawal of life-support. Nor does it even require a transition from a situation in which physicians do not kill patients to one in which they do, if I am right in holding that they do kill patients when they withhold care in order to end life.

This is not the whole story, however. The strong resistance to voluntary active euthanasia and assisted suicide that some physicians express will not simply dissipate in the light of philosophical analysis. It has other sources than a failure to recognize that withdrawing life-support can be killing and that the same values of self-determination and well-being that support it can support more direct forms of killing as well. In part, physicians' opposition to voluntary active euthanasia and assisted suicide may stem from a very understandable uneasiness, not about what they will be permitted to do, but rather about what they may be required to do.[21]

With some simplification it can be said that we have witnessed in the past 15 years or so, not just the recognition of a right to die, but the transformation of that right from a purely negative right against intrusive medical procedures to a positive right to determine the manner of one's dying.[22] It is true that advance directives were first developed as mechanisms for ensuring that the negative right against intrusion was not violated by over aggressive physicians. But the emphasis on patient self-determination which was invoked to establish the negative right inevitably pointed toward the need for giving patients more positive control over the dying process. Not without reason, therefore, physicians may fear that an expansive, positive right to die may result in a redefinition of the physician's role to include the idea that he is obligated to perform voluntary active euthanasia or to assist the patient in committing suicide. Physicians may fear that what began as a struggle to free patients from unwanted control by physicians will result in patients exercising excessive control over physicians.

This fear, though understandable, does not provide a reason for refusing to allow further, responsible, institutionally safe-guarded exceptions to the prohibition against intentional killing by physicians—to allow killing by lethal injection, for example, in addition to killing by removal of life-support. The proper conclusion to be drawn, rather, is that any sound public policy allowing intentional killing in medicine must recognize the patient's right of self-determination is not a right of unlimited, nonconsensual authority over others.

A morally acceptable public policy allowing intentional killing in medicine would have to be based on clear distinctions among the following rights: (1) the patient's right of self-determination, as a right against unwanted medical intrusions; (2) the patient's right to seek voluntary active euthanasia or assistance in suicide (subject to appropriate safeguards) without interference from the law or medical personnel; and (3) the physician's right to refuse to participate in intentional killings (other than withdrawal of care) that are recognized as legitimate by sound public policy.

The first right carries a corresponding obligation on the part of the physician, but only a negative one—the obligation not to subject the patient to unwanted intrusions. Fulfilling this negative obligation, however, can require positive actions, such as killing by withdrawing life-support, as well as allowing to die by not starting life-support.

The second right carries no obligation on the part of the physician to participate in voluntary active euthanasia or assisted suicide. All it guarantees is that those patients who seek these forms of intentional killing and those physicians who agree to participate will not be interfered with or held liable (so long as they operate within prescribed institutional safeguards).

The third right, which might be called a physician autonomy right or a right of conscientious refusal, allows the physician to limit his role in patient care so as to exclude voluntary active euthanasia or assisted suicide. Physicians who fear the imposition of an obligation to kill should take heart from the fact that there is already widespread recognition of a right of conscientious refusal in at least two other areas of medicine having to do with life and death decisions: the right of a physician not to participate in abortions and the right not to participate in some forms of withdrawal of care, in particular, termination of feeding and hydration. Effective institutionalization of all three of these rights is a necessary condition for a morally acceptable public policy allowing intentional death in medicine, at least for our society at this time.[23] Whether such a policy can be morally justified will depend on whether an adequate account of principled exceptions to the fundamental legal and moral prohibition against intentionally killing human beings can be articulated. In the next and final section such an account will be sketched.

PRINCIPLED EXCEPTIONS TO THE PROHIBITION ON INTENTIONAL KILLING OR REPLACEMENT OF THE PROHIBITION?

The last strategy for dealing with the conflict between our deeply felt allegiance to the prohibition on intentionally killing human beings and the growing conviction that there are some cases in which voluntary active euthanasia and assisted suicide are morally justifiable is to affirm the prohibition, but then provide a convincing, principled account of legitimate exceptions to it in such a way as to accommodate our most confident intuitions concerning justified intentional killing. The chief outlines of such an account have already been drawn: the same fundamental values of individual self-determination and well-being whose recognition have led to the acknowledgment of the right to refuse life-support also speak in favor of allowing voluntary active euthanasia and assisted suicide.

As Cases 1 and 2 show, there are circumstances in which these values will not be served adequately by the right to refuse life-support. First, there are situations where merely not starting or withdrawing life-support will not enable the patient to avoid futile pain. Although the number of cases in which adequate pain relief cannot be achieved if the best available techniques for pain control are employed may not be great, such cases do occur. Moreover, it is a sad fact that many patients do not receive the best pain control that is technically available. Further, our ability to ameliorate suffering does not match our technology for pain control. People who are faced with an incurable degenerative disease experience what they find to be intolerable suffering–severe psychological distress–even if they are not in extreme pain, and even the best psychiatric care may not provide adequate relief, at least in the eyes of the sufferer himself. This is not surprising, especially in cases in which the individual cannot be comforted with the thought that the condition causing the psychological distress will only be a transient phase. Consequently, even if it were true that in virtually all cases adequate pain control is possible, this would not solve the problem of suffering. A second, and much more frequently occurring situation is one in which pain can be controlled, but at the price of rendering the patient virtually unconscious, and the patient regards the prolongation of life in such a condition unacceptable. The third case in which the values of individual well-being and self-determination speak in favor of allowing intentional killing, if the patient requests it, is where the patient, though not choosing between extreme pain and virtual unconsciousness, nevertheless concludes that he no longer wishes to live, because continued care will be a great burden on his family or on public resources, and because he finds no compensating benefit to offset that burden, given his impaired condition. (This may well describe the condition of the woman with Alzheimer's dementia whose suicide was assisted by Dr. Kevorkian in Michigan.) In each of these three types of situations the values of individual self-determination and well-being support intentional killing–if the legitimate concerns about fallibility and abuse stressed by the prudent public policy argument are addressed by adequate safeguards.

In some instances, as continuing controversies over the justifiability of paternalism attest, self-determination and well-being conflict. They often do not conflict, however, chiefly because, at least for competent, informed individuals, the individual is likely to be the best judge of his or her interests, especially an interest in sustaining an acceptable quality of life. This (albeit imperfect) congruence between the competent, informed individual's well-being and one's own judgement concerning what is conducive to it is due to two factors: the likelihood that the individual will be more highly motivated to preserve his or her own good and more concretely aware of his or her own wants and needs and the conditions for their satisfaction, and the fact that, especially with regard to the question of the quality of one's own life, well-being is to some extent subjective, that is, constituted in part by the individual's own conception of what life has been and what it should be. For these reasons, regardless of whether we view self-determination and well-being as distinct, coordinate values, or view self-determination as being valuable only because it tends to promote well-being, we will best promote both values if the competent, informed patient is allowed to determine whether to continue living.

It should now be clear that the justifications given for intentional killing in the preceding sorts of cases do not apply in the cases of intentional killing which we all regard as morally unacceptable and against which the prohibition on intentional killing is at least primarily directed. Nonetheless, to make a convincing case that allowing voluntary active euthanasia or assisted suicide in such cases would constitute principled exceptions to the general prohibition, it is necessary to provide an account of what is morally wrong with intentional killing when it is wrong, and then show that the features that constitute the moral wrong do not exist in the exceptional cases. The justification for the exceptions will be especially strong if the same values that are shown to support the exceptions also support the general prohibition itself.

They do. At least in a secular account of what is wrong with intentional killing, the values of individual self-determination and well-being must be paramount. What makes killing a human being morally bad, in the first instance at least, quite aside from indirect consequences, is that it deprives the person of any form of well-being and puts an end to self-determination. Furthermore, most intentional killings are not committed with consent and hence cannot be viewed as promoting self-determination.

A plausible secular interpretation of the reverence for human life, as distinct for a reverence for mere physiological life, is that it consists at least in large part in concern for individual well-being and self-determination. In that sense it is true that the prohibition on intentional killing expresses a reverence for life.

Some religious interpretations of the prohibition against intentional killing would take a different stance. Human beings would be thought of as being under a strict injunction from their creator to refrain from intentionally killing themselves or their fellows–an injunction which cannot be waived by the consent or request of a mere human being. This, in fact, has been a prominent strain in Christian religious ethics, one that has been invoked to condemn suicide, assisted suicide, and voluntary active euthanasia. On one construal, this is the idea that in killing ourselves or other human beings we are destroying god's property. On a less demeaning interpretation–one that does not see human beings as things owned by God–it is the view that God alone has the rightful authority to decide when we may "quit our stations." There are two serious difficulties with invoking any such notion to justify a strict prohibition on intentional killing in medicine. First, the religious view justifies too much: not only a ban on destroying God's property or quitting one's station by killing, but by refusing or withdrawing life-support as well. In other words, if it is wrong for a human being to decide to shorten one's life by killing or having another person do the killing, why is it not wrong deciding to shorten life by refusing life-support? Or, conversely, if respect for God's property in us or authority over us is compatible with our shortening our life by refusing life-support, why is it not also compatible with shortening our lives by taking a lethal injection? In either case we take it on ourselves to decide when to end our lives, and either we have a right to make such a decision or we do not. Some proponents of a religious interpretation of the prohibition against intentional killing might contend that neither the God's property view nor the God's authority view is the true basis of their belief that consent can never justify intentional killing. Instead, they would hold that there are certain types of actions–intentional killing of innocent human beings being one of them–that are wrong in themselves and that if the action in itself is wrong, then the fact that it is consented cannot alter its moral status. It seems to me that such a stance faces a dilemma. If asked to justify the claim that such actions are wrong in themselves, those who hold this view can either appeal to revelation, saying that God has decreed these actions to be wrong in themselves; or they can attempt to give a substantive account of why these actions are wrong in themselves. The former reply not only faces all the familiar epistemological objections to appeals to alleged divinely revealed truths generally, but also runs counter to the assumption that we must confine ourselves to a secular, public ethical discourse suitable for a pluralistic society. The latter strategy seems unpromising as well. As I have argued, the most plausible substantive account of what is wrong with intentional killing (when it is wrong) relies on broadly accepted values of self-determination and well-being, and those values support not only withdrawing care but voluntary active euthanasia and assisted suicide as well, if adequate institutional safeguards are in place.

What makes intentionally killing a human being a moral wrong for which the killer is to be condemned is that the killer did this morally bad thing not inadvertently or even negligently, but with conscious purpose–with eyes open and a will directed toward that very object. But if a particular instance of intentional killing does not deprive a person of well-being, but rather relieves that person of what deprives of well-being, and is an exercise of autonomy, rather than a thwarting of it, then there is no basis for saying that this act was morally bad, at least in terms of the values of individual self-determination and well-being. And if the act is not morally bad, then it is hard to see how the fact that it is done intentionally can make it a wrong.

Of course, this qualifier "in the first instance" is extremely important. As proponents of the prudent public policy argument rightly note, certain types of acts, some instances of which are not wrong, nevertheless ought sometimes to be prohibited because a policy of allowing this type of act will lead to unacceptable consequences either for those directly involved or for others. But given the fundamental character of the values that speak in favor of allowing exceptions to the prohibition on intentional killing–the *same values that are the primary justification for the prohibition itself*, at least in public, secular moral discourse–the burden of argument to be borne by the prudent public policy argument is onerous. For reasons indicated earlier, I do not believe that this burden has been successfully borne. The case against allowing limited instances of intentional killing in medicine is greatly weakened as soon as these three points are acknowledged. First, since physicians already justifiably engage in intentional killing by withdrawing life-support in some cases, intentional killing per se is not incompatible with a proper conception of the physician's role. Second, merely allowing physicians to perform voluntary active euthanasia or to assist with suicide in certain cases does not place an obligation on physicians to engage in such practices. Third, the principled exceptions to the prohibition against intentional killing are deeply principled, that is, they spring from the same basic values that support the prohibition itself.[24]

There is, however, a more radical conclusion to be drawn from these reflections on principled exceptions to the prohibition against intentionally killing innocent persons. We might conclude, not that there are valid exceptions to the principle that it is wrong intentionally to kill innocent human beings, but that the principle itself ought to be abandoned, not qualified, and replaced with one that makes clearer the nature of the wrong that is committed in those cases in which intentional killing is wrong. The principled exception strategy's emphasis on consent points toward this other principle, and in doing so points beyond itself to a replacement for the prohibition against intentional killing, rather than to a qualification of it.

My suggestion is that the best account of the nature of the wrong that we do when we do wrong in intentionally killing is that we *violate an innocent human being's right to life*.[25] This enables us to explain why cases in which there is consent to being killed are justifiable: the right has been waived by the act of consenting. More important, perhaps, including a principle that articulates a right to life, rather than one which prohibits intentional killing, focuses on *the individual who is killed*, and this better accords with the secular account of why intentional killing is wrong when it is wrong, an account which, as I have suggested, is based on respect for the individual's self-determination and concern for well-being. In contrast, the principle that intentional killing is wrong makes no connection with any features of the victim at all, much less any which could serve to justify the prohibition.[26] In other words, the principle that it is wrong intentionally to kill innocent persons suggests that the wrongness of the act is to be understood by reference to the perpetrator, not the victim.

Reliance on the principle that intentional killing is wrong makes more sense, then, in an ethical theory that views the prohibition as an *agent-centered constraint* on action, while the principle that innocent human beings have a right to life fits better into an ethical theory that is *subject-centered* and takes certain features of individuals, namely their capacities for well-being and self-determination, as the source of moral constraints on the agency of others. Thus, we might conclude that the best solution to the problem of intentional killing–the one that makes the structure of the morality of intentional killing most perspicuous–is one which resolves the conflict between allegiance to the general prohibition and the conviction that some cases of intentional killing are justified by abandoning the prohibition and replacing it with the principle that innocent persons have a right to life.[27]

NOTES

1. It is instructive to note that the First Commandment is "Thou shalt not kill," not "Thou shalt not kill an innocent person," or "Thou shalt not kill except under such and such circumstances."

2. Treason is a possible exception.

3. For the distinction between excuse and justification, see H.L.A. Hart, *Punishment and Responsibility.* Oxford: Oxford University Press, 1968, pp. 28–53.

4. More specifically, all that may be needed in second degree murder is intention to do the act, with a high degree of foreseeability that a death may result. Wayne R. LaFave and Austin W. Scott, Jr., *Substantive Criminal Law*, vol. 1. St. Paul: West Publishing, 1986, pp. 303–305.

5. LaFave and Scott, vol. 2, pp. 248–251.

6. By one who is sane and over the age of legal discretion. LaFave and Scott, vol. 2, p. 246.

7. Sanford Kadish, "Authorizing Death," in Jules Coleman and Allen Buchanan, eds. *In Harm's Way.* New York: Cambridge University Press, 1993.

8. For a useful presentation of a number of official ethical statements by various health care professional groups, see *Ethics in Emergency Medicine,* Iserson et al., eds. Baltimore: Williams & Wilkens, 1986, pp. 240–262.

9. However, even if they are not powerful enough to solve the problem of intending death, these two approaches are not without moral implications. Under certain conditions, each would reduce the scope of the contradiction between the general prohibition and intuitions concerning particular cases. If a cognitivist conception of death came to be accepted, the first strategy would provide a clear and uncontroversial justification for administering lethal injections to anencephalics or permanently unconscious patients, without in any way restricting the generality of the prohibition against intentionally killing human beings. Similarly, if, as the second strategy advocates, we restrict the scope of the prohibition against intending death to human beings who have interests, and if the idea that those who are permanently bereft of all awareness lack interests, then killing such beings would not offend against the prohibition.

   Whether either of the changes that would be needed to give the first and second strategies moral bite will occur is a matter of speculation. In my opinion, wide acceptance of the view that basic moral principles generally apply only to human beings with interests and that the permanently unconscious have no interests is much more likely, at least in the near term, than the adoption of a cognitivist conception of death. However, the former change might well be a way-station on the path to the second. Quite independently of these possible developments, the first and second strategies are worth at least a brief consideration, if only because both point toward what is really at issue in the problem of intending death: What it is about a life—about the quality or character of life—that makes intentionally ending a life wrong, when it is wrong?

10. P. Foot, "The Problem of Abortion and the Doctrine of the Double Effect," *Oxford Review* 5; 1967: 5–15, reprinted in Bonnie Steinbock, ed. *Killing and Letting Die.* Englewood City, NJ: Prentice Hall, 1980, pp. 156–165.

11. Both versions of the conditions are cited in Donald B. Marquis, "Four Versions of Double Effect," *The Journal of Medicine and Philosophy*, 16; 1991: 516–517.

12. Nor do either (1) or (2), singly or in conjunction, entail that (3) It is always permissible to bring about a death, so long as it is merely foreseen and not intended. The latter principle, of course, is patently unacceptable, as a familiar example clearly shows. Suppose an unscrupulous merchant intends to make a profit by selling poison oil to unsuspecting customers. He merely foresees their deaths and does not intend them, either as an end or as a means. His action is still wrong.

13. Foot, *Ibid* 157–160.

14. This is not to say that such a view and, indeed, any view that relies heavily on a distinction between positive and negative duties, is without problems of its own. In particular, it must develop an adequate account of "levels" of duties, distinguishing basic from nonbasic duties, if the ordering principles noted are to be at all plausible. For example, it would not do to say that negative duties, no matter whether they are basic or not, always override positive ones. This would commit one to the wrongheaded view that the negative duty not to lie could never be overridden by a positive duty, for example, the duty to help save millions of lives.

15. Warren Quinn, "Reply to Boyle's 'Who is Entitled To Double-Effect?'" *The Journal of Medicine and Philosophy*, 16; 1991: 511–514.

16. This example is due to Dan Brock. It might be argued, of course, that once we add other conditions, such as proportionality, that is, that there is a good effect of such importance as to justify the evil, then the doctrine of double effect will only permit foreseen deaths in just those cases in which the Kantian injunction to treat persons as ends in themselves would permit them. I am not convinced that the addition of such conditions would produce a perfect congruence, but even if it did, it seems that the use of the doctrine of double effect would be redundant. If the point is to treat persons as ends in themselves, why should one think that it is either necessary or permissible to explicate this fundamentally anticonsequentialist notion in terms of apparently consequentialist considerations such as the proportionality between the magnitude of the evil that is foreseen and the good that is intended?

17. James Rachels, "Active and Passive Euthanasia," reprinted in *Contemporary Issues in Bioethics*, Tom L. Beauchamp and LeRoy Walters, eds. Encino, CA: Dickenson, 1978, pp. 291–294; also reprinted in Bonnie Steinbock, ed. *Killing and Letting Die.* Englewood Cliffs, NJ: Prentice-Hall, 1980; pp. 63–68. Originally appeared in *The New England Journal of Medicine*, 292, no. 2; 1975: 78–80.

18. My discussion of the positive and negative consequences of a policy of allowing some forms of intentional killing has benefited from a more detailed analysis of these issues by Dan W. Brock, "Voluntary Active Euthanasia," *Hastings Center Report*, 22, no. 2; 1992: 10.

19. See Allen Buchanan, Dan W. Brock, *Deciding For Others*. Cambridge: Cambridge University Press, 1989, pp. 29–40.

20. This is not to assume that the same institutional arrangements that would work there simply could be transferred to other cultures.

21. This fear is not merely speculative. In totalitarian regimes, physicians have become executioners, as in Hitler's "euthanasia" program.

22. Daniel Wikler makes this point as well (personal communication).

23. This is not to say that including an *obligation* to perform voluntary active euthanasia or to assist in suicide is incompatible with the role of physician—an essence, as it were, of physicianhood, a universal set of normative components of the role, valid for all times and places. What the proper normative constitution of a social role is can only be determined by complex moral reasoning that takes into account not only basic moral values but also the nature of the concrete social conventions and above all the social division of labor in a given historical setting. My suggestion is only that at this time, in our society, acknowledging the physician's right of conscientious refusal is morally and practically necessary, both as a matter of respecting the autonomy of physicians as individuals and in order to secure their cooperation in devising and effectively implementing adequate safeguards for voluntary active euthanasia and assisted suicide.

24. A more comprehensive discussion of the desiderata for a sound public policy allowing voluntary active euthanasia and assisted suicide would have to address the issue of the context in which such actions would be deemed legitimate. My opinion is that the strongest case for the claim that adequate safeguards can be developed will require that voluntary active euthanasia and physician-assisted suicide take place within medical institutions. It is an important feature of modern medical institutions that decisionmaking within them is to a large extent (a) public and (b) collective. These two features serve as significant constraints on decisionmaking and provide a foothold for adequate procedural safeguards and other checks on abuse and error. To put the same point differently, the prudent public policy argument is much more powerful against a policy that allows extrainstitutional voluntary active euthanasia and assisted suicide, than against a policy that allows them only within appropriate institutional contexts.

25. My own view is that rights principles are conclusions to be supported by complex arguments whose premises include reference to a plurality of fundamental values, such as individual well-being and self-determination, and contingent empirical assumptions about social institutions, some features of which are substantially conventional. In other words, accepting the proposal to replace the prohibition on intentional killing with a principle that human beings or innocent human beings have a right to life does not commit oneself either to a rights-based or a consequentialist ethical theory.

26. Albert Jonsen has pointed out to me that the prohibition, at least as it is stated in Catholic moral theology, always includes the qualification that the individual is innocent and that the traditional notion of innocence identifies it with harmlessness rather than lack of guilt. If this is so, then the prohibition, at least in those versions that include the qualifier "innocent," does point toward something about the victim that can be relevant to the wrongness of the act. However, by so doing, the prohibition opens itself to demands for an account of why innocence alone—as opposed say, to innocence and absence of consent—is the only feature of the victim that is morally relevant.

27. I am indebted to Dan Brock and Albert Jonsen for their perceptive comments on an earlier version of this paper.

Criteria That Make Intentional Killing Unjustified: Morally Unjustified Acts of Killing That Have Been Sometimes Declared Justified

ALBERT R. JONSEN

University of Washington, Seattle, Washington

The moral history of homicide is written at the very frontier of human morality, the definitive and deliberate ending of a human life. That frontier, like the front lines in a military conflict, advances and retreats continuously with the ebb and flow of beliefs and arguments that now broaden, now limit the ethical justifications for killing. The history of warfare, from the earliest protocols of Roman military law through the just war doctrines of medieval and renaissance Christianity to the mutual annihilation theories of the nuclear age, provide an apt example of the tides of moral justification and limitation on killing.

Teachings on the morality of suicide provide another. A vigorous debate between Platonists and Stoics in antiquity opened a spectrum of opinions. St. Augustine firmly repudiated that spectrum of opinions and issued a condemnation of suicide that was absolute: indeed, in his eyes, Judas's hanging himself was a more serious, more unforgivable sin than his betrayal of Jesus.[1] Under the dominance of Augustinian thought, Christian writers maintained an unbroken tradition that suicide was unconditionally sinful until 1647, when the idiosyncratic Dean of St. Paul's, John Donne, dared write his *Biathanatos. A Declaration of the Paradox or Thesis That*

Self-Homicide Is Not So Naturally a Sin That It May Never Be Otherwise.

Donne's subtitle nicely expresses the topic of this essay: When might something that is sinful (or as we in our more antiseptic secularism say, "unethical") be otherwise? My topic is, "Criteria that make intentional killing unjustified: Morally unjustified acts of killing that have been sometimes declared justified." I take for granted, as the premise of my discussion, that intentional killing is prima facie wrong. My task is to give an account of those circumstances under which the prima facie duty not to kill intentionally allows of exception or yields to another duty which, in given circumstances, appears more stringent. I intend to recall one historical case of an "unjustified act of killing that has sometimes been declared justified," place that case in its own historical setting of premises and arguments, and then reflect on its relevance for the current question of medical killing.

During the first five centuries of the Christian era, the Fathers of the Church almost unanimously repudiated killing for any reason whatsoever: even killing in self-defense was illicit. They interpreted Jesus' rebuke to Peter, "Put up your sword: they that use the sword shall perish by the sword," as an absolute prohibition of violence. As the Church became more fully integrated in the political life of the Empire, Christians were allowed to engage in military activities and thus to kill in the pursuit of "just wars." In the eighth and ninth centuries, the Church vigorously opposed those forms of private revenge killings that were customary in the Germanic lands, substituting judicially authorized killing. From the fifth to the twelfth centuries, defense of one's life under attack, within limits of necessity, was admitted for laity but not for clerics. In the twelfth century, the theological doctrine of "holy war" fueled the Crusades, and linked a divine command, mediated by a papal voice, to the previously accepted criteria for killing in a just war. From that time onward, a creeping tolerance opened the restrained definitions of most of the accepted justifications. Self-defense came to include defense of property, and then, in a peculiar eddy of moral confusion in the seventeenth century, to defense of personal honor. This justification was defended by arguing that honor was analogous to property, since some persons, such as noblemen and military officers, made a living on their honor. Shame or tarnished reputation literally might put them out of work. Thus, for some 50 years, between 1600 and 1650, it was a common, though not universal teaching of moral theologians, that an insulted gentleman could rectify a serious insult, in the absence of any lesser remedy, by killing his accuser.

Blaise Pascal, in his blistering critique of Jesuit casuistry, *The Provincial Letters*, was outraged by this teaching. In his diatribe against it, he singled out the Jesuit doctrine of "directing the intention" as the target of his attack. Pascal has his genial but naive mouthpiece, The Good Jesuit Father, explain,

> You should know then that this marvelous principle is our great method of directing the intention ... I want to show you this great principle in all its luster, on the subject of homicide, which it justifies in innumerable circumstances.... This method

of directing the intention consists in setting up as the purpose of one's action some lawful object ... when we cannot prevent the action, at least we purify the intention and thus we correct the viciousness of the means by the purity of the end ... this is how our Fathers have found a way to permit the acts of violence commonly practised in the defence of honor. For it is only a question of deflecting one's intention from the desire for vengeance, which is criminal, and applying it to the desire to defend one's honor, which is lawful.[2] (*Provincial Letters*, VII)

This passage is a malicious piece of Pascalian satire. Pascal pushes the "Good Father" into hyperbole, having him extol the "method of directing the intention" as an ethical device for "justifying homicide in innumerable circumstances." The method is, of course, a debased version of the doctrine of double effect. St. Thomas Aquinas was, I believe, the first to state that doctrine in precise terms. In response to the question, "Is it legitimate to kill in self-defense," he writes, "it is possible that one action has two effects, one of which is intended (*in intentione*), the other beyond intention (*praeter intentionem*). An act receives its moral quality from that which is intended, not from that which is beyond intention."[3] To introduce and insistently repeat the phrase, "directing the intention" as Pascal does, subtly changes the meaning which Aquinas, and subsequent theologians, appear to have given to the word "intention." For them, intention refers to the subjective appreciation of the nature of an action, its purpose, and the means required to attain it. In their view, there were certain intrinsically good or bad moral objects which agents might voluntarily adopt as goals and direct their energies toward accomplishing. Thus, defense of one's own life was such a morally good objective and one may take proportionate means to accomplish it. The means must be designed in such a way as to avoid killing the assailant if possible, but the aggressor's death is permissible if unavoidable. Above all, the death of the assailant must be "incidental" to the intention of saving one's own life.

Pascal's formulation, "directing the intention" suggests that the Jesuit casuists were claiming that an agent could change the nature of the action by merely shifting one's way of thinking about it: I now believe this action is sinful intentional killing; but now I believe it is a defense of my honor and so not sinful. Intention becomes a kind of cerebral spotlight that one can turn and illuminate one title of action and then another. In this view, intention begins to resemble another, quite different component of moral action, namely motive. It should be clear to all moralists, medieval or modern, that an agent can do an act of a certain sort which would be generally recognized as good or bad and have a motive that is contradictory: people do good things for bad motives and bad things for good motives. That, however, is not the issue here.

The more serious distortion in the passage, however, lies in the suggestion that "directing the intention" justifies homicide "in innumerable circumstances." This suggests that the Jesuit casuists found in that "method" precisely what Allen Buchanan has described in this volume as his "third strategy" for resolving the contradiction between the general prohibition of intentional killing and conflicting intuitions in particular cases. Buchanan correctly notes that the proposal to justify the killing of a person by arguing that the death was foreseen but not intended "offer[s a] partial solution to the problem.... But [does not come] close to providing a reconciliation across the whole range of intuitively justified cases" (p. 26). The partial solution consists in the fact that double effect argumentation does reconcile the general prohibition with some intuitions about the justifiablility of intending death. Indeed, Buchanan comments that the attempt to redescribe certain cases so that the double effect doctrine can be invoked amounts to "sheer sophistry," for example, a patient's intention is "not to die but to avoid futile suffering" (p. 28). This is exactly the sophistry that Pascal accused the casuists of perpetrating.

Buchanan, unlike Pascal, proposes several acute criticisms of the doctrine of double effect. He does admit that the doctrine has some plausibility in certain cases of killing, but proposes that other forms of ethical argument are more plausible. Still, Buchanan might be pleased to find that the originator of the double effect argument never offered it as a way of reconciling the prohibition against killing with our intuitions of its permissibility in certain cases. Aquinas drafted eight articles in his Question about Homicide. Only in the seventh, concerning self-defense, does he introduce the double effect argument. In the previous articles, he affirms that "in itself, it is never permissible to kill anyone since every person has a nature given by God, which we are bound to love and which we violate by killing." This is his statement of the general prohibition: "in itself" means "in principle." However, he argues in article two, that it is permissible to kill "sinners" insofar as they are "dangerous and corruptive" to the common good of the community. This elimination of corrupting elements is permissible only to those who are legitimate rulers acting according to law. It is never, he states in article six, permissible to kill "innocent person[s]," whose lives "conserve and promote the common good." In the final article, he points out that killing can be blameworthy only if it is "intended and voluntary." Thus, the eight articles constitute a defense of the general prohibition: it is wrong intentionally to take an innocent human life. On the contrary, it is permissible for civil authorities to take the life of those who corrupt the community.[4]

What is striking about Aquinas's treatise is the emphasis on "innocence." While the harsh totalitarian tone of his argument about the permissibility of judicial killing of sinners is offensive to our modern sensibilities, the general thrust of his argument is that deliberate killing is justified only if a person is a "nocens," that is, one who causes grievous harm to the community. "Innocent," to a Latin speaker, meant not "guiltless," but "harmless." He does not, in these texts, carefully define what "sinner" means, other than saying that the sinner corrupts the community. In his time, this may have included proselytizing but peaceable heretics; in our times, it might be limited to Saddam Hussein. In his time, it might include violent miscreants who roamed the dark alleys of Paris and for whom there were no penal institutions; in our time, we prefer to "put such people away" rather than kill them. Nevertheless, the killing of the innocent, that is, the innocuous, the harmless, is what Aquinas unequivocally condemned. "In no way is it permitted to harm the innocent (*nocere innocentem*)."

The introduction of the double effect argument in the seventh question about self-defense is necessitated by the restriction against private killing. Aquinas has allowed the killing of the harmful only by judicial officers. This had been painfully introduced into European law after the eighth century in the obstinate effort to abolish the customs of private revenge killing prevalent in the Germanic tribes. Intentional killing was, in Aquinas's view and that of most canon and civil lawyers, the business of the state and the state alone.

Self-defense, then, posed a problem. First, there had been a long Christian tradition that prohibited it as contrary to the Gospel injunction to turn the other cheek to violent attack. Second, as Aquinas himself notes, all men are given their life by God and we are bound to love them. Finally, the sense of "sinner" and "innocent" invoked in the earlier articles refers, it seems, to those who harm the common good, not the private good. (So, while an assailant can be described as potentially harmful, he is not harmful in the requisite sense that Aquinas has stated, namely, as *corruptivus boni communitatis*. Indeed, the assailant may not be a "sinner," in the sense of one who maliciously does harm to the common good (we note that Aquinas, unlike his later commentators, does not use the term "unjust aggressor" in this text.) Indeed, it is possible that the attacker does not "intend" harm but is, say, attempting to escape from some harm himself and you are in the way. Thus, presumably, a private person has no right to kill one who attacks him.

Yet, it appears odd to require a person to love, and thus, to refrain from harming someone who attacks him, since the victim is equally bound to love himself: love thy neighbor as thyself. Why must we prefer another's life to our own? In light of this reasoning, self-defense requires a special justification and the peculiar device of "*in intentione*," "*praeter intentionem*" is trundled out. It is, I think, a very limited device: it works well only on the paradoxical cases in which moral evil and moral good seem inextricably mixed: if I preserve my life, which is right, I take an innocent life, which is wrong; if I refrain from killing innocent life, which is right, I allow myself to be killed, which is wrong. Of course, in such paradoxical situations, either solution is equally blameless or blameful: thus, the one who defends oneself is permitted to take the life of the assailant, but equally is permitted to give up his or her life. Thus, it was common doctrine that clerics and monks who were bound to a higher virtue, should not defend themselves but permit themselves to be killed. The double effect argument seems only to be permission granted to those who choose to defend rather than die.

Now to the point of all this medievalia. The traditional arguments against intentional homicide, as they were developed through the Middle Ages, centered on the prohibition against killing the innocent, that is, the harmless. Those who did serious harm to the public good could be judicially killed. Self-defense was seen as posing a moral paradox, resolved as best it could be, by permitting the death of the assailant incidentally or "*praeter intentionem*." I propose that this set of ideas has constituted the dominant paradigm regarding the morality of killing from at least the thirteenth century until our own times.

The fault of the lax casuists whom Pascal castigated was not to have departed from the paradigm, but to have extended it too far. They remained within the paradigm that justified killing the harmful and within its analogy that allowed self-defense: they simply pushed the limits of self-defense onto indefensible grounds, the vindication of damaged reputation. Rightly, then, did Pascal excoriate them and rightly did their own casuistic colleagues view their opinion with skepticism, according it at best the status of "speculatively possible, but not permissible in practice;" their version of Buchanan's Prudent Public Policy strategy.

The case of the insulted gentleman, then, offers an example of a morally unjustified act that was sometimes declared justified. Its brief enjoyment of justification, however, was because of a culturally conditioned linkage between honor and livelihood and an exaggerated, but already decaying, exaltation of personal honor. Insofar as it stayed within the paradigm of prohibition of killing the harmless, it broke no radically new moral ground. The criticism to which it eventually succumbed was a criticism of the exaggerated exaltation of honor.

It is possible, however, to undertake quite a different form of justification of an action. This consists not in the extension of the characteristics of a paradigm case but in the proposal of an unprecedented paradigm. By unprecedented, I mean a paradigm that, although it might have been known both as a practice in a culture and as a problem known to the philosophers of that culture, it had never achieved prominence as a way of thinking about the moral justification of a certain action. Although espoused by some, it failed to make the cut as a favored, persuasive argument with the majority of people or of philosophers.

Allen Buchanan again offers an instructive example. He calls his fifth strategy, "the principled exception strategy" (p. 26). He proposes that legitimate exceptions to the general prohibition on intentionally killing the innocent may be grounded in the values of individual self-determination and well-being. What makes killing a human being morally bad, he says, "is that it deprives him of any form of well-being and puts an end to his self-determination." An act of intentional killing that "does not deprive a person of well-being, but rather relieves him of what deprives him of well-being, and is an exercise of one's autonomy, rather than a thwarting of it, then there is no basis for saying that this act was morally bad" (p. 37).

Buchanan offers a provocative thesis. When worked out in detail, it will give philosophical sophistication to the popular assertion that consent, voluntarily and consciously given, should suffice to justify active euthanasia. The Washington State Proposition 119 and California Initiative 161 were firmly founded in that belief: they legally authorized a physician to provide "aid-in-dying," that is, a painless and swift death, when a patient who was mentally competent freely and consciously requested it. An appeal to personal freedom and self-determination is highly persuasive in our culture. Had it not been for more persuasive "prudent public policy" reasons, the appeal to self-determination would very likely have prevailed with the voters.

The appeal to self-determination is, however, an appeal to an unprecedented paradigm. It departs radically from the long accepted paradigm for killing that centered on the concept of the innocuous. It asks for a new paradigm to move to the center of consideration about homicide. Buchanan, speaking of the weakness of the doctrine of double effect, notes that "what is striking and disturbing is that the doctrine is utterly blind to the whole question of consent" (pp. 29–30). In the context of its historical development and within the paradigm of innocuousness, this ought not to be surprising. The consent of the noxious person to be killed by judicial authority is clearly irrelevant as is the consent of the assailant. It is sufficient that they be noxious and aggressive. Consent, within that paradigm, simply plays no part. Thus, we find the legal maxim, which grew up along with the paradigm, that the consent of one killed does not constitute a defense against a charge of homicide.

Consent has become in recent times, a respectable justification for self-killing in the popular mind and has been endorsed by many philosophers and theologians. Consent, however, has never achieved the same status with regard to intentional killing of others. A new paradigm that replaced the innocuous subject with the self-determining, autonomous agent, was not effectively promoted in the public consciousness, nor did the philosophers who had transformed the doctrine on suicide by grounding it in consent, do the same for the killing of others. In actuality, there is little incentive to do so. Suicide is perpetually fascinating to philosophers: from Seneca to Camus, it has been considered a central, indeed, the only real philosophical problem. Homicide, on the other hand, is repellant and crude. Also, only the rarest cases raise the issue of whether consent is morally relevant: May a police officer shoot to death a person trapped in a burning truck who pleads for death? May survivors of a shipwreck accept the voluntary death of one of their number in order to lighten the boat? These are interesting, perplexing questions, but not of great philosophical interest.

The issue of medical killing, raised so acutely by the life-sustaining power of medical technologies, has provided the first real opportunity to formulate and push to center stage a new paradigm. Buchanan has begun to sketch the new paradigm in his paper. Others will follow his line of thought. I wish to offer some reflections on what happens when a long standing moral paradigm is under pressure from a new paradigm. While Buchanan's proposal is plausible, it is not unproblematic. In these concluding pages, I will suggest the problems that it raises.

When we are asked about criteria that will or will not justify action, we can trace argument from judgment back to rules, to principles and to theories, and then we can defend or demolish theories. However, this entire effort seems to me quite unidimensional. It is a kind of linear logic in a modal world. The real world of moral action and judgment is a world of probabilities and possibilities, optatives and subjunctives, necessities and contingencies. Any question about criteria ought to be articulated against this background.

The background itself is on two different but related scales: on the large scale of culture and history and on the small scale of cases. Social practices are those actions that have specified moral meanings in a given culture. For example, killing a human being is not a social practice; it is a physical event. In effect, a killing pure and simple never happens. What happens is a revenge killing, a defensive killing, a sacrificial killing, a punitive killing, and so forth. The adjective invokes a cluster of socially and historically beliefs that are proposed and defended (or assumed) in similarly social and historical ways. When such practices are called into question (and the reasons that they are called into question are various), the criteria for judgment must come from reflections about the culture that cultivated the practice.

This line of thought leads us to a problem, which some would consider a dead end. Moral actions of agents are measured against social practices, but what are social practices measured against? If nothing but themselves, how can they be called moral or be the measure of morality? It hardly seems a solution to enlarge the screen and say, as I have done, a coherent pattern of social practices, for this leaves us with the same question. What then can measure social practices other than principles? If so, why object, as I have done above, to the linear logic of practice to principle?

I suggest that the measure of a social practice is the moral paradigm that is embedded within it. A paradigm is, literally, an example and an example is, literally, a sample or a pattern. A moral paradigm is an abbreviated story that has few but striking details. It also incorporates a moral value that can be expressed as a principle. A paradigm can be "parsed," that is, its elements can be sorted out in such a way as to show their relationship to each other. One way to parse a paradigm is to set out the "claims," or assertions offered for general acceptance, the "grounds," or the specific facts about a situation that are offered to make good the claim, the "warrants," or general statements and maxims that authorize the rational moves between claims and grounds and, finally, the "backing," the body of reasoned experience relied on to validate warrant.[5]

The question of intentional killing now has, in our culture, a long preserved paradigm, that of prohibition on killing the innocent, to which the consent of the killed has no relevance, and an emerging paradigm, the permissibility of killing the voluntarily consenting. Each of these paradigms consists of claims, grounds, warrants, and backing. Each of them fits, either snugly or uncomfortably, into a culture that consists of many other practices with their paradigms. These other paradigms may or may not be "consistent" with the paradigm under consideration. Consistency, here, refers not to any absolute coherence, but rather a loose relationship in which a culture easily accommodates a paradigm or finds it a striking contrast with the prevailing mores. In other words, I am suggesting that the focus on principles exclusively as a mode for justification of practices is inadequate (just as, in my opinion, is the focus on consequences). A unitary approach to paradigms, which sees them as a cluster of circumstances, consequences, principles, and values, may takes us farther along the road of moral justification and will give us, I believe, a more exciting journey.

The problems may be illustrated by reflecting on the different formulations of paradigms that could arise from the assertion of self-determination as the central principle. The first formulation would be the broadest: anyone may kill any other person of sound mind when competently requested to do so. This paradigm only offers one characteristic of the parties involved, namely, a competent person competently requesting. A second formulation would be more descriptive: a physician may kill a competent person when competently requested to do so. Here, the agent is described as a physician. A third formulation might be: a physician may kill a competent patient who competently requests. The requester must, in this paradigm, be a patient of the physician. A fourth formulation might add other characteristics, such as a terminal condition or unrelieved pain. The Washington State and California "Aid-in Dying" proposals worked with a form of this fourth paradigm: A physician is permitted to kill a competent patient who competently requests and is in a terminal condition. The Dutch practice adds to terminal condition evidence of a persistent request and of intractable pain.

These different descriptions of agents and patients in these paradigms constitute what we have called the *grounds* when the paradigm is parsed. The challenge posed to ethical analysis is to show why these grounds, which are essentially circumstances of the case, support the claim that the killing is justified. Thus, the description of the agent as a physician must have some relevance to the claim that could not be sustained if the agent was merely described as a person. Similarly, it must be shown why qualifiers such as "terminal condition" and "intractable pain" are relevant to the support of the claim.

Buchanan's unprecedented paradigm, self-determination as the justification for intentional killing, seems compatible with the first, most broad formulation. Yet few of those who have supported active euthanasia have taken this position. Most supporters, it appears, embrace the third or fourth formulation: A physician may kill a competent patient who requests or who requests and is terminal and/or in pain. If these latter formulations are preferred, one might wonder why the characteristics of being physician, being patient, being in pain and terminal are part of the paradigm which, in its abstract formulation rests so heavily on self-determination.

If being a patient is considered important to the paradigm, then presumably some sort of formal relationship between agent and patient is required for a reason that is intrinsic to the justification of the act. That formal relationship, namely being a patient of a physician, is culturally and historically defined and, in our culture, that definition is quite "thick." It involves a range of understandings and expectations that are complex and layered and is textured with intersecting obligations. The introduction of a newly formulated paradigm challenges the cultural and historical paradigm. Already, that paradigm has been strongly challenged and significantly modified by the introduction of the concept of the autonomous patient. However, the autonomous patient is not entirely strange to the history of medicine (recall Plato's discussion of the free and slave physician) and it may be that the overturning of medical paternalism, which we consider a triumph of modern bioethics, is not as stunning a victory as we like to think. There may be enough in the cultural and historical tradition of medicine to accommodate the change. The question to be asked of the new paradigm of killing is whether it also can be accommodated within the understanding of the relationship or whether it will radically modify that understanding. This speculative problem is echoed in the remarks of physicians who say, when confronted with the prospect of being active euthanizers, "that's not what being a doctor is all about" or something similar.

If qualifiers such as terminal condition or intractable pain are introduced, it may be asked why these empirical states are added to self-determination pure and simple. They seem to be limitations of freedom and, in the nature of things, call for assessment by someone other than the self-determining party who requests to be killed. Thus, if we say that intractable pain is a condition, a physician who is asked to kill a patient must make a professional judgment that pain is present and is indeed intractable. This appears to introduce another self-determining party who could veto the self-determining request of the patient. If so, we appear to have something more than a principle of self-determination as the basis of the paradigm.

I shall not pursue this investigation any further. I offer it merely to demonstrate how a paradigm approach might differ from a principle approach to the problem of medical killing. As one moves from assertion of principle to the exposition of the grounds and warrants for a claim, questions other than the linear relationship between act and principle arise. In my view, these questions are not merely matters of prudent public policy, but are intrinsic to the moral structure of the problem.

The contemporary proposals for assisted suicide or medical killing are, in essence, proposals to inaugurate a social practice. It is misleading, I think, to say that they have the intention of alleviating pain; this is a motive, not an intention. The intention is the innovative moral practice itself, or rather the architecture of the practice, whereby medical care, already accepted as a moral good, is given an expanded definition of its task and practitioners are charged with a responsibility they have not previously had. The proposal is to endorse medical killing as a practice integral to the practice of medicine (which, we may recall, more than once had to be justified as a social practice itself). This is analogous to other historical proposals about killing: defensive killing was slowly endorsed; tyrannicide was tentatively endorsed and still has its defenders; honor killing was briefly endorsed, then thoroughly repudiated.

When medical killing is proposed as a candidate for acceptance as a social practice, two features deserve attention. The first is the conception and reality of modern medicine that seems to inform the intention behind medical killing, namely, the apparent absence of humaneness as an almost intrinsic aspect of technological, scientific medicine. Arguments that favor assisted suicide inevitably affirm that this practice would remedy the inhumane condition of dying within technological medicine. This claim undoubtedly has rhetorical appeal. The second feature is the invocation of autonomy as a justification of assisted suicide. The intention is to advance the realm of autonomy. This is not, as we have noted, an entirely new idea. In the ancient debates over suicide, almost all philosophical sects admitted the moral legitimacy of suicide and, among these the Stoics, and in particular Seneca, affirmed sovereign freedom as the moral justification. Still, in that debate, most ancient authors, with the exception of Seneca, did not simply assert sovereign freedom as the justification of self-killing: rather the circumstances and the motive were crucial in determining whether suicide was "noble" or "ignoble." In other words, the principle of autonomy needed to be supplemented by the convergence of many values. The "grounds" were as important as the "warrant" of freedom.

Both of these features constitute aspects of the intention in medical killing. The question is whether one or both of them have more than a rhetorical appeal, but can be fitted into a social, cultural setting, immune to critiques that call that setting into question. The repudiation of killing for honor came at a time when the Renaissance ideology of glory and valor was already deteriorating; it may be ironic that proposals for medical killing appear at a time when the critique of technological medicine is well underway and when the briefly undisputed sway of the principle of autonomy is waning. Indeed, the principle of autonomy itself, which has in recent times pushed almost all other moral principles to the side of the stage, may be the object of some skepticism from philosophers who begin to wonder whether it is strong enough to bear the weight of an entire morality.

NOTES

1. ST. AUGUSTINE, *The City of God*, [1.17]. Translated by John Healey. New York: E.P. Dutton Publishers, 1945.

2. BLAISE PASCAL, *The Provincial Letters*. Translated by A. Krailsheimer. London: Penguin Books, 1967.

3. ST. THOMAS AQUINAS, *Summa Theologiae*. II-II, 64, 7. Latin text and English translation, Introductions, Notes, Appendices and Glossaries. New York: McGraw-Hill, 1962–1989, vol. 38.

4. AQUINAS, *Summa Theologiae*. II-II, 64, 1–8.

5. ALBERT R. JONSEN, STEPHEN E. TOULMIN, *The Abuse of Casuistry. A History of Moral Reasoning*. Berkeley: University of California Press, 1988, pp. 321–326.

What Makes Intentional Killing Unjustified?

RUTH MACKLIN

Albert Einstein College of Medicine, Bronx, New York

It is beyond serious doubt that morally unjustified acts of killing have at some times been declared justified in various societies or groups, but this claim is more complicated than it first appears. Do such acts include those declared justified by a very small minority of people, despite the fact that the acts have been widely condemned as morally unjustified by most people at other times and places? Some examples might be killing as a form of ritual sacrifice and hanging women for witchcraft by the Puritans in colonial New England. Do such acts include those declared justified during a brief historical period, despite the fact that the acts were condemned before or after that time? This is Albert Jonsen's example (in this volume)–that of a nobleman or gentleman whose intentional killing of a person who had insulted him was morally justified during the period between 1600 and 1650. Do such acts include intentional killings that were approved by many people yet were clear instances of racial bigotry, such as the lynching of African Americans in the American South? And do they include examples from the Holocaust, the Nazi euthanasia program as well as the gassing of millions of Jews, Gypsies, homosexuals, and others viewed as enemies of the Third Reich?

One complicating factor in the claim that morally unjustified acts of killing have sometimes been declared justified is the word "sometimes." How many times, by how many people, when and where must an act of killing have been declared justified in order for the declaration to be taken seriously? Jonsen's example of justified killing to defend one's honor spanned a period of only 50 years. Killing women

accused of witchcraft was carried out in a small area of New England for a short period of time. Our inclination is to dismiss these cases as aberrant, failed attempts at
moral justification.

A second complicating factor lies in the presuppositions embedded in the
phrase "morally unjustified acts of killing." The phrase presupposes that criteria for
unjustified acts of killing can be identified and will most likely be acknowledged
once they are spelled out.

All of the examples I just gave accurately fit the description of acts of killing
that have sometimes–by however few people and for however short a time–been
declared justified. They also presystematically fit the description of morally unjustified acts of killing because no one is likely today to question that moral judgment
even in the absence of providing the criteria that would make them unjustified.

These examples can serve as paradigms precisely because they help us locate
the criteria that make intentional killing unjustified. Other examples, which I will discuss in more detail later, cannot serve as paradigms although I will maintain that they
are also instances of morally unjustified intentional killing. These examples include
capital punishment and the killing of a woman or her lover by the woman's husband
who discovers the adulterous affair. I will conclude with a discussion of my only
extended example of intending death in medicine, the Nazis' so-called euthanasia
program. I hope to show that the criteria that make intentional killing unjustified in
the paradigm cases are also sound and appropriate for use in the medical context.

I begin with the paradigms. What makes them paradigm cases of unjustified
acts of killing that have sometimes been declared justified? In each case, the circumstances under which the acts have been declared justified rest on beliefs that are either
demonstrably false or highly questionable but unprovable, and also on values that are
"off the scale" of what is held to be acceptable in civilized society.[1] Mention of "civilized society" raises one more complicating factor. We have to grant an additional
premise in order to accept any examples as paradigms of unjustified acts of killing:
the premise that the thesis of cultural ethical relativism is mistaken.

There is insufficient space here to discuss that premise fully, but I need to make
clear which thesis I am rejecting. It is the view that ethics are inherently relative to
time and place, that ethical rightness and wrongness are simply products of the cultural and historical milieu from which they emanate, and that whatever members of a
society approve of is right, whatever they disapprove of is wrong. Anyone who
accepts the thesis of cultural ethical relativism cannot be critical on moral grounds of
acts of intentionally killing human beings in religious sacrifice, ritual killing in cultures practicing that rite, hanging women for witchcraft in Salem in the seventeenth
century, intentional killing in the years 1600 to 1650 by a nobleman or gentleman by
a person who had insulted him, lynchings of African Americans by whites in the
South, and the gassing of millions of Jews, Gypsies, and others viewed as enemies of
the Third Reich. All these acts of killing were products of a cultural milieu, of shared
values at a certain time in history or in a particular geographical locale. Even if not

everyone in that culture, nation, or era accepted the acts as morally justified, a sufficient number of people held them to be justified for the practice to endure. To accept the thesis of cultural ethical relativism would be to render these acts immune from moral criticism. If ethical relativism were a logically coherent position, it would follow that members of one culture or historical era could never criticize on moral grounds the socially approved practices of another time or place.[2]

According to what criterion was the killing of his insulter by a nobleman or military officer declared justified in the years between 1600 and 1650? Jonsen's example is interesting precisely because the proffered justification, when applied properly, does count as a moral justification of intentional killing. That justification was self-defense, which is accepted as morally valid by all but thoroughgoing pacifists.

So it was not the justification itself that constituted this peculiar moral confusion, as Jonsen views it, but rather the expanded application of the principle "killing in self-defense is morally justified" to instances of personal honor. As Jonsen notes, self-defense was first broadened to include defense of property and then to embrace defense of personal honor. Reasoning by analogy, the theologians who held this view argued that honor was analogous to property since people like noblemen and military officers "made a living on their honor." What was wrong with this justification was not the underlying moral principle that killing in self-defense is morally permissible, but the weakness of the analogy between loss of life, loss of property, and loss of honor. As Jonsen notes, those who made the analogy "pushed the limits of self-defense onto indefensible grounds, the vindication of damaged reputation" (Jonsen, p. 47).

Acts of hanging women in New England for witchcraft in the colonial period rested on a justification of an entirely different sort. That practice rested on a false metaphysical belief conjoined with a particular value held by the Puritans. The false belief was that the women who were accused as witches actually possessed some evil supernatural powers. The value was that possession of those powers was sufficient grounds for state-sanctioned killing. The value alone is not sufficiently off-scale to condemn killing alleged witches, since another example of state-authorized killing, capital punishment, has been held justifiable for people convicted of murder and treason, and proposed even for drug dealers. Although I believe capital punishment is morally unjustifiable, that form of intentional killing does not have the status of a paradigm of unjustified killing. In order to be a paradigm, a case has to be a clear, undisputed example. What makes the killing of women in Salem accused of witchcraft a paradigm is not the value alone–that the state may kill its citizens for crimes–but that value conjoined with the false imputation of evil supernatural powers to ordinary citizens in the community.

If the term *justification* can be applied at all to bias-related killings, it is different from the ones just cited for the first two paradigm cases. Racial and religious bigots rest their actions on a blend of beliefs and values, typically beginning with the idea that the despised minority is in some way inferior, not fully human, or deserving of treatment that would be held morally wrong if the victims were members of the majority's racial or religious group. Lynching African Americans in the South was surely motivated by racial hatred and bigotry, but the intention, as I understand Jonsen's account, was to ratify a social practice in which whites could take the law into their own hands in which African Americans were concerned. Hence, intentional killing could only be justified by the judgment that African Americans did not deserve the rights accorded to whites, specifically, the Constitutional protections of due process.

The criterion that makes bias-related acts of killing wrong is the morally obtuse belief system of bigots. They consider skin color, ethnicity, or religion a characteristic that renders the minority group inferior to them. The value corresponding to that belief is that members of those racial, ethnic, or religious groups are sufficiently inferior to justify intentionally killing them. That, by the way, is the same justification used to defend the killing of nonhuman animals for food, clothing, or biomedical research.

To identify an alleged justification for Hitler's killing of millions of Jews would be to dignify the Holocaust by assimilating it to behavior that could admit of justification. Whether the Nazis believed that Jews were a threat to the racial purity of Aryans or to the monetary interests of German business and banking concerns, those beliefs pale by comparison with the off-scale values that enabled physicians, as well as government and military officials in a modern civilized state to commit large-scale acts of genocide.

What do these paradigms of unjustified acts of killing that have sometimes been declared justified tell us about criteria that make intentional killing unjustified? I have said that the circumstances under which the acts have been declared justified rest on beliefs that are either demonstrably false or highly questionable but unprovable, and on values that are "off the scale" of what is held to be acceptable in civilized society. Metaphysical beliefs are problematic because empirical justification is impossible. How can one prove that there are no real witches, or humans possessed with evil supernatural powers? Killing people as a religious sacrifice–because the act is ordained by the gods–rests on two unprovable metaphysical assumptions, that there are gods and that those gods ordain such intentional killings.

Hanging or burning women for witchcraft rests on the metaphysical assumptions that evil supernatural powers exist and that some people are possessed with those powers. However, the correlative value–that the state may kill its citizens for reasons the state deems appropriate–is the same value that operates in the justification for capital punishment. There are no doubt people who maintain that capital punishment is justified, at least for some crimes, yet who would reject as unjustified the killing of women thought to be witches. Rejecting the latter as unjustified could, in turn, rest on a belief or a value. A defender of capital punishment might dismiss the notion that there are witches, and for that reason reject the practice. Or the defender might take the value stance that the state may kill citizens for some reasons but not for others, for example, for premeditated murder but not for drug dealing or witch-craft.

Unlike the paradigms of unjustified acts of killing that have sometimes been declared justified, the second set of examples on my list does not involve false or bizarre beliefs conjoined with values. It is the values alone that are presumed to jus-tify the killings, without any accompanying false or metaphysical beliefs, beliefs about racial inferiority, or errors of analogical reasoning such as assimilating liveli-hood to life. The nonparadigmatic examples include capital punishment and the killing of a woman or her lover by the woman's husband who discovers the adulter-ous affair. I will examine each example briefly.

The main difference between proponents and opponents of capital punishment lies in the value they place on the life of individuals found guilty of murder or other capital crimes. Defenders of capital punishment typically accept a retributive justifi-cation for capital punishment, thereby accepting the notion that one who has com-mitted a crime justly deserves punishment similar in kind and degree: Murderers deserve to die. Opponents of capital punishment typically reject the retributive justi-fication.

As for the justification based on deterrence, opponents of capital punishment usually marshall statistics that tend to show it has no deterrent value. Murder rates are higher in states that have executed convicted murderers, or some such facts. Yet even if capital punishment were shown to have some deterrent value, that would not auto-matically lead opponents of capital punishment to change their view about its per-missibility. The value involved in state-sanctioned killing would remain unacceptable to many who hold that practice to be unjustified. Each year that Mario Cuomo was the New York Governor, he vetoed the state legislature's bills proposing reinstate-ment of capital punishment in New York, but he favored life imprisonment without parole for those convicted of capital crimes.

There may still be laws on the books of some states that do not classify as homi-cide the killing by a husband of his adulterous wife or her lover. (Perhaps such acts are classified as justifiable homicide.) These so-called "crimes of passion" have been seen as justified, under the circumstances, in numerous cultures at various times in history including the present. Although killing by a cuckolded husband is morally unjustified, I must establish, why it does not count as a paradigm. The value that would permit such killing with impunity is off-scale in all but those cultures whose religious code specifies killing as a punishment for adultery. There is no secular eth-ical principle or standard that could sanction killing as a fitting response to adultery. A society or legal system that does sanction such killing would have to hold that it is a reasonable response on the part of a man who discovers his wife in an adulterous affair. The "reasonable cuckold" standard is not one that can be publicly and impar-tially endorsed.

A man's killing his adulterous wife or her lover is not a reasonable response to discovering the affair, but rather goes to an irrational extreme. The very irrationality

of the act prompts a question about the state of mind of the perpetrator. If cuckolded
husbands can be viewed as so blinded with rage that their condition is akin to "temporary insanity," there is a moral (as well as legal) defense that can operate at least as
a mitigating factor. Although I think it is a mistake to impute that mental state to all
husbands who discover their wives' extramarital affairs and subsequently kill the
woman or her lover, it may be true of some. That would entitle such killers, on a case-
by-case basis, to a lesser charge than intentional homicide. The result, however,
would not be to declare the acts of killing justified, but rather to hold the killer less
culpable because of diminished capacity, temporary insanity, or other mental defect
at the time of the killing. It is this uncertainty that renders this class of action nonparadigmatic. Although they are not paradigms, they do belong in the category of
unjustified acts of killing that have sometimes been declared justified.

Before concluding this exploration of criteria that make intentional killing
unjustified, I want to turn to a discussion of Hitler's so-called euthanasia program.[4]
(I say "so-called," since it is obvious that the intentional killings were not "mercy
killings" in any sense of that term, nor were they motivated by a desire to relieve suffering.) In an examination of morally unjustified acts of killing that have sometimes
been declared justified, it is important to make a clear distinction between the Nazis'
mass killings of Jews in gas chambers and the Nazi euthanasia program. The former
acts arose from such off-scale values as not to allow anything to count as a justification for intentional killing. The misnamed euthanasia program, on the other hand,
rested on a justification that is dangerously close to one adopted by some people
today: intending or permitting death in order to conserve resources.

The first phase of the Nazi euthanasia program was known as the "children's
euthanasia program." In August 1939, a circular issued by the Reich Interior Ministry
mandated a "duty to report deformed births." All newborn infants "suspected of suffering from the following congenital defects" were to be registered: (1) Idiocy and
Mongolism (particularly cases which involve blindness and deafness); (2)
Microcephalie; (3) Hydrocephalus of a serious or progressive nature; (4) Deformities
of every kind, in particular the absence of limbs, spina bifida, etc.; (5) Paralysis
including Little's disease.[5] Some of these infants were identified by "assessors" (who
did not actually examine them) and marked for death. This group was transferred to
special "pediatric clinics," where they were either starved to death, given lethal injections, or died of diseases caused by malnutrition.[6]

Thus, some of these children marked for death were actively killed, while others were simply allowed to die. Their parents were pressured to allow the infants to
be transferred to the special clinics on the grounds that they would be given "optimum treatment." The stated reason was an obvious falsehood, clearly intended to
deceive the parents about the purpose of the transfer.[7] Although it was possible for
parents to refuse, they had to sign a declaration committing themselves to remove the
children from the hospital, and provide supervision and care.[8]

Again in order to deceive, the cause of death was listed as "a more or less ordinary disease such as pneumonia, which could even have [a] kernel of truth...."[9] Parenthetically, we may wonder, from a moral point of view, how much this misrepresentation of the cause of death differs from that of Dr. Timothy Quill in the case of his patient, Diane. She died from a self-administered overdose of narcotics supplied by Dr. Quill. He listed the cause of death as "acute leukemia." Quill noted in his published article that although that was the truth, "it was not the whole story."[10]

Hitler's adult euthanasia program had a separate organization and history from the children's program. It began with a statement in August 1939 by Philipp Bouhler, then head of the Party Chancellery, that the purpose of eliminating persons having a "life unworthy of life" was not only to continue the "struggle against genetic disease" but also to free up hospital beds and personnel for the coming war.[11]

The focus of the adult euthanasia program was on adult chronic patients, especially mental patients. Implementation of the program involved virtually the entire psychiatric community, as well as physicians from the general medical community.[12] In a later phase of the program—referred to in Nazi documents as "wild euthanasia"—physicians were empowered to act on their own initiative regarding who would live or die.[13]

At a meeting of the steering group in October 1939, the statement of purpose was translated into a cost-benefit assessment of how many would be killed.

> The number is arrived at through a calculation on the basis of a ratio of 1000:10:5:1. That means out of 1000 people 10 require psychiatric treatment; of these 5 in residential form. And, of these, 1 patient will come under the programme. If one applies this to the population of the greater German Reich, then one must reckon with 65–75,000 cases.[14]

The program proceeded according to schedule, and by the end of August 1941, when the gassing phase was ended, 70,273 people had been killed.[15]

When the question was posed of how the killings would be done, the initial answer was again arrived at by a cost-benefit analysis.

> The number referred to by Party Comrade Brack also tallies with [Heyde's] own estimation. It makes the proposed method of injections put forward by Professor Nitsche unviable. For the same reason, the use of doses of medicine is also impossible.... The question has been discussed with the director of the Reich Criminal Police Department.... We are in agreement with him that CO (Carbon Monoxide) is the best method.[16]

As for just which inmates of psychiatric asylums were to be selected for the euthanasia program, "the criteria for assessment were ... periodically adjusted."[17] Initially, patients who could perform useful work were to be excluded from this action, as well as people who had had a stroke and had become "mentally defective," and "war disabled who had suffered some kind of mental damage."[18] By 1941, the exclusion criterion of war service was eliminated.

The final set of criteria for assessment of candidates for the adult euthanasia program was issued in March 1941, before the official ending of the program. The document explicitly excluded senility as a criterion: "Extreme caution in cases of senility. Only urgent cases, for example, criminals or asocials are to be included.... This reference to senile patients does not apply to aged patients with psychoses, such as schizophrenia, epilepsy, and so forth, who are basically included in the programme."[19]

Two recent commentators note the centrality of the economic justification in the Nazi euthanasia program and suggest that our own society may be only a small step away from that slide down the slippery slope.

Laurence McCullough argues that the accuracy of the comparison between the Nazi euthanasia program and our own biomedical practices depends on which features are taken to be relevantly similar or different.

> We see that what got German society on the slippery slope, indeed what characterized the slope, was the racist attitudes already in place. It is a reasonable defence and distinguishes our case from theirs, for us to say that we don't have those attitudes.... *Our* slippery slope might yet be analogous to Germany's in a more abstract way. If we consider the rationale which gives social utility or economic returns precedence over individual freedom, then we might see how our society could approach the kind of thinking that underlay the Nazi experience. There, racism overrode personal autonomy; here, it might be an economic rationale—the attitude that we won't spend so much per year to keep somebody alive on the slim chance of recovery.[20]

This view is echoed and reinforced by Alan Weisbard and Mark Siegler, who observe that the slide down one slippery slope has already begun, and now is the time to be vigilant. Their particular concern is withholding food and fluids from dying patients, conjoined with recent furious efforts to control the costs of medical care.

> We have witnessed too much history to disregard how easily society disvalues the lives of the "unproductive"—the retarded, the disabled, the senile, the institutionalized, the elderly—of those who in another time and place were referred to as "useless eaters." The confluence of the emerging stream of medical and ethical opinion favoring legitimation of withholding fluids and nutrition with the torrent of public and governmental concern over the costs of medical care ... powerfully reinforces our discomfort.[21]

It is easy to see how withholding food and water can be assimilated to Nazi practices. The Nazi doctor, Hermann Pfannmuller, was credited with the policy of starving to death those selected for the children's euthanasia program, rather than wasting medication on them.[22] According to the account of a visitor to the institution Pfannmuller directed, he said:

> "We do not kill ... with poison, injections, etc.; ... No, our method is much simpler and more natural, as you see." ... The murderer explained further then, that sudden withdrawal of food was not employed, rather gradual decrease of the rations. A lady who was also part of the tour asked–her outrage suppressed with difficulty–whether a quicker death with injections, etc., would not at least be more merciful.[23]

The irony of the visitor's question serves as a reminder that intentional killing by lethal injection would probably have brought about a more "merciful" death than starvation for these children. But unlike patients in the last throes of terminal illness, the children in the Nazi euthanasia program were deliberately selected to die. It is a cruel irony to voice an ethical indictment of the mode of death, when it is the very fact of death that constitutes the moral outrage.

The same can be said for the cases of Baby Doe in Bloomington, Indiana, and the Johns Hopkins baby immortalized in the bioethics classic film, "Who Should Survive?" The fact that the babies were not fed, and hence starved to death, renders these cases unjustified intentional killings. Both infants would have lived if their parents had not refused to consent to surgery to correct their intestinal malformation. And both would have lived had a court order been sought and granted to override parental refusal. Any defense of the form, "we didn't intentionally kill these babies, we just let them die" is identical to that offered by the doctors who engineered Hitler's children's euthanasia program.

How far removed are we today from the justification used by the Nazis for intentional killing and intending death by withdrawal of treatment in their euthanasia program? Consider a statement made in 1984 by a physician, following the passage of amendments to the Child Abuse and Neglect Prevention and Treatment Act and ensuing federal regulations.

> The law now states that in obstetrical units, babies must be fed and given full support regardless of how extensive and hopeless their congenital malformations.... These [issues] must be viewed not only in the light of the individual's right to life, but in that of society's right for its members to have pleasant and productive lives, not to be lived mainly to support the growing numbers of hopelessly disabled, often unconscious people whose costly existence is consuming so much of the gross national product.[24]

The author of this article is careful to point out that he is not referring to defects that can be treated (the author cites harelips, spina bifidas, or deformities of the extremities). He does, however, include "totally incurable and accurately diagnosable brain defects" such as Down's syndrome, stating that "No child with Down's syndrome ever grew up to be self-sustaining."

It is clear that this physician was not endorsing intentional killing by active means of infants with Down's syndrome or other groups for whom he claims "there should be no reason to support life artificially," such as "oldsters with mental deterioration from stroke or Alzheimer's disease [who have] become totally incompetent to care for themselves." However, he does assert that "there should be no support from the community or the state" to keep such people alive. It is worth recalling that in 1939, under the children's euthanasia program fashioned by the Nazis, it was possible for parents to refuse to have their children transferred to the special "pediatric clinics" if they signed a declaration committing themselves to remove the children from the hospital and provide supervision and care.

The primary, economic intention of the Nazi euthanasia program was identical to what is being proposed by many in the United States today for curtailing medical treatment. If we think that Hitler's euthanasia program was a morally unjustified instance of intending death, we need to identify the criterion that made those acts wrong. It would be odd, if not dishonest, to conclude that what made the Nazi euthanasia program morally unjustified was that the practice included cases of intentional killing. What made the practice unjustified was the judgment that some lives were not worth living—"lives unworthy of life," along with the judgment that conserving resources is a more important value than preserving life.

The Nazi example is one of several paradigms used to illustrate my main thesis: What makes intentional killing unjustified is not the intention alone, but the intention conjoined with false or unprovable beliefs or off-scale values—or both. Killing a person who threatens one's life is intentional killing, yet it can be justified on grounds of self-defense. But when the notion of self-defense is expanded to include defense of one's honor, then the killing is unjustified because the value of preserving one's honor is incommensurate with the value of human life. Hanging women accused of being witches is intentional killing grounded in a false or unprovable belief (that the women possessed evil supernatural powers) conjoined with the value that permits state-sanctioned killing. The moral permissibility of state-sanctioned killing of murderers and those who commit high treason is a matter on which reasonable people disagree, but the imputation of evil, supernatural powers to ordinary citizens cannot meet the evidentiary standards required for a just system of punishment.

The criteria that make intentional killing unjustified in these paradigm cases are also sound and appropriate for use in the medical context. Thus, a false belief on the part of a physician or a relative who kills a patient (for example, the belief that the patient wanted to be killed) or an unprovable belief (that the patient would be better off in the afterlife) would make the intentional killing unjustified. Killing a patient either by active euthanasia or by removing life supports on the grounds that continuing to treat the patient costs society too much money is also unjustified because the

No Consent

justification rests on the off-scale value that the worth of human life can be measured in monetary terms.

It is more difficult, however, to determine what might make intentional killing justified in the medical context. The paradigms of justified intentional killing, that is, killing in self-defense when one's life is threatened or killing enemy soldiers in a just war, have no analogue in the medical setting. The converse of the criteria that make intentional killing unjustified cannot do the job by themselves. The presence of true or provable beliefs, conjoined with accepted, "on-scale" values, is not sufficient to serve as a justification for the intentional killing of patients.

NOTES

1. For a discussion of "off-scale" values, see M. P. Battin, *Ethics in the Sanctuary*. New Haven: Yale University Press, 1990.

2. See Bernard Williams, *Morality: An Introduction to Ethics*. New York: Harper & Row, 1972, for a persuasive statement of the view that ethical relativism is logically incoherent.

3. Islamic law contains this penalty for adultery, and it is imposed in some fundamentalist Islamic societies.

4. Portions of the remainder of this paper are adapted from my "Which Way Down the Slippery Slope? Nazi Medical Killing and Euthanasia Today," in Arthur L. Caplan, ed. *When Medicine Went Mad: Bioethics and the Holocaust*. Clifton, NJ: Humana Press, 1992, pp. 173–200.

5. J. Noakes, G. Pridham eds., *Nazism 1919–1945*, vol. 3, *Foreign Policy, War and Racial Extermination*, Exeter Studies in History, No. 13, Exeter: Exeter University Publications, 1988, p. 1006.

6. Noakes and Pridham, *Nazism 1919–1945*, p. 1007.

7. Robert Jay Lifton, *The Nazi Doctors: Medical Killing and the Psychology of Genocide*. New York: Basic Books, 1986, p. 54.

8. Noakes and Pridham, *Nazism 1919–1945*, p. 1007.

9. Lifton, *The Nazi Doctors*, p. 55.

10. Timothy E. Quill, "Death and Dignity: A Case of Individualized Decision Making," *New England Journal of Medicine* 324; March 7, 1991: 691–694.

11. Robert N. Proctor, *Racial Hygiene: Medicine Under the Nazis*. Cambridge, MA: Harvard University Press, 1988, p. 182.

12. Lifton, *The Nazi Doctors*, p. 65.

13. Lifton, *The Nazi Doctors*, p. 96.

14. Noakes and Pridham, *Nazism 1919–1945*, p. 1010.

15. Proctor, *Racial Hygiene*, p. 191.

16. Noakes and Pridham, *Nazism 1919–1945*, pp. 1010–1011.

17. Noakes and Pridham, *Nazism 1919–1945*, p. 1017.

18. Noakes and Pridham, *Nazism 1919–1945*, p. 1013.

19. Noakes and Pridham, *Nazism 1919–1945*, p. 1018.

20. Laurence McCullough, cited in David Lamb, *Down the Slippery Slope: Arguing in Applied Ethics*. New York: Croom Helm, 1988, p. 29.

21. Alan J. Weisbard, Mark Siegler, "On Killing Patients with Kindness: An Appeal for Caution," in John D. Arras and Nancy K. Rhoden,. eds. *Ethical Issues in Modern Medicine*, 3rd ed. Mountain View, CA: Mayfield Publishing Company, 1989, p. 218.

22. Lifton, *The Nazi Doctors*, p. 62.

23. Lifton, *The Nazi Doctors*, p. 62.

24. George Crile, Jr., "The Right to Life," *Medical Tribune*, December 19, 1984, p. 27.

Intention, Foresight, and Killing

RAYMOND G. FREY

Bowling Green State University, Bowling Green, Ohio

There is no issue more vexing in substantive ethics generally and in medical ethics in particular than that of whether a genuine distinction can be drawn between intending death and merely foreseeing death as a side-effect of one's act and, if such a distinction can be drawn, whether it can be used to mark off moral differences between cases. This issue haunts discussions of killing, in cases of abortion, euthanasia, self-defense, suicide, and physician-assisted suicide. It has been one of the main bones of contention among parties to the debate over the viability of the doctrine of double effect; and it is, when allied with a whole array of concerns having to do with whether the act/omission (killing/letting die) and active/passive distinctions are morally significant ones, part of the central battleground between consequentialists (whether or not utilitarians) and their deontological opponents. Much has been written on the intention/foresight issue, and I myself, in my paper, "Some Aspects to the Doctrine of Double Effect,"[1] have previously discussed it. There, I denied that a genuine distinction between intending death and merely foreseeing death as a consequence of one's act could be drawn if death were an inevitable or inseparable or certain consequence of one's act, and I could find no causal or moral differences between cases that proponents of the distinction purported to find. I then set out what I thought to be the crucial issue, the causal notion of control responsibility, that was involved in various prominent cases involving, for example, physicians and the intention/foresight issue. I wrote from a consequentialist or utilitarian perspective in normative theory, but nothing of moment in my paper turned on this fact.

I should like here to return to several facets of the intention or foresight debate; for I now believe that there is a more direct way of getting to the important causal

66

questions, including issues to do with control responsibility, that seem to me to determine morally what we say about the cases in question. My conclusion about the intention/foresight distinction comes out as before. Once again, I do not think my consequentialist or utilitarian perspective in normative theory affects my claims, though it will be apparent that such a perspective lies in the background. (I might note that, as a general project, I hope to show as the cumulative result of several papers to do with intention that this notion does not play the role in determining what we say morally about cases that deontologists of nearly all shades have taken it to play.[2])

Because a great deal in the intention/foresight, act/omission, and activity/passivity debates will be very familiar to readers, I propose to go straight to my central concerns and to forego the kind of extended preliminary discussion that these distinctions and the extraordinary variety of issues they touch on usually require, whether in medical contexts or elsewhere.

What concerns me is the reason that some give for drawing a moral difference between certain cases. A familiar example can be used to illustrate the point. With a patient who has required ever larger doses of a pain-killer, a physician now proposes to administer the minimum dosage necessary to relieve pain, in the knowledge, however, that the drug at that dosage will prove fatal or at least hasten death. Is the physician's act permissible? According to some, it is permissible, since the physician directly intends the relief of pain, not death, and only foresees as a side effect of the act that death will ensue or be hastened. Were the doctor directly to intend the patient's death, that is, were the intention to aim at that death either as end or as means, the act would be on completion, not tantamount to, but in fact murder. In this way, then, some want to distinguish morally between the doctor's intentionally killing the patient and knowingly bringing about the patient's death. Others, myself included, have strong doubts that any such moral distinction on this basis can be drawn.

It is sometimes said by critics that what supporters of the moral difference view want is a way of bringing about indirectly what they are forbidden, by their acceptance of the intrinsic wrongness of some acts,[3] to bring about directly. Whatever the truth of this remark, and I am sympathetic towards it in the cases of those who espouse the absolute and intrinsic wrongness of acts, irrespective of consequences, it does not, however, engage the moral difference view at the point of concern. Rather, it focuses attention on whether one can or cannot bring oneself to accept that there are some acts that it would always be wrong to perform, irrespective of consequences. Our point of concern is whether a distinction between intention and foresight can play the moral role it is given in the moral difference view, namely, that it can be used to distinguish morally between two doctors, one of whom intentionally kills the patient, the other of whom knowingly brings about the patient's death. I think it cannot, because it fails to take into account important causal considerations; put differently, I think it is causality, not intention, that matters in our moral pronouncements on the case at hand and others like it.

Nothing here turns on the fact that there can be degrees of foresight of consequences. Even if we were to agree that consequences can be foreseen as possible or barely probable, the fact is that our doctor foresees as very highly probable or as certain that the patient's death will ensue or be hastened. The doctor's whole training tells that, if he or she proceeds with this dosage of this drug, death or hastened death will ensue, and he or she would be a bad doctor *qua* doctor, were he or she ignorant of this fact. Again, nothing here is affected by the claim that an agent can fail to foresee certain consequences and that we can say that this doctor ought to have foreseen them. No party to our dispute is arguing that our doctor is negligent or reckless and so, as it were, can be condemned, independently of the decision made in the patient's case. Indeed, it is precisely because the doctor is not negligent or reckless, precisely because no claim is made of ignorance through deficient medical training with regard to the drug in question, that the decision whether to go ahead and administer the drug bears the moral interest it has for us.

The example of the doctor is drawn in terms of permissibility of actions, not responsibility for them, and it can seem that this is an important point for two reasons. The first is that adherents to the moral difference view need not be committed to certain dubious claims about responsibility. For example, they need not be committed to the view that agents are responsible only for what they intend and not for what they foresee as a certain consequence of their act, and such a view is, of course, very dubious. The proverbial terrorist who throws a bomb into a crowd intending to kill the head of state is certainly responsible for others who are killed. Nor is the adherent of the moral difference view committed to the claim that the degree of responsibility the terrorist has for the deaths of these others is somehow less than the responsibility for the death of the head of state. Again, and much more important, one cannot argue that the terrorist is only responsible for consequences which he foresees and wants. Even if it is true that he foresees but does not want or desire the deaths of the others, he does not thereby shed responsibility for them, if they are killed by the bomb. Similarly, even if it is true that our doctor neither intends nor wants the death of the patient, if the drug is administered, the doctor seems no less to bear responsibility for that death. The suggestion that one is not responsible for foreseen but unwanted consequences is very dubious at best, and adherents to the moral difference view may, but need not, be committed to it.

The second reason I think it important to be at least aware of a distinction between permissibility and responsibility in the doctor's case is that I think talk of permissibility gives the doctor *a guide to action* that tells that, if the drug is administered, the doctor's character will not be tainted. In other words, I think that, at bottom, what the moral difference view comes to is just this: though the acts of both doctors produce death, the doctor who intentionally kills the patient is a worse person than one who knowingly brings about the patient's death. Talk of responsibility at this level can possibly overlook this point about character. That is, the doctor in our case can know that he or she will be responsible for a death *whichever way he or she decides* but that the doctor's character will not be tainted, *only if* he or she decides one way rather than the other. Since from murder can emanate a considerable taint, this piece of knowledge can seem important for the doctor to have.

I take it as obvious that, to the supporters of the moral difference view that I am concerned with, no moral equivalent of a "dirty hands" defense is available to the doctor who directly intends the patient's death. To them, we may not do that which can be construed as compromise with evil,[4] even if we do come to acknowledge guilt for having done so and even if this guilt is conceded to be evidence of our realization that we have violated certain deontological requirements.[5] Thus, for example, if one truly may not lie to save lives, then one cannot incur the charge of dirty hands; only someone prepared to relax the deontological requirement not to do evil in order to produce good can incur this charge. And it is precisely this requirement that adherents to the moral difference view will not permit the doctor to relax. A doctor may bring about a death, but cannot bring it about in such a way that the act represents a compromise with evil. Murder represents just such a compromise in the doctor's case, and he or she murders the patient if the patient's death is directly intended and the doctor proceeded accordingly.

An important question now arises: Can one withhold intending that which one knows in fact will occur? The doctor is pondering what to do and trying to think through the case morally. The doctor's training tells him or her, and this fact is brought before his or her mind and considers it, that death is inevitably or inseparably or certainly linked to this dosage of this drug. To be sure, if death were foreseen as only possible, perhaps the doctor could withhold intending it; but can he or she withhold intending that which is certain will occur? It must be the view of those who find a moral difference in character between intentional killing and knowingly bringing about death that the doctor can do so.

The question here is not whether doctors, knowing death will ensue or be hastened, desire or want that result. That is, I am not assuming, in asking whether they can withhold intending patients' deaths that they know are certain to occur, that they desire that which they intend. In many attacks on the doctrine of double effect, I concede that just such an assumption has often been made. It is, however, a false assumption, even if it is true, as it surely is, that one typically desires that which one intends. Typically, when I intend to go to the theater, I desire to go, and when I intend to annoy someone, I want to annoy them. In other cases, however, it may not be true that I desire what I intend. I intend to repay the $5 I owe you, but I do not really want to do so; I intend to mark several graduate essays on my return home this evening, but I certainly do not desire to do so; and I intend to declare on my taxes a recent honorarium, though paying up is far from something I (heartily) desire to do.[6]

The question before us, however, is not, and must not be confused to be, whether doctors must desire that which they intend. It is rather whether they can withhold intending that which they know will certainly occur, if they administer the drug. In short, the question is about, not the relation between intention and desire, but the relation between intention and foresight.

It now seems to me fairly clear that one need not intend that which one foresees even as a highly probable or certain consequence of one's act; at least, there are examples where this seems to be so. At a dinner party, I may foresee full well that my rather poor eating habits, which I have tried unsuccessfully to break, are very likely to put people off their food; but I do not intend—and I do not want—that they be so affected. Again, I may foresee as a virtual certainty that my views on the morality of suicide will be annoying or offensive to many of my closest friends, but I do not intend to annoy or offend them. And while I foresee as an absolute certainty that constant use of my books will damage them, I do not intend that they be damaged. Accordingly, I think we must affirm, even though it may be true that we usually intend that which we foresee as a certain consequence of our acts, that a genuine distinction can be drawn between intention and foresight.[7] In the doctor's case, then, I do not believe that we can simply conclude from the fact that the doctor foresees as a certainty that the patient will die if the drug is administered either that he or she intends the patient's death or that he or she cannot withhold intending that death.

It should be noted that the point here about intention and foresight applies in the case of the legal maxim that one intends the natural and probable consequences of one's act. That maxim must be dubious, if we cannot conclude from the fact that a consequence is (natural and) foreseen by the agent as probable or highly probable that the agent intends it. Such doubt must in turn infect "reasonable man" standards of (tests of) intention at law, since those standards uniformly appeal to what reasonable people *would foresee* in the circumstances. (Much more needs to be said about this role of foresight in law and in "reasonable man" standards, some of which I attempt in my paper, "Intention, Foresight, and Appeal to Reasonable Man Standards."[8])

In the examples mentioned of intention and foresight, the agent foresees *but does not want* the consequence at issue; but what if the agent foresees *and wants* that consequence? In this event, it might be held that the agent has come to will the consequence, either as means or as end, and that, therefore, he or she intends it. Because of this, in the case of our doctors, it can seem important that they foresee but do not want the death that will inevitably ensue from their acts of administering drugs.

The way forward, I think, turns on understanding why one is tempted to raise the question of the doctor's withholding intending the patient's death in the first place. (What is true here is true of all the interesting medical cases, e.g., the craniotomy case, involving doctors who decide what befalls their patients.)

The doctor foresees the death of the patient as certain to occur, if he or she goes forward with the drug, and, if he or she does go forward, the doctor *in full knowledge* brings about that death. Under these circumstances, the reason we press the question about withholding intention is that the doctor seems the agent of the patient's death, in the sense that, if he or she chooses one way rather than the other, the death of the patient ensues. (It should be evident here what I mean by control responsibility on the doctor's part, a matter to which I return.) Now it would be a woefully inadequate account of the doctor's case simply to say that the drug killed the patient. It only kills the patient if the doctor chooses to administer it. Similarly, in the ectopic pregnancy cases, it will not do simply to say that the mother and fetus die: they both die only if the doctor chooses not to crush the skull of the fetus. The temptation to collapse the intention/foresight distinction arises because we want to try to capture this agency on the doctor's part, and we try to do this by building it into the doctor's intention, as if it is only through intention, the content of an intention, that agency can manifest itself in the case. We have seen that we must resist the temptation to collapse the intention or foresight distinction, yet we still do want to take account of this point about agency. So how do we express the matter?⁹

Suppose the doctor chooses to administer the drug and knowingly brings about the patient's death. What shall we say about this "bringing about"? We cannot say that the patient's death was the result of an accident, a mistake, or ignorance; we cannot say that it was the result of negligence or recklessness; and we cannot say that it was not a product of choice or decision. It seems intentional or deliberate; but this way of speaking runs the risk of causing confusion through it being assumed that, therefore, the patient's death was part of the doctor's intention. I shall speak, then, of the patient's death as "chosen" or "decided," or "the product of choice or decision." We can now explain why we are tempted to collapse the intention/foresight distinction. For what we want to affirm as an integral part of the doctor's case is that the patient's death is chosen or decided, that the doctor is an agent in that death, and that no account of the doctor's situation can ignore this fact of agency. Certainly, the choice or decision by the doctor cannot be ignored in describing what happened in the patient's case, since that choice or decision in part determines what happens in that case. And we want to affirm this, even if it is true that the death of the patient forms no part of the doctor's intention. Were we thinking morally about all of this, the point would be that it is simply false that the only way morality can, as it were, be injected into the doctor's case is through what is intended; for that fails to take account of the fact that the patient's death is chosen or decided, in the sense described. We can, in addition to holding the doctor responsible for this choice or decision, morally assess what he or she took into account and what he or she left out in making it.

What sort of agency am I attributing to the doctor? In my earlier article on double effect, I cashed out this notion of agency in terms of control responsibility. Consider the craniotomy case. Does the doctor perform the craniotomy and save the mother, or is the child delivered by Caesarean section after the mother's death? To crush the fetus's skull is directly to intend its death, and this is murder and so forbidden. Whereas to refrain from crushing its skull and, in the jargon, "permitting" the mother to die, is to foresee the mother's death as a consequence of not operating, and this "permitting" or "allowing" the mother to die, or, as it is sometimes put, of "letting nature take its course" is, though a tragic affair, not forbidden. But talk of the mother being "permitted" or "allowed" to die will not do: she is permitted or allowed to die by the doctor. Only if the doctor decides one way as opposed to the other does the mother die, and over this decision the doctor has control. As a result of this control, he or she is answerable for what ensues in the woman's case through the decision.[10] The mother need not have died, but, then again, the fetus need not have had its head crushed. Whichever of these alternatives ensues is traced directly to how the doctor chose to exercise the control over the decision whether or not to operate on the fetus, and, through this control, bears responsibility for that decision.

In my earlier article, I distinguished three senses of responsibility: to be responsible for P is (1) to be guilty of having done P, (2) to be the cause of P, and (3) to be answerable for P, in the sense that there is a case to be put and so a case to be answered. While guilt is not attributed in this last sense, we shall assess and weigh the answer that is forthcoming. In saying of the doctor in the craniotomy case that he or she bore responsibility for whether or not to operate on the fetus, so that he or she was responsible for what ensued whichever way was chosen, I construed the sense of responsibility at issue to be that of answerability. It now seems to me that this view, while true, is not the whole truth; at least, it needs to be understood in a particular light.

For what is the doctor answerable? The doctor is answerable for being a causal factor in the fetus's or the mother's death; the doctor is answerable, that is, for that of which he or she is a cause. This explains what is really so misleading about expressions like "permitting" or "allowing" to die or "letting nature take its course": they all suggest that, if the doctor does not operate and the mother dies, he or she is not a causal factor in effecting her death. And this is simply false. Whether the mother lives or dies depends on how the doctor exercises control over the decision whether or not to operate. She dies only if the doctor exercises control one way rather than the other, and this substantive point is true of the death of the fetus as well. The truth is that, causally, the doctor is between the devil and the deep blue sea. The doctor is a causal factor in whichever death ensues as the result of control over the decision whether or not to operate. The doctor is not, or not yet, charged with being guilty of anything, but is answerable for what he or she caused, and this can, and very well may expose him or her to the charge of guilt. Whether it does or not will depend on what we make, morally, of the reasons for exercising control one way as opposed to the other. (In this regard, suppose that the doctor opposes abortion, "permits" the mother and fetus to die, yet has very powerful evidence that the delivered child will die shortly after birth in any event. This piece of information about the fetus seems obviously morally relevant to the decision whether to operate. If the doctor chooses to set this evidence aside and so, as the result of this choice, to lose two lives instead of one, many people may well begin to suspect that the doctor is guilty with respect to the mother's death.)

Here, too, is an area where distinctions between act/omission, acting/refraining, and activity/passivity can fail to do significant work.[11] For it is a mistake to think that a doctor's control of a situation can only manifest itself through acting and intervening and never through not acting or not intervening. Whether or not the doctor intervenes is his or her decision. The doctor can choose to crush the fetus's skull or to refrain from doing so. But it is wrong to think that failures to act or refrainings or passivity are, because they are noninterventions, causally inert. Suppose I omit to feed the baby or refrain from doing so, suppose further that there is no one else to feed the baby, and suppose the baby dies. Surely my omission or refraining is a causal factor in the baby's death? To be sure, certain other conditions about the world (e. g., the absence of other people) and about the baby (e. g., malnourishment) may have to be present, but that does not mean that my omitting to feed the baby was not a causal factor in the baby's death. Again, it would be a seriously impoverished account of what befell the baby to delete reference to my omission; for it would then appear that starvation overtook the baby in the natural course of events, when it is certain that, had I not omitted to feed the baby, the baby would not have starved. Equally, when one chooses to walk past an infant drowning in a few inches of water, it is a very impoverished account of what befell the infant to delete reference to one's choice; for the infant only drowns if it is "permitted" to do so by one's choice.[12] The point of these examples matters enormously, since those who find a moral difference between directly intending a death and knowingly bringing about a death nearly always insist that it is not the doctor in the craniotomy case who produces the deaths of mother and fetus; nature does this. But it is the doctor's choice not to intervene, and two deaths, not one, ensue; in this respect, then, the decision not to intervene is not causally inert.[13]

I shifted to the craniotomy case, in order to set out the notion of control responsibility, which formed the terms in which I understood the agency of the doctor in the drug case, with respect to the patient's death. The doctor in that case bears control responsibility for the decision whether to administer the drug, and, if he or she decides to go ahead, then he or she is a causal factor in a death, *whether* he or she directly intends the patient's death or knowingly brings it about. The doctor is answerable for what he or she causes, and we need to go into the reasons given for exercising this control. In the absence of this examination, we cannot say whether a doctor who directly intends a patient's death is a worse person than one who knowingly brings about a patient's death. Each causes, or is a causal factor in, a death, and in neither case is that the result of a mistake, an accident, ignorance, negligence, or recklessness; rather, each death is a chosen or decided one, and each doctor bears control responsibility for that choice or decision.

The doctor does not escape the net of control responsibility by surrendering the decision about what to do in the drug case to some list of intrinsically wrong acts that forbids, for example, directly intending a person's death. One bears control responsibility for surrendering one's decision about what to do to such a list, no matter to what moral authority that list may be imputed or traced. Moreover, the decision to act on the verdict given by the list or the authority clearly remains the doctor's. Finally, to say in, for example, the craniotomy case that there really is no choice at all, that since crushing the fetus's skull is absolutely proscribed it cannot be one term of a choice situation, is still to leave us with the question of why one surrendered control over

decisions in this case to this list or authority. (The answer to this question is very likely to take us off into rather remote areas of metaphysics.) Control over this kind of
surrender of control remains firmly in one's own hands.

Now there is an objection to all this talk of causality that I want to consider; in
so doing, I want to say something about the notion of causality I have in mind in this
discussion, when I speak of "causal factors." The objection consists, in what I have
claimed was an ubiquitous feature of one camp's discussion of cases, in simply insisting that the doctor's decision to exercise control one way rather than the other causes nothing. If this is so, then I cannot use responsibility in the causal sense as a
ground, given that further assessments are forthcoming, for ascribing responsibility
in the moral or guilt sense.[14]

Consider the craniotomy case. If the doctor decides to operate and crush the
fetus's skull, he or she intervenes and causes a death; if, however, he or she decides
not to operate and so not to intervene, he or she does not cause the mother's death.
Nature, or the disorder in question, it might be said, causes her death. This line of
argument can be employed in a similar way in numerous other cases. In the case of a
newborn with multiple, serious complaints, the doctor can intervene and kill or try to
save the infant. The doctor can, on the other hand, choose not to intervene and so
withhold treatment. If treatment is withheld, the doctor might go on to claim that the
infant's death was caused by the maladies in question. (The drug case, of course, is a
bit different; there, if the doctor does not intervene, he or she perpetuates the patient's
suffering, whereas if he or she does intervene and administers the drug, then the doctor is a causal factor in the patient's death.) In the craniotomy and withholding or
withdrawing treatment cases, noninterventions are being regarded as causally inert;
nature, or the malady in question, it might be said, is being left to run its course, and
it does the killing. I have rejected this line of argument, in connection with omissions,
refrainings, and passivity; I return to it now, in order to sketch an alternative to it.

Interestingly, Kant has something to say on an issue very like ours.[15] In his
essay, "On a Supposed Right to Lie from Altruistic Motives,"[16] Kant presents his
famous (or infamous) example of the murderer, to whom the truth must be told, if one
speaks at all, when he seeks information as to the whereabouts of his intended victim.
What Kant has to say about this example is ignored today, but it relates directly to our
present concern.

In response to the question of whether, if one reveals the victim's whereabouts
to the murderer and the murderer brings off the deed, one is causally responsible for
the victim's death, Kant answers in the negative. That is, if one tells the murderer that
his intended victim is within one's house, and this is in fact the case, then even if the
murderer kills his intended victim through employing the information one gives him,
one is still not the cause, Kant holds, of the victim's death. Kant writes: "Each man
has not only a right but even the strict duty to be truthful in statements he cannot
avoid making, whether he harm himself or others. In so doing, he does not do harm
to him who suffers as a consequence; accident causes this harm."[17] For Kant, then,

one is not causally responsible for the victim's death: it is not truth-telling but the use to which the truth is put that causes his death, and it is simply an accident of truth-telling in this case that it is put to that use. This view seems to me quite wrong; I suggest instead that one is a part cause of the victim's death. And this is what I want to maintain about the doctor's decision not to intervene in, for example, the craniotomy and withholding treatment cases. What view do I take, then, of part causes?

In order to establish causal responsibility for an outcome in the world, I espouse a contributory theory of causation, according to which S is a cause of P if it helps to produce or contributes to the occurrence of P.[18] Suppose it takes six men pushing to get a car up the hill, six men are present, all push, and the car reaches the top of the hill: I want to say that each act of pushing considered singly is "a part cause" of the car's reaching the top of the hill, since each act helps to produce that outcome, whereas all six acts of pushing considered collectively are "the cause" or "the whole cause" of the car's reaching the top of the hill. Thus, to specify what caused or brought about P, we need to compile a list of the contributory or part causes of P. In the present case, I want to say that the victim's death has two part causes, one's telling the murderer the truth and the use to which this information is put by the murderer. Jointly, these two causal factors provide "the cause" or "the whole cause" of the victim's death.

Now I think it must be conceded that conditional analyses can be given of part causes in my example.

Necessary Conditions. In my example, in which all six men must push to produce the outcome and all six push, then each act of pushing can be seen as a necessary condition for the occurrence of the effect. All six acts considered jointly can be seen as the totality of the separately necessary conditions for the car's reaching the top of the hill. Put in these terms, a part cause may be regarded as a necessary condition (or necessary in the circumstances) and a whole cause as the totality of necessary conditions (which, in the circumstances, may jointly suffice) for the occurrence of the effect.

Sufficient Conditions. In my example, in which all six acts of pushing are required to produce the outcome, the whole cause of this outcome consists in several (logically) independent factors (each act of pushing) which jointly are sufficient to get the car up the hill. This sufficiency view of whole causes then devolves on part causes: each act of pushing thus becomes part of a sufficient condition for the occurrence of the effect in question.

As I say, these conditional analyses of part causes are possible. I have elsewhere argued against them.[19] On this score, I have space for only a brief word here.

On a contributory theory, a part cause is going to be anything that helps to produce, that stands in a productive relation to anything else. The focus is entirely on the productive aspects of events and so on the specific productive aspects of the events that preceded the particular event in question. This type of construal of causation does indeed cast a very wide net, but such scope is, I think, precisely what we want. Suppose the high-rise walkways in a hotel lobby collapse. What we want to know is what all the contributory factors were that produced this event, not the answer to the narrower question of what the necessary and/or sufficient conditions were of the crash. Indeed, notice how such a narrower focus can produce a counterintuitive result. Factor A must be either a necessary or part of a sufficient condition for the collapse, if it is to be a part cause of the collapse at all; if it is neither of these things, then *even if* it contributes to and helps to produce the crash, it cannot be a part cause of it. (Causally overdetermined, as well as nonoverdetermined, cases can be used to make the point.)

In a list of factors that contributed to the collapse of the walkways, one factor may be judged so important to the occurrence of the collapse, for example, structural defects in the steel girders, that it may come to be spoken of as "the cause" of the collapse. In other words, these defects in the girders were judged to have made a much greater contribution to the collapse than any other single factor, indeed, perhaps greater than all the other factors combined. On the other hand, it is possible that the contribution of a factor can be so slight that it ceases to be spoken of as "a cause" at all. Had a person been walking across the walkways at the moment of collapse, we might judge their contribution to the outcome to be so negligible that we ignore it.

I do not deny that there is a relative inexactness in all this that would have to be ironed out in more detailed work. But I think it quite clear, for example, that all kinds of Boards of Inquiry into various disasters wield a contributory theory of causation and operate in the way I have described.

Now what of Kant's example. In telling the murderer the truth, is your contribution to the victim's death so slight that we can ignore it and focus exclusively on the murderer? I do not believe your contribution is so slight. Your telling the murderer the truth leads him to his intended victim, it enables him to accomplish his purpose. Moreover, if you *know* the whereabouts of the intended victim, then in telling the murderer the truth, you *know* you are leading him straight to his victim. And if you *know* you are leading the murderer straight to his intended victim, then in telling the murderer the truth, you must be prepared to *put* the murderer onto his intended victim. Under these conditions, I really cannot see how we can avoid concluding that you are at least prepared to see the victim murdered. As for the character of a person who is prepared to allow this, what a person is prepared to permit or allow or see happen is every bit as much a part of his or her character as what he or she is prepared to do or directly intend. In one of Ibsen's plays, a fanatical truth-teller destroys the world of one small family, but he does not really know or realize (except at the end) what he is doing; Kant's truth-teller knows full well what he is doing.

It is a version of this line of argument that I should use in, for example, the craniotomy and withholding treatment cases both to rebut the claim that doctors who do not intervene in the course of events do not cause anything and, taking them, therefore, to be part causes of the deaths in question, to query any assumption that, because they do not intervene, they are somehow per se morally better persons than doctors who do intervene. It may turn out that they are morally better persons, but it will not be on *this* basis, unless such a claim can be anchored firmly to differences in causal structure in the examples. This is what I am querying and cannot find, especially on the assumption that "permitting," "allowing," or "letting nature take its course" removes one as a causal factor in the cases at hand. Accordingly, armed with a contributory theory of causation, I reject the view that, in our cases, the doctor's decision not to intervene removes him or her as a causal factor in the deaths in question and so removes him or her from answerability, and through answerability, the *possibility* of the ascription of guilt, for those deaths. The doctor cannot, moreover, pass the buck to nature, to claim that the maladies of the patient were what killed the person; for the decision not to intervene is a part cause of the person's death. To say anything else is to treat the doctor as a *spectator* on the natural course of events, when in truth he or she is an *actor* in what will befall the patient, and he or she bears control responsibility for the choices or decisions made. More important, control responsibility for outcomes anchors our doctors to the category of actors, not spectators.

What, finally, am I claiming about the intention or foresight distinction? Essentially, I am claiming that it fails to pick out important causal concerns that go towards determining what we say, morally, in the cases of our doctors. These concerns lie outside a distinction between intending a death and bringing about a death and are not captured by it. Yet, these very causal concerns show how morality can enter into the discussion of the doctors' cases, even if one concedes a genuine distinction between intention and foresight. To repeat, the doctor in the craniotomy case cannot be allowed to describe him or herself as a spectator on what befalls the mother; the natural course of events takes the course it does because of the doctor's decision not to intervene, for which he or she bears control responsibility. It is through this notion, in the way I have described, that we can inject morality into our discussion of the doctor's decision, whatever the state of play with respect to the distinction between intention and foresight.

NOTES

1. R.G. Frey, "Some Aspects to the Doctrine of Double Effect," *Canadian Journal of Philosophy* IV; 1975: 259–283. A slightly amended version of this paper appears in my *Rights, Killing, and Suffering*. Oxford: Basil Blackwell, 1983 as Chapter 13, "Killing and the Doctrine of Double Effect."

2. In this regard, see my, *The Nature of Suicide*. Oxford: Basil Blackwell, forthcoming.

3. Among many deontologists, for example, Catholic moral theologians, the moral difference view has almost always gone hand-in-glove with the view that some acts are intrinsically (or nonconsequentially) wrong. The source of such a list of acts, and why that source should be taken as authoritative, can clearly be matters of controversy; but even more controversial has been the inclusion of certain kinds of acts (idolatry, blasphemy, masturbation, for example) on that list. There cannot be degrees of wrongness with intrinsically wrong acts, so murder and masturbation are equally wrong.

4. This is in essence the point of G.E.M. Anscombe's attack on consequentialist accounts of rightness. See her "Modern Moral Philosophy," *Philosophy* 43;1958:1–19. See also Roy Holland, "Absolutist Ethics, Mathematics and the Impossibility of Politics," *Against Empiricism*. Oxford: Basil Blackwell, 1980, pp. 126–142.

5. The acknowledgment of these points is something that Michael Walzer has stressed. See his "Political Action: The Problem of Dirty Hands," *Philosophy and Public Affairs* 2; 1973, pp. 160–180. See also H. Oberdiek, "Clean and Dirty Hands in Politics," *International Journal of Moral and Social Studies* 1; 1986:41–60; Steven Lukes, "Marxism and Dirty Hands," *Social Philosophy and Policy* 3; 1986: 204–223.

6. For elaborations of the distinction between intention and desire, see Alan R. White, *Grounds of Liability*. Oxford: Clarendon Press, 1985, pp. 75–82; John Finnis, "Intention and Side-Effects" in R.G. Frey, and Christopher W. Morris, eds. *Liability and Responsibility: Essays in Law and Morals*. Cambridge: Cambridge University Press, 1991, pp. 34–64; R.A. Duff, *Intention, Agency, and Criminal Liability*. Oxford: Basil Blackwell, 1990, pp. 52–73.

7. In this regard, see White, *Grounds of Liability*, pp. 82–91; Finnis, "Intention and Side-Effects," pp. 74–81.

8. R.G. Frey, "Intention, Foresight, and Appeal to Reasonable Man Standards," *The Nature of Suicide*.

9. I do not imply that what follows is the only way to capture the doctor's agency; as will become apparent, however, it does capture rather nicely the control the doctor has over what befalls the patient.

10. I assume, of course, that the patient does not die unexpectedly from some reason unconnected with her pregnancy.

11. In this connection, see my "Acts and Omissions," in Lawrence Becker, and

Charlotte Becker, eds. *Encyclopedia of Ethics*. New York: Garland, 1992, pp. 14–15.

12. This is Peter Singer's example, used by him in another context.

13. In this regard, see Joel Feinberg, *Harm to Others*. Oxford: Oxford University Press, 1984, pp. 171–186.

14. At this point, all three senses of responsiblity come together. One is answerable at the very least for what one causes, and the reasons one had for choosing that way, can always form a ground for imputing responsibility in the moral or guilt sense.

15. In the discussion that follows, I draw on an earlier piece of mine, "Causal Responsibility and Contributory Causation," *Philosophy and Phenomenological Research*, XXXIX; 1978: 106–119.

16. Lewis White Beck, ed. and trans., in *Critique of Practical Reason and Other Writings in Moral Philosophy*. Chicago: University of Chicago Press, 1949, pp. 346–350.

17. Beck, *Critique of Practical Reason*, p. 349.

18. For further dicsussion of the contributory theory, see my "On Causal Consequences," *Canadian Journal of Philosophy*, IV; 1974:161–180.

19. That is, I have argued against conditional analyses where what is under consideration is responsibility, as opposed to the prospective task of trying to decide what to do. See the works referred to in notes 1, 2, and 18.

Causal Responsibility and Moral Culpability

ALISA L. CARSE

Georgetown University, Washington, D.C.

In "Intention, Foresight, and Killing," Raymond Frey rejects what he calls the *moral-difference view*, the view that the distinction between intention and foresight can serve "to mark off moral differences between cases." Frey is not denying that a distinction exists between intending and merely foreseeing an outcome such as death, even in cases in which, for example, we foresee that death is a highly likely or certain outcome of what we are doing. Rather, he claims that moral assessment, both of actions and of agents, cuts across this distinction. In addition, and more positively, Frey asserts that it is "causality, not intention, that matters in our moral pronouncements" on cases. We are to "use responsibility in the causal sense," or what he terms control responsibility, "as a *ground* ... for ascribing responsibility in the moral or guilt sense" (my emphasis). It is not physicians' intentions, then, but the causal roles they play in their patients' deaths, that is to determine the status of their acts.

Frey's position brings to light important conceptual challenges facing those who would maintain the moral-difference view that he rejects. At the same time, Frey does not so much offer an argument against the moral-difference view as an alternative to it. I will argue that this alternative leaves unanswered the crucial question how we should construe the relation between conditions for the ascription of responsibility in the *causal* sense and conditions for the ascription of responsibility–or culpability—in the *moral* sense. I also raise doubts about any approach that would give causal considerations the determinative role in assessing moral culpability.

At the center of Frey's position is his notion of "control responsibility." It is, he

Tim...

Just thought I'd
say hello 😊 😊

so....

Bonjour 😊

Hallo 😊

Have fun in lab.

😊

Merideth

This method requires more than one
full adder per bit, because multiple
sums and carries can be generated.
This can be avoided by adding partial
products as soon as they appear. The
rules for shifting remain unchanged.
Now there are only two digits in each
column, and only one adder is needed.

```
                    1 0 0 1 1
                  x 1 1 0 1
                  ---------
```

1st product		1 0 0 1 1
2nd product	1 0 0 1 1	
Sum		1 0 1 1 1 1 1
3rd product	1 0 0 1 1	
Total sum		1 1 1 0 1 1 1

With an expanded COMP-U-KIT system,
we can do multiplication. It requires
full adder circuits, a shift register,
one or more auxiliary storage registers,
and some control logic circuitry. The
complexity of the circuits will depend
upon such factors as the length of the
numbers, and whether serial (one bit at
a time) or parallel (several bits at a
time) addition is used.

STEP FOUR - DIVISION
Division is normally performed by
using multiplication. It can be done
without multiplication by simply sub-
tracting. This is true for any number

claims, in virtue of our control over choices of action that we are to be held responsible, or "answerable," for the causal outcomes of our acts. In the case of the physician who administers an analgesic that she foresees will hasten the death of her patient, Frey writes, "it would be a woefully inadequate account of the doctor's case simply to say that the drug killed the patient; it only kills the patient if the doctor chooses to administer it" (pp. 72–73). In the craniotomy case, in which a physician decides not to intervene and crush the fetus's skull knowing that the mother's death will result, we cannot, according to Frey, simply say that the doctor "permitted" or "allowed" the mother to die, "letting nature take its course," because the doctor decides to "permit" or to "allow" the death, *choosing* to "let nature take its course." In both cases, the doctors exercise control through their choices and are therefore answerable for the deaths they help cause, *whatever their intentions might be.*

Frey emphasizes that control responsibility establishes no more than "answerability." Answerability does not entail guilt; it puts one in a position to be answerable for what happened, to owe a justification. Guilt is determined as a result of our assessment of the answer one gives, "what we make, morally, of his reasons for exercising his control one way as opposed to the other." Thus, an agent who is answerable is at most shown to be responsible in the causal sense and thus to be a candidate for moral appraisal.

If we accept this account of control responsibility, we might ask what, if anything, follows from it for the moral status of the intention/foresight distinction. This distinction is not, after all, taken by its proponents to address causal responsibility. It is taken to address the moral permissibility or impermissibility of actions, and, by implication, moral responsibility or culpability.

At the heart of Frey's case against the moral-difference theorist appears to be his denial that intention demarcates the scope of moral agency. In the case of the doctor who foresees but does not intend his patient's death, Frey writes that it is "simply false that the only way morality can, as it were, be injected into the doctor's case is through what he intends." Frey's argument is best taken, then, as directed against the deontologist who holds that an agent's acts are defined by his or her intentions, which are to be distinguished morally from foreseen consequences the agent merely "permits" or "allows." As Thomas Nagel expresses this view, "[Although] it is also possible to foresee that one's actions will cause or fail to prevent a harm that one does not intend to bring about or permit ... [this] is *not*, in the relevant sense, something that one does and [it] *does* not come under a deontological constraint."[1] On this deontological account of action, an agent is a candidate for moral assessment only for what she does, and thus, by definition, for what she intends to do, not for all that she causes (or helps to cause) through her actions. Frey's notion of control responsibility in effect amounts to a denial that what we do is defined by what we intend to do. Correlatively, his account extends the scope of answerability (and thus, in principle, moral responsibility) to those outcomes caused by the acts over which we have control through our choices, whatever our intended ends might be in choosing to act as we do. Essentially, Frey is asserting that even if one does not intend the harm one foresees as a likely outcome of one's action, one is at least answerable for that harm, and possibly morally culpable for it, insofar as one's chosen course of action plays a causal role in bringing it about.

What is Frey's argument for delineating the scope of responsibility in this way and, more important, can it count as an argument against the moral-difference view?

Frey appears to advocate a shift in moral focus away from agents' intentions because he holds that the causal implications of our actions rather than our intentions in acting matter in moral assessments of actions. He suggests that in cases in which the harm done through an action is foreseen but unintended by the agent, the action is not thereby rendered "causally inert";[2] he insists that we do not, through our intentions remove ourselves as "causal factor[s]" in bringing about harm.

But if this is right, then Frey's argument does not directly engage the moral-difference view, which need not hold that our choices of actions with foreseen but unintended consequences are causally inert. The proponent of the moral-difference view is interested in distinguishing what we, as agents, merely cause from what we can be said, in the morally relevant sense, to do, and it is deemed a virtue rather than a fault of the intention/foresight distinction that it would have us drive a wedge between these. As N. Ann Davis puts it, "many deontologists ... have appealed to a distinction between intention and mere foresight *in order* to distinguish between the things that an agent does and the things that an agent is properly said only to have caused or to have failed to prevent. What an agent *does*, in the relevant sense, is a function of what the agent *intends*: One violates the deontological constraint against lying or the constraint against killing the innocent only if one utters a falsehood or causes a death intentionally."[3] Frey is flatly asserting what proponents of the moral-difference view deny, namely, that the causal role of voluntary actions renders them candidates for moral assessment, and determines what we say morally about them. What Frey has offered, therefore, is less an argument against the moral-difference view than a rejection of it.

Of course, even if Frey's argument does not succeed in engaging the moral-difference view directly, there might be compelling reasons for embracing his alternative. What is needed is independent motivation for the claim that the causal role our chosen actions play should be our moral focus, rather than our intentions in acting. I want, therefore, to turn to an examination of Frey's positive view, both to see where its motivations might lie and to raise further questions about it.

As Frey points out, the physicians in the kinds of cases at issue are not flies on the wall, or mere spectators, but agents, considering possible courses of action and committing to one or more over others, even when the courses chosen by them are noninterventionist or involve foreseen but unintended death. Indeed, a significant virtue of Frey's account might be found in its insistence that we do not opt out of being answerable for the foreseen consequences of our actions, simply because they are not our intended ends. There seem grounds for attributing answerability to an agent even for unintended harm he or she knowingly and voluntarily brings about in acting.

Accepting this much, broad questions arise: First, how, on Frey's positive view, are we to understand the conditions for the appropriate attribution of answerability? And, second, how are we to understand the relation between the conditions for the attribution of answerability–or responsibility in the causal sense–and the conditions for the ascription of culpability–or responsibility in the moral sense?

As I have noted, Frey is clear that in moving from judgments of answerability to judgments of culpability, we need to invoke independent moral considerations. I want to suggest that moral considerations are needed as well in determining an agent's answerability. Why? Because a myriad of actions play causal roles in producing any given state of affairs, and every action has many consequences–even infinitely many. Surely, not all of these consequences are properly to be understood to fall within the scope of an agent's responsibility. We therefore need some normative basis on which to determine which causal facts are relevant to our answerability ascriptions and which are not.

It is not clear that Frey would recognize this as a need. In the craniotomy case, he claims that the physician is answerable "for being a causal factor in the fetus's or the mother's death; he is answerable, that is, for that for which he is a partial or whole cause." He advocates what he calls "a contributory theory of causation, according to which S is a cause of P if it helps to produce or contributes to the occurrence of P." Thus, in effect one is to be held answerable not just for the contributory causal role one plays in bringing about an outcome, but for the outcome one contributes to bringing about. Frey admits that his conception of causal responsibility "casts a wide net," but sees this as a virtue. I think this conception is more problematic than Frey recognizes. Seeing why can help make clear why determining answerability is a fundamentally normative–even moral–matter.

Consider the following story. Cappy is 6 years old. Mattie is his mother. They live on a relatively unpopulated peninsula, with little traffic, at least after Labor Day. Their house is in a remote part of the peninsula on a piece of land flanked by a road on which occasional cars and even more occasional trucks travel, and then often at quite high speeds. At the edge of their land by the road are trees that make their house and yard a private enclave. It is a school day. Cappy is dawdling and late for the school bus. Mattie is annoyed. "You'll miss the bus!" she urges, "Stop goofing around and tie your shoes!" "Get going!" Cappy grabs his lunch and without a "goodbye" races out the door to the road by the trees. Just as he emerges from the trees, the truck zooming around the bend hits him. He is left severely and permanently brain-damaged. Mattie cares for him and blames herself for what happened.

Surely, many of us would regard such a case as a terrible tragedy. We might see it as appropriately eliciting sadness, even horror, at the twists life can take. But we might think recrimination or (more neutrally) demands for justification are inappropriate responses to a case such as this. Yet no one can deny that Mattie's nudging played a causal role in what happened to Cappy. Of course so did the decision she and Cappy's father made not to cut down the trees, and the driver's decision not to stop for donuts. We would, on Frey's account, say that Mattie, Cappy's father, and the bus driver are all answerable for what happened. But on Frey's account we would also, consistently, have to deem answerable many others whose choices and actions contributed in some (arguably necessary) way, however remotely, to what occurred–the truck driver's boss who determined the route to be driven that day, the gas station attendant, who spotted and repaired the truck's flat tire, the school administrator, who decided what time school would begin in the morning, even the obstetrician who safely delivered Cappy into this world 6 years prior to the accident.

The point is a familiar one: A genuine challenge faces any "causal" account of responsibility regarding how we are to determine which of the many causes contributing to the production of an outcome are relevant to our ascriptions of responsibility for that outcome and just what their relevance is.

Of course, Frey focusses only on those causes that are agents' chosen acts, and hence (arguably) under agents' control, but this focus doesn't avoid the problem. As the Cappy story shows, Frey's account of control responsibility gives us no way to distinguish those choices that are properly regarded grounds for attributing answerability and those that are not. As Arthur Ripstein argues in a different context, "When something goes wrong, there seem to be too many causes, including too many voluntary human acts, that need to come together in order for the accident to happen ... merely being part of the broader causal story is not sufficient to establish one person's responsibility ... responsibility ... cannot be ... reduced to quasi-empirical measures such as control."[4] The grounds for imputing responsibility must, Ripstein claims, be found in "a prior standard of what is owed whom."[5]

Ripstein's claim is illuminating. Standards "of what is owed whom"—including the obligations we take ourselves to have, the expectations we are entitled to embrace in our relations with each other, the way we conceive the responsibilities attached to our roles, and the like, are crucial not only to our moral assessments of responsibility, but also to our decisions about which of the many actions that contribute causally to an outcome are *legitimate candidates* for moral assessment, and thus are grounds for the attribution of answerability. However we understand the normative criteria to be formulated, some such criteria are needed, because without any, we would have no nonarbitrary, "causal" basis on which to ascribe answerability.

It is worth noting that this need may appear less obvious in Frey's discussion than in other contexts, because his focus is on types of cases in which agents' roles are already broadly defined–cases, that is, arising between physicians and their patients. Moreover, his focus is on cases in which the candidate for moral assessment is already assumed to be the physician. But from the perspective of Frey's control-responsibility account, who the candidates for moral assessment are properly to be, and how we are properly to understand the responsibilities between physicians and patients are both open issues. At the very least, a normative account is clearly required in determining the region of focus to which Frey's "causal" account is even to be applied, let alone in determining who is answerable.

This brings us to the second problem, namely, how we are to understand the relation between attributions of answerability and attributions of culpability on Frey's account. Frey claims that the difference between intention and foresight makes no moral difference because the distinction itself cuts across the causal roles agents play in bringing about harm. To make this claim stick, Frey would ultimately need to show that the distinction between intention and foresight cannot, in his words, be "anchored firmly" to differences that make a moral difference in the causal structure of cases, and, moreover, that the causal structures of cases in some significant sense "determine" our moral assessments of them. In order to do justice to Frey's account, we would, of course, have to wait for a fuller specification of just how the causal structure is to be morally "determinative," especially once it is joined to a moral account, as Frey intimates it must be. I want to set out some of preliminary questions for such an account, particularly if it is to be at all motivated for those broadly sympathetic to the moral-difference view.

First, let us imagine a revised Cappy story. In this version, the causal contributions of Mattie's actions are the same as in the first version, but Mattie intends the outcome of Cappy's injury. In nudging Cappy, she is attempting to provoke him into running out the door and into traffic. Many of us would have a radically different moral assessment of Mattie's actions (and Mattie) on this version of the story. We would likely take Mattie's intention to harm her son to define her actions as morally horrific acts of malevolence, rather than unfortunate expressions of annoyance. Correlatively, Mattie would likely appear to us an evil, looming figure, not a hapless and stressed-out, but caring, parent. We would, that is, regard Mattie's intention as crucial to how we are to understand the actions she is performing, and thus to how we are to judge her actions (and her person), even if the causal contributions of her actions are the same as those of actions performed with a fundamentally different intention.

The problem, then, is how one might account for the seemingly dramatic moral differences in the two versions of the story on Frey's account, in which the moral focus is not to be the agent's intentions in acting, but the outcome her action contributes causally to producing.

Frey might respond by insisting that an agent's intentions can, on his account, make a difference to our moral assessments. His point is not that intentions are morally irrelevant, but that the intention/foresight distinction is morally irrelevant; it does not as such reveal moral differences between cases. He might then pose the following question: Had Mattie *known* her nudging would likely prompt Cappy to dart out of the door and into a truck, had she decided *with foresight* to nudge him anyway, would we not deeply condemn her decision, *whatever her intentions in acting*? If so, we have an example in which mere foresight appears sufficient to determine culpability, and thus, in which the intention/foresight distinction is not "anchored" to differences that make a moral difference in the causal structure of the various stories.

This imaginary dialogue invites the question whether we can, contrary to the assumption behind Frey's (imaginary) question, legitimately judge agents morally culpable for harm they "merely" foresee on grounds other than causal grounds. The answer, I would maintain, is clearly "yes." If, for example, Mattie were to have foreseen Cappy's accident as the likely consequence of her provocations, and yet to have provoked him anyway, our judgment that she is culpable need not be grounded in the causal role her provocations played in bringing the accident about, though it would doubtless be motivated by the causal role they played. Rather, our judgment might be grounded in a conception of responsible and loving parenting, in virtue of which we find it morally alarming—even repugnant—that Mattie, who is to cherish and protect her children from harm, should knowingly undertake such a risk with her son. Similarly, if we were to assert of Mattie that she should have foreseen that her child might dart out of the house and into the street; or of the driver that he should have foreseen the possibility that a child might dart out from behind the trees, and each in turn have altered their actions so as to avoid such a consequence, we may be invoking, not a causal analysis of responsibility, but a normative conception of what we are entitled to expect of others—minimally responsible and attuned parenting, say, or competent and observant driving. The intention/foresight distinction may not be alone determinative of proper ascriptions of negligence (or any other form of culpability), but it doesn't follow that it is the causal structure of cases that is morally determinative. Quite to the contrary, appeal to the bald causal facts of cases cannot get us far without an accompanying normative construal of which causal facts are relevant and which have moral import and why. Few of us would, for example, think a strong case exists for ascribing culpability to the obstetrician who contributed causally (however remotely) to Cappy's tragedy by ensuring his successful birth 6 years earlier.

Even if we grant that the causal roles actions play can make a difference to our moral assessments of those actions and the agents who perform them, we need a way to determine which causal roles make a difference, and what moral difference they make. It is the moral account rather than the causal facts that will determine both which causal facts are morally relevant to our ascriptions of responsibility, and what their moral relevance is.

The Cappy case is not the sort of case in which the intention/foresight distinction has traditionally been invoked. The traditional invocation of the intention/foresight distinction, at least in conjunction with the doctrine of double effect, has been endorsed specifically in guiding decisions arising in morally dicey situations in which the application of a strenuous moral injunction would preclude action for which there are compelling moral grounds, grounds good enough to outweigh the bad that will result as a concomitant of our action.[6] For this reason many deontologists have resorted to accepting the view that it is on occasion permissible to bring about (or permit) as a foreseen side effect of one's intended action an outcome it would be impermissible to bring about (or allow) as one's intended end or means to one's end. I would suggest, however, that the questions I have raised for Frey's account become even more pressing in the sorts of cases in which the doctrine of double effect and the intention/foresight distinction have traditionally been invoked. These are characteristically cases in which bad effects will normally ensue no matter what the agent's course of action. The possible outcomes between which agents must choose are severely and unfortunately limited, and thus the room within which agents exert control over what happens is highly confined by the exigencies of the situation.

Frey's notion of control responsibility confronts a problem endemic to many consequentialist accounts, namely, how a robust conception of moral agency and moral responsibility are to be retained through an approach that understands agency principally as a form of causal intervention in the world, and the agent as a locus of such intervention.[7] Such a framework cannot of itself invite us to understand as morally relevant the way the agent construes the complex of circumstances and evaluations that prompt the course of action he or she undertakes, and help define its purpose or end. Frey insists that we will, in assessing culpability, ultimately need to ask what the agent's reasons are for acting as he or she does. The challenge, then, will be to show how we are to tie an evaluation of agents' reasons to a broader account in which the causal structure of cases is still in some significant sense determinative of our moral assessments of the agent's actions.

Having said all this, it would be disingenuous to proceed as if the intention/foresight distinction is itself an uncontroversial and unproblematic distinction. The doctrine of double effect, in conjunction with which this distinction is classically invoked, raises many puzzles that I cannot address here.[8] And there continues to be little agreement in the literature about how precisely we are to define and understand the notions of intention and foresight. If we are to accept that the "intentions" with which we act are to play a key role, either in determining the permissibility of our actions or in assessing the virtue of our characters, we must work for more clarity and consensus on what these notions mean, and determine how, if at all, we are definitively to distinguish the intended from foreseen but unintended outcomes of action in particular cases.[9]

Though some cases will seem quite transparent in this regard, a close look at the process of intention-ascription suggests, as N. Ann Davis points out, that it is a highly interpretive, even imaginative process, leaving a great deal of leeway for description and redescription of the facts about what our intentions and motivations are in a given case, thus opening us up in a general way to the risks of (self-)deception and unwarranted permissiveness.[10] This may reflect no more than the general difficulty of developing moral interpretations of actions and agents, rather any peculiar complication that arises through the invocation of a nonreductive mentalism, but it is good not to be more sanguine than is realistic about meeting this challenge.

The challenge becomes more strenuous if we are to take to heart Frey's insight that we are not mere spectators but active agents who are implicated in the unintended consequences to which our chosen actions causally contribute. If we are to preserve this insight, we would do well to abandon the view that what we do is defined by what we intend, and instead employ a broader and richer account of agency, on which, at the very least, the actions we deliberately and knowingly choose to perform and what we intend in acting are both to be included in what we do, and yet to be distinguished both phenomenologically and morally.[11] More work still needs to be done on the moral relation between choice and intention in agency if the moral-difference view is to serve as a legitimate and clarifying justificational tool.[12]

Whatever we say about the viability of the intention/foresight distinction and the appropriate use to which it is put, either as a moral action guide, or as a guide to our assessment of culpability after the fact, the appeal to this distinction has represented one way of recognizing the exceedingly important fact that we sometimes must, through our choices, consent to bring about as side effects outcomes we do not endorse bringing about in and of themselves, and that we must do so because of the practical constraints of the situations in which we find ourselves. The need for recognition of this sort is acute in health-care contexts, in which situations of extreme exigency and conflict are commonplace. As Joseph Boyle writes, "[i]n health care general norms such as preserving life and relieving pain are often placed at risk no matter what one's choice of action, for example, whether to save the fetus' life or, by abortion, to save the mother's, or to reduce one harm, of pain, by risking another, of shortening life by the analgesic."[13]

Whether the distinction between what we intend and what we merely foresee in acting maps on to moral assessment in the way proponents of the moral-difference view believe it does is largely, in the end, a matter of the general moral-justificational framework one embraces. I have attempted to show some of the dangers inherent in an approach that would place moral focus on the causal effects of our actions. Martha Nussbaum has recently argued that judicious moral judgment requires a view of the world as one of "imperfect human efforts and of complex obstacles to doing well ... of scarcity and accident."[14] What is required of the moral judge, she says, "is a gentle art of particular perception." One of the dangers inherent in a causal approach is that it risks separating our moral judgments of actions and agents from the springs and purposes of the actions and agents being judged, as well as from the exigencies and limitations of our world that affect all of us as actors, by constraining the options open to us. Whether or not the moral-difference view can in the end ensure judicious judgment by directing us to the right particulars, I have attempted to show that causal accounts, left alone, clearly cannot.

NOTES

1. Thomas Nagel, "The Limits of Objectivity," in S. McMurrin, ed., *The Tanner Lectures on Human Values*, vol. 1. Cambridge: Cambridge University Press, 1980, p. 130 (my emphasis); as quoted in N. Ann Davis, "The Doctrine of Double Effect: Problems of Interpretation," *Pacific Philosophical Quarterly* 65; 1984: 107–123, p. 108.

2. This point is made explicitly in connection with acts of nonintervention, but Frey's arguments about the moral status of the intention/foresight distinction are most often framed in terms of the causal contributions of acts of nonintervention (allowing, permitting).

3. N. Ann Davis, "The Doctrine of Double Effect," p. 108, emphasis added.

4. Arthur Ripstein, "Equality, Luck, and Responsibility," *Philosophy and Public Affairs* 23; Winter 1994: 3–23, pp. 6–7.

5. Ripstein, "Equality, Luck, and Responsibility," pp. 6–7.

6. Whether the doctrine of double effect and the moral difference view central to it are essentially bound to absolutist views is a debated matter. See, for example, Joseph Boyle, "Who Is Entitled to Double Effect?" and "Further Thoughts on Double Effects: Some Preliminary Responses," *The Journal of Medicine and Philosophy* 16; October 1991: 475–494, 565–570; Frances M. Kamm, "The Doctrine of Double Effect: Reflections on Theoretical and Practical Issues," *The Journal of Medicine and Philosophy* 16; October 1991: 571–585.

7. This is Bernard Williams's metaphor in "A Critique of Utilitarianism," in J. J. C. Smart and Williams, *Utilitarianism: For and Against.* Cambridge: Cambridge University Press, 1973, p. 96.

8. For recent, detailed discussions of the doctrine of double effect, see *The Journal of Medicine and Philosophy* 16; October 1991, which is devoted in its entirety to this issue.

9. N. Ann Davis rigorously takes on this issue in "The Doctrine of Double Effect."

10. See N. Ann Davis's contribution in the present volume.

11. Michael Bratman makes important strides in this direction in *Intention, Plans, and Practical Reason.* Cambridge, MA: Harvard University Press, 1987; see especially Chapter 10.

12. See Bratman, *Intention, Plans, and Practical Reason*, pp. 152ff, esp. pp. 163–164.

13. See Boyle, "Who Is Entitled to Double Effect?" p. 476.

14. Martha Nussbaum, "Equity and Mercy," *Philosophy and Public Affairs* 22; Spring 1993: 91–2, 103.

Withdrawal of Treatment versus Killing of Patients

BARUCH BRODY

Baylor College of Medicine and Rice University, Houston, Texas

In a very important study published in The Lancet,[1] van der Maas and his colleagues presented information on events surrounding the death of Dutch patients. According to their data, 17.5 percent of the patients who died had received such high dosages of opioids to alleviate pain and other symptoms that their lives might have been shortened. Mostly, the shortening of life involved hours or days, but it sometimes involved weeks or months. In 6 percent of these cases, life-termination was the primary goal. According to their data, another 17.5 percent of the patients who died had life prolonging therapy withheld or withdrawn from them. The resulting nonprolongation of life was an explicit goal in half of these cases, and the estimate of the amount of life foregone was considerably greater than in the cases of patients receiving high dosages of opioids. Finally, according to their data, administering lethal drugs at the patient's request occurred in 1.8 percent of all deaths, and occurred without an explicit request just before the administration of the lethal drugs in 0.8 percent of all deaths. The authors introduced a new term, a medical decision concerning the end of life (MDEL), meant to cover all three of these decisions, and summarized their report with the claim that MDELs deserve much more attention in research, teaching, and public debate since they occur in 38 percent of all deaths.

Some will find this new term very useful. Whatever type of decision is made (to provide the opioids, to withhold or withdraw care, to administer the lethal drugs), the decision is probably followed in each case by the death of the patient at an earlier time than the time the patient would have died but for the decision, and the decision is made with the recognition that this would probably happen. Others will find this new term unhelpful, precisely because it lumps the three types of cases together, disregarding important moral distinctions between them, distinctions having to do with the intentions of the parties involved, with the cause of the death (or with the explanation of the death's occurring earlier), or with the nature of the actions carrying out the decision. This paper is an attempt to examine at least some of the issues raised by these conflicting perceptions of this new term.

My main focus will be on the question of whether, from the moral perspective, the withholding or withdrawing of life-preserving therapy is significantly different than the administration of lethal drugs. To avoid extra complications, I will confine my attention to these cases, and leave out issues raised by the usage of high dosages of opioids. In the first section, I will present two familiar arguments, resting on common intuitions, one suggesting that there is no significant moral difference between the two types of cases and the other suggesting that there is. I will also present my reasons for supposing that the second argument is more persuasive. In the second section, I will offer my reasons for not drawing many of the conclusions that are normally drawn by people who do accept the moral significance of the distinction between the cases. Finally, in the last part of the paper, I will look at two attempts to explain the difference between the two cases and argue that one is preferable to the other. The conclusion for which I will be arguing is that there is a morally significant distinction between administering lethal drugs to patients and withholding/withdrawing therapy from them, a distinction based on the distinction between killing and letting die, but that both the meaning of those distinctions and their implications requires much further analysis.

TWO ARGUMENTS

The first of the two arguments was offered by James Rachels in a now classic article which appeared in 1975.[2] The argument has been restated on other occasions by Rachels and others, but I think that it is useful to begin with the original presentation of it. The argument runs as follows:

One reason why so many think that there is an important moral difference between active and passive euthanasia is that they think killing someone is morally worse than letting someone die. But is it? Is killing, in itself, worse than letting die? To investigate this issue, two cases may be considered that are exactly alike except that one involves killing whereas the other one involves letting someone die ... Let us consider this pair of cases. In the first, Smith stands to gain a large inheritance if anything should happen to his 6-year-old cousin. One evening while the child is taking his bath, Smith sneaks into the bathroom and drowns the child, and then arranges things so that it will look like an accident. In the second, Jones also stands to gain if anything should happen to his 6-year-old cousin. Like Smith, Jones sneaks in planning to drown the child in his bath. However, just as he enters the bathroom

Jones sees the child slip and hit his head, and fall face down in the water. Jones is delighted; he stands by, ready to push the child's head back under if it is necessary, but it is not necessary.... Now Smith killed the child, whereas Jones "merely" let the child die. That is the only difference between them. Did either man behave better, from a moral point of view? If the distinction between killing and letting die were in itself a morally important matter, one should say that Jones's behavior was less reprehensible than Smith's. But does one really want to say that? I think not.

The second of the arguments we will be considering was my own, offered in the course of a discussion of abortions when the mother's life is threatened:3

The obligation not to take a life is clearly of a higher priority than the obligation to save lives and is present in a great many cases in which the latter is not. After all, while I am normally under an obligation to another person not to take his life even when my own life or my own well being is at stake, I certainly am not normally under an obligation to another person to save his life at the cost of my own life (or even at the cost of a significant impairment of my well-being).

Each of these arguments needs to be restated so as to make them applicable to our issue and then each needs to be evaluated.

I offer the following as a reconstruction of Rachels's argument.

1. If there is a morally significant difference between administering lethal drugs and withholding or withdrawing life preserving therapy, it is because the former involves killing while the latter involves letting someone die, and there is a morally significant difference between those two;

2. If there is a morally significant difference between killing and letting someone die in at least some cases, that would be a sufficiently important difference so that it would make a morally significant difference in every case;

3. The only difference between the behavior of Smith and Jones is that one involves a killing while the other involves letting someone die;

4. Intuitively, however, their behavior is equally bad, so this is a case in which the difference between killing and letting die makes no morally significant difference;

5. Consequently, there is no morally significant difference in any case between killing and letting die and between administering lethal drugs and withholding or withdrawing life-preserving therapy.

Many have offered good criticisms of this argument.[4] They have pointed out that no arguments are offered in support of (2), and that it may well be that there is a morally significant difference between killing and letting someone die in some cases even if there is no such difference in cases like that of Smith and Jones. Others have challenged (4), either claiming that our intuitions are not fine enough to discriminate among two very evil forms of behavior, even if one is worse than another, and that is why we mistakenly judge that the two are equally bad even when one is worse than the other, or claiming that our intuitions are really only telling us that Jones and Smith are equally bad people for doing what they did, even if what one did was worse than what the other did, and that (4) confuses the intuitive judgment about the people with the very different judgment about their behavior.

While these familiar criticisms are correct, I think that they don't address another fundamental problem which needs to be emphasized. The problem is that the concept of making a morally significant difference has been given insufficient attention in the debate. There are, after all, many ways in which a distinction can make a morally significant difference. The distinction can make a morally significant difference as to when different moral obligations are present, as to the strength of the different obligations in relation to other obligations or to each other, as to the extent of the sacrifices we are called on to make to satisfy the differing obligations, as to the degree of condemnation called for by violations of the different obligations, and so forth. Now what is being claimed when it is said in (4) that there is no morally significant difference between Smith's behavior and Jones's behavior? I would suggest that the intuition being appealed to is that the behavior of the two are deserving of equal condemnation. Suppose that this is true. By itself, this tells us nothing, even for that one case, about other morally significant differences between the behaviors in question. It certainly tells us nothing about these other morally significant differences in other cases. In order for the argument to go through, (2) would have to be strengthened even further to become (2*):

2*. If the distinction between killing and letting die makes a morally significant difference in some way in at least one case, then that would be such an important distinction that it would make a morally significant difference in all relevant ways in all cases.

There is even less reason to believe (2*) than there is to believe (2).

The point of this last set of remarks is not just to add one more criticism to an already ample list, although it certainly does do that. I want to be making the more general point that we need to be very attentive to the many different ways in which a distinction may make a morally significant difference as we discuss the question of whether or not the distinction between killing and letting die makes a morally significant difference.

With this understanding in mind, let us turn to a reconstruction of the argument I offered for the moral significance of the distinctions in question. I would offer the following as a reconstruction (with some modifications to make it directly applicable to the discussion in this paper).

1. There are many cases in which we face certain decisions which, if made, will result in significant sacrifices on our part and which, if not made, will mean that people die earlier than they would have but for our not making the decision.

2. Even if those decisions result in our own death or a significant diminution of our wellbeing, we are morally obligated in at least some cases to make those decisions if not doing so means that we will kill innocent human beings.

3. In parallel circumstances, we are not obligated to make those decisions, precisely because of the sacrifices they entail, if not making those decisions only means that we will let some innocent human beings die.

4. This shows that there is at least one morally important distinction between killing and letting someone die.

5. Since administering lethal drugs involves killing someone while withholding or withdrawing life-sustaining therapy only involves letting someone die, this also shows that there is at least one morally important difference between administering lethal drugs and withholding or withdrawing life-sustaining therapy.

Premises (2) and (3) can be supported by reference to simple threat cases. Even if a third party holds a gun to my head and convincingly threatens to kill me unless I kill you, I am still obliged not to kill you. I am certainly not obliged, however, to not let you die if in similar circumstances a third party convincingly threatens to kill me if I do not let you die. Naturally, there are more complex types of threat cases (e.g., innocent shields, people to whom I have fiduciary obligations) which require much further analysis, but the difficult questions raised by such cases should not prevent us from recognizing that simple threat cases validate (2) and (3).

There has been considerable recent literature devoted to criticizing these intuitive claims about appeals to costs and sacrifices justifying certain options such as the option to let the person die. Perhaps the most sustained critic of these intuitive claims is Shelly Kagan.[5] I will not here attempt to respond fully to his arguments, since a full response would lie beyond the scope of this paper. Let me only say that I would challenge his arguments on methodological grounds. The thrust of Kagan's sustained argument (in his Chapters 7–9) against options based on the appeal to costs is that moderates are unable to provide a certain type of justificatory argument for the existence of options, and I would challenge his claim that such an argument is needed.

In my original presentation of the above-cited argument, I went on to draw certain conclusions about other ways in which the distinction is morally significant, namely, the claim that in cases where the two obligations are in conflict with each other, the obligation not to kill takes precedence over the obligation not to let someone die. The validity of that additional step, and others like it, will be the topic of the next section of this paper, where we will attempt to explore the full extent of the moral significance of the distinction.

THE SIGNIFICANCE OF ACCEPTING THE DISTINCTION

Let us suppose then that there are good reasons for believing that there is at least one morally significant distinction between killing and letting someone die and consequently between our obligation not to kill someone and our obligation not to let someone die. The former obligation is more demanding than the latter obligation in that we are required to make greater sacrifices to insure that we respect the former obligation than we are required to make to insure that we respect the latter obligation.

This point has an important clinical implication. The suggestion has sometimes been advanced[6] that there are modalities of therapy that are sufficiently expensive that our society is not obliged to provide them to certain patients even if a failure to provide them means that patients will die earlier than they would have died if they had received that form of therapy. Such a suggestion is actually quite consonant with our observations about the limited extent of the sacrifices we are obliged to make in order to avoid letting people die. To be sure, those observations referred only to the limited extent of our individual obligations to make sacrifices to save lives, as opposed to our obligations as part of an organized society, but in the end social obligations can only be met by imposing financial burdens on individual taxpayers, so those observations need to be carried over to the obligations of an organized society. I must confess that I am often quite surprised[7] by the vehemence with which such suggestions are rejected. However, because we are required to make far greater sacrifices to avoid killing people, those economic considerations would almost certainly never, by themselves, justify a policy of killing such patients. So the one distinction between killing and letting die which we have defended has important clinical significance.

Are there other important moral distinctions between killing and letting die and the associated obligations not to do either? Most crucially, is there a difference in the implications of the fact that the person in question wants to be allowed to die or wants to be killed? These questions bring us to the heart of the debate about active and passive voluntary euthanasia.

The discussions in our society about advance directives, do not resuscitate (DNR) orders, and death with dignity have led to a broadly shared consensus that the moral obligation to not let someone die does not exist when the person who would die is a competent adult and refuses life-prolonging therapy. Those who oppose voluntary active euthanasia often[8] argue that the consensus should not be extended to voluntary active euthanasia precisely because there is a morally significant difference between killing and letting someone die. Those who advocate the licitness of voluntary active euthanasia often[9] argue that it should be extended to voluntary active euthanasia because there really is no morally significant difference between letting someone die and killing them. I would like to suggest that both lines of argumentation are flawed.

The former line of argumentation in the active euthanasia debate is flawed precisely because the existence of one morally significant difference between the two does not mean that the two are different in all important respects. Let us say that an obligation is waivable providing that it no longer exists when the individual to whom it is owed waives that obligation. Let us grant the truth of the consensus view that the obligation not to let someone die is waivable by that person. Finally, let us accept the conclusion of the first part of this paper that the obligation not to kill is more demanding than the obligation not to let someone die, so that there is a morally significant difference between killing and letting someone die. What follows from all of this about the waivability of the obligation not to kill? As far as I can see, nothing follows, since it has not been shown that more demanding obligations cannot be as waivable as less demanding obligations. Moreover, there are intuitive reasons for thinking that the issue of whether an obligation is waivable is quite different from the issue of how demanding is the obligation. The question of waivability has to do with whether the obligation is at all present, as is evidenced by the fact that there is usually no moral merit in performing a waived obligation, while the question of how demanding is the obligation has to do with the justification for not performing an obligation which is present, as is evidenced by the fact that respecting the obligation in a very demanding situation is often a highly commendable supererogatory act. Given the very different nature of these issues, there is little reason to expect that more demanding obligations will be less waivable than less demanding obligations.

This last point is consonant with a point made by Frances Kamm in an extremely important article.[10] In that article, she distinguished what she called the *effort standard* for comparing the stringency of obligations (this being our notion of how demanding is an obligation) from what she called the *precedence standard* (this being the question of which obligation must be fulfilled when it is impossible to fulfill both), and argued that one obligation might be more stringent than another on one standard while less stringent than another on the other standard. Her argument, if successful, would, of course, undercut my conclusion in my work on abortion that the obligation not to kill takes precedence over the obligation not to let someone die because the latter obligation is less demanding than the former. Our conclusions in the area of euthanasia are however quite consonant, for we are both arguing that great care must be taken not to draw unwarranted conclusions from the premise that there is a morally significant difference between killing and letting someone die in that the obligation not to do the former is more demanding than the obligation not to do the latter.

The latter line of argumentation in the active euthanasia debate, that active euthanasia is justified because there really is no difference between killing and letting die, is flawed because it denies the moral significance of a distinction whose moral significance has been established. But it is also flawed by the fact that those who offer it have misunderstood the dialectical situation; supporters of voluntary active euthanasia on the grounds that the individual has waived any obligation not to be killed can maintain that support even if they concede that there are significant moral differences between letting someone die and killing someone.

In short, then, I believe that we should grant that the distinction between killing and letting die is a clinically relevant and morally significant distinction but insist that the existence of such a distinction does not settle the question of the licitness of voluntary active euthanasia. How then should that question of licitness be decided? While a full answer lies beyond the scope of this paper, I would offer two lines of enquiry which seem to me to be fruitful.[11]

The first addresses the issue of whether there are bases for the wrongness of killings other than the obligation to the person not to kill him or her, bases that may mean that killings remain wrong even if the person in question requests that he or she be killed so that the obligation to him or her has been waived. The second addresses the issue of whether there are nonwaivable obligations, so that killing may be wrong in cases of voluntary euthanasia, even if the person in question requests that he or she be killed, precisely because it violates a nonwaivable obligation to the person in question. These are to my mind the issues that deserve attention, and they remain perplexing even if we grant the existence of a morally significant distinction between killing and letting die.

TWO WAYS OF DRAWING THE DISTINCTION

We have so far focused on whether or not there is a morally significant distinction between killing and letting someone die and on what is the significance of the existence of such a distinction, if there is one, for the discussion of active euthanasia. We have not until now said anything about the nature of the distinction; that is the topic for this section. We will consider two accounts, the intending the death account and the causing the death account, and we shall note various problems faced by each. Our conclusion will be that the latter account is more promising than the former, but that much work is required by the causing the death account because it is far from satisfactory at this point. When the causing the death account, or some other account, is developed in a fully satisfactory manner, it may shed light on some of the crucial issues identified but left unresolved in the first two sections of this paper.

It is important to remember that we are dealing with decisions that are such that but for the decision the patient would probably have died at a later point in time than the patient did die. The decision is then a necessary condition of the patient's having died at the earlier time. The intending the death account claims that the decision constitutes a decision to kill if the earlier death of the patient is intended as an end, or as a means to attain an end, for which the decision is made, and constitutes a decision to let die if the earlier death of the patient is foreseen but not intended in either way. The causing the death account claims that the decision constitutes a decision to kill if it causes the earlier death of the patient and constitutes a decision to let die if it is no more than a necessary condition of the earlier death.

The intending the death account was employed by Grisez and Boyle[12] in their discussion of killing by omission.

> On the analysis of this sort of omission which we just now stated it clearly is possible to kill in the strict sense by deliberately letting someone die. If one adopts the proposal to bring about a person's death [their language for intending the death of the person] and realizes this proposal by not behaving as one otherwise would behave, then one is committed to the state of affairs which includes the person's

death. This commitment, although carried out by a nonperformance, is morally speaking an act of killing.

As a result of adopting this approach, these authors concluded that:[13]

> The moral legitimacy of refusing treatment in some cases on some such grounds certainly was part of what Pius XII was indicating by his famous distinction between ordinary and extraordinary means of treatment.... The conception of extraordinary means is abused, however, when the proposal is to bring about death by the omission of treatment, and the difficulties of the treatment are pointed to by way of rationalizing the murderous act. If it is decided that a person would be better off dead and that treatment which would be given to another will be withheld because of the poor quality of the life to be preserved, then the focus in decision is not upon the means and its disadvantageous consequences.

I understand the authors to be saying that such withholdings are morally illicit cases of killing by omission (something which is possible once you focus on intentions) precisely because the resulting earlier death of the patient is an intended end of the decision, as the patient's continued existence is judged a loss (because "the person would be better off dead"). They would, however, approve such withholdings as morally licit if it is the treatment which is found to be excessively burdensome, for in such cases, the earlier death of the patient is not the intended end of the decision, which is made to avoid the burden of the treatment, nor is it even an intended means to attain the end.

    I find this way of drawing the distinction troubling. One way of explaining why is to return to some of the data presented in the above-cited Dutch study. In about half of the cases of the withholding or withdrawal of therapy, "not prolonging the patient's life was an explicit goal,"[14] The authors presented little information about the modalities of therapy involved, but they presumably ranged over the usual, including CPR, intubation, dialysis, blood products, antibiotics, and so forth. Such decisions, regardless of the intention, are normally taken as paradigms of decisions to let patients die, rather than as decisions to kill. On the intending the death account, however, they may be, depending on the intention, decisions to kill, and would be morally licit only if active euthanasia was licit. This seems wrong. It would seem at least possible to deny the moral licitness of killing patients while accepting as licit the decisions described in the Dutch study even if the death of the patient was an explicit goal. Perhaps there are other ways of allowing for this position, but it seems that the best way would be to deny that those decisions constituted decisions to kill, regardless of the intentions. But to say this is to reject the intending the death account of the distinction in question, which can be upheld only if one is willing to condemn many of these decisions which are normally seen as morally licit.

To my mind, the clinical importance of this point cannot be overemphasized. As pointed out, those who offer the intending the death account usually claim that decisions to withhold or withdraw therapy are justified because the death of the patient is not intended either as the end of the decision or as the means to attain the end. On their account, the end is avoiding the burdens of the treatment, and the death of the patient is not even the means to attain that end, as is evidenced by the fact that the decision makers would not oppose the patient's continuing to live if the burden-some treatments could be avoided. On this account, the death is at most a foreseen side effect. That account is not consonant with much of my clinical experience, which is similar in this respect to what the Dutch investigators found. In many cases of with-holding or withdrawing therapy, it is the continued existence of the patient in the condition in which they are in which is found burdensome, not the treatment itself. "Mama wouldn't have wanted to live this way" is the common refrain, and with-holdings or withdrawings of therapy are undertaken in response to that refrain. The death may be the intended end for which the decision is made, or, more plausibly, the intended means to avoid the continued suffering and indignity of living that way. It is certainly not a mere foreseen side effect. We want an account of the distinction between killing and letting die that sees most of the resulting withholdings or with-drawings of care as cases of letting die, and the intending the death account does not provide such an account.

Let us turn from the intending the death account to the causing the death account. That account distinguishes necessary conditions of the earlier death from causes of the earlier death, and describes decisions which are no more than the for-mer as decisions to allow someone to die and decisions which are the latter as deci-sions to kill.

The causing the death account is not vulnerable to the objections we raised to the intending the death account. It says that even if the decision to withhold or with-draw care has as its end, or as an intended means to attain its end, the death of the patient, it is merely a decision to let the patient die because it is merely a necessary condition of the earlier death of the patient and not a cause of the earlier death of the patient. The cause of the earlier death of the patient remains the patient's underlying disease condition.

Will this move work? There are two potential problems with it. The first is that it presupposes the possibility of distinguishing causes from necessary conditions in such a way that normal cases of witholding or withdrawing care will turn out to be necessary conditions and not causes. The second is that all of this needs to be done for the earlier death of the patient, not just the death of the patient, and that seems even more problematic. Let me elaborate on both of these potential problems, and on possible responses to them.

While the theory of causes as necessary conditions is not without adherents, most authors reject it, in part because there are causes which are not necessary con-ditions (as in the case of causal overdetermination) but primarily because many necessary conditions seem too remote from the effect to be considered its cause.[15] So the very existence of the distinction between causes and necessary conditions (which is presupposed by the causing the death account), while needing further elaboration, is not by itself the first potential problem. The problem is that it is far from certain that elaborations of the distinction will result in withholdings or withdrawings being categorized for the most part as necessary conditions and as allowings to die rather than as causes and as killings. My first concern is not based on my belief that all withholdings or withdrawings must be categorized as mere allowings to die. I have elsewhere[16] suggested that there are intuitive reasons for supposing that the withholding or withdrawing of nutrition and/or hydration might in some cases actually be a cause of death and a killing. This is particularly plausible in cases where the patient could, even if with difficulty, swallow food if it were provided, so that it is hard to say that the patient's disease process caused the death if the patient dies from starvation. Rather, my concern is based on the belief that most withholdings or withdrawings should be so categorized, and until the cause–necessary condition distinction is adequately drawn, we have no way of being sure that its use to ground the killing–allowing to die distinction will produce the intuitively appropriate results, the very results that the intending the death account failed to produce.

My second concern arises out of the following argument that is sometimes presented to me by clinical colleagues hesitating about withholding or withdrawing of care: while the cause of the death of the patient may be the patient's underlying illness, the proposed withholding or withdrawing of care certainly causes the patient to die sooner than the patient would otherwise die. That is enough to make it a killing rather than an allowing to die. So how can it be justified unless active euthanasia is justified? In effect, they are claiming that the causing the death account should distinguish killings from allowings to die by distinguishing causes and necessary conditions of *the earlier death of the patient*, not just of *the death of the patient*, and the proposed withholdings or withdrawings of care are the causes of the former even if they are not the causes of the latter. So we must either treat normal DNR orders and other such decisions as killings or find another account to replace the causing the death account of the killing/allowing to die distinction. I believe that this is a serious concern, but that it can be met by a plausible set of metaphysical moves. The first is the claim that the death of the patient and the earlier death of the patient are the same event. The second is the claim that causality is an extensional relation, so that if e* and e** are the same events, they must have the same cause. If these two claims are true,[17] then any cause of the earlier death of the patient would have to be a cause of the patient's death. From the perspective of logic, this means that my colleagues must conclude that the withholding or withdrawing in question either is the cause of both the death and the earlier death or of neither. From the dialectical perspective, given that they began by conceding that it is not the cause of the death, they must conclude that it is also not the cause of the earlier death. At most, they can say that the decision explains why the patient died sooner than he or she would have otherwise died, but that is compatible with its not being the cause either of the death or of the earlier death, and therefore, on the causing the death account, with its not being a killing. So this second concern may be resolvable by these metaphysical reflections, but further consideration of their adequacy is certainly needed.

Let me summarize the argument of this section as follows: we need a distinction between killing and allowing to die that treats the usual decisions to write DNR orders, to withhold antibiotics and even to extubate nonweanable patients as allowings to die and not as killings. Since these usual decisions are often made with the death of the patient as the intended end or as an intended means, the intending the death account will not do. The causing the death account may work, but that depends on needed further analysis both of the distinction between causes and necessary conditions and of the metaphysics of causality.

Shelly Kagan is far less optimistic that the causing the death account of the distinction will work, and he offers a series of arguments for that pessimism in Chapter 3 of his book.[18] Some of them involve his demand for a certain type of justificatory argument, a demand that I have already indicated I would reject on methodological grounds. Others (such as the opening paralysis argument) can be met in ways that Kagan himself indicates. But there are two very troubling types of cases[19] which cannot be so quickly dismissed. I want to focus on the first type of case, since it is directly relevant to our discussion.

Kagan asks us to contrast a normal case in which a physician disconnects a dying patient from a respirator from a case in which a stranger does so in order that a rival will die in time for the stranger to win a reward. Kagan says that we would describe the physician's act as allowing the patient to die while we would describe the stranger's act as killing the patient. But how could this differential description be justified, Kagan asks, on the causing the death account? After all, the causal connection in the two cases between the action and the death is clearly the same. Note, by the way, that adherents of the intending the death account should take no solace from this objection, since the doctor may well be intending the death of the patient as much as the stranger (even if for very different motives), so both cases might well be killings on that account as well. In any event, does not this type of case show that the causing the death account of the distinction will not work?

I can think of no response that is entirely satisfactory, but the following at least offers the possibility of partially reconciling our intuitions about the case of the stranger with an otherwise attractive theoretical account of an important distinction: the stranger's actions are as morally reprehensible as if he had killed the patient even if in fact he did not kill the patient. The claim that he did not kill the patient is required to reconcile the case with our theoretical account of the killing–allowing to die distinction, while the claim that what he did was as reprehensible as if he had killed the patient is required to at least partially capture our intuitions about the case.

If he did not kill the patient, what did he do which is just as morally reprehensible? To begin with, he brought about the conditions in which the patient's underlying medical problem caused the patient's death, and did so for reprehensible motives. There is no reason why doing that with those motives could not be as reprehensible as killing, even if doing that with very different motives (as in the case of the doctor) is neither a killing nor even a morally reprehensible act. Second, having done so, he allowed the patient to die, and did so for reprehensible motives. Remembering our earlier discussion, there is no reason why we cannot say that some allowings to die (particularly those done for reprehensible motives) are as reprehensible as killings, even if there is a morally significant difference between killings and allowings to die.

Is this response satisfactory? I think that in the end the answer to that question depends upon one's methodology. If, as I do, you view moral theorizing as an attempt to systematize and explain particular intuitions in the way in which scientific theorizing is an attempt to systematize and explain particular observations, and if you accept the resulting legitimacy of the moral theorist modifying or even rejecting anomalous intuitions, then perhaps it is. But other approaches to moral theorizing might find it less satisfactory. Again, this is a matter for further thought.

CONCLUSIONS

I have attempted to argue for a number of conclusions and to suggest a number of areas for further investigation. The conclusions are that there is a morally significant difference between killing and letting die (and therefore between administering lethal drugs and withholding or withdrawing life sustaining therapy), a distinction based on the distinction between a cause and a necessary condition, but that the existence of this distinction does not settle the issue of the licitness of active euthanasia. The areas for further investigation include the relation between various possible differences between killing and letting die, why it is wrong to kill, whether all obligations are waivable, and what is the causality–necessary condition distinction.

In the end, we may or may not conclude that voluntary active euthanasia is at least sometimes morally licit. But even if we conclude that it is, its licitness raises many issues of great complexity not necessarily raised in the discussion of passive euthanasia. It is not helpful, therefore, to lump a wide variety of morally different types of decisions under this new rubric of a medical decision concerning the end of life (MDEL).[20]

NOTES

1. P.J. van der Maas et al., "Euthanasia and Other Medical Decisions Concerning the End of Life," *Lancet* 338; 1991: 669–674.

2. J. Rachels, "Active and Passive Euthanasia," *New England Journal of Medicine* 292; 1975: 78–80.

3. B.A. Brody, *Abortion and the Sanctity of Human Life*. Cambridge, MA: M.I.T. Press, 1975, p. 17.

4. See, for example, the papers collected in or cited in B. Steinbock, *Killing and Letting Die*. Englewood Cliffs, NJ: Prentice Hall, 1980.

5. S. Kagan, *The Limits of Morality*. New York: Oxford University Press, 1989.

6. Most notably by the defenders of Oregon-style rationing. See, for example, H.G. Welch, "Health Care Tickets for the Uninsured," *New England Journal of Medicine* 321; 1989: 1261–1265.

7. Some of that surprise, directed against those in the Jewish tradition who have vehemently rejected the suggestion, is found in B.A. Brody, "The Economics of the Laws of Rodef," *Svara* 1; 1990: 67–69.

8. This is the crux of the argument offered in Chapters 11 and 12 of G. Grisez and J. Boyle, *Life and Death with Liberty and Justice*. Notre Dame, IN: University of Notre Dame Press, 1979. The way in which they understand that distinction will be discussed below.

9. See, for example, P. Singer, *Practical Ethics*. Cambridge: Cambridge University Press, 1979, pp. 150–151.

10. F. Kamm, "Supererogation and Obligation," *Journal of Philosophy* 82; 1985: 118–138.

11. I first raised both of these issues in B. Brody, "Voluntary Euthanasia and the Law," in M. Kohl ed. *Beneficent Euthanasia*. Buffalo, NY: Prometheus Books, 1975, pp. 218–232.

12. Grisez and Boyle, *Life and Death*, p. 415.

13. Grisez and Boyle, *Life and Death*, p. 418.

14. van der Mass, "Euthanasia and Other Medical Decisions," p. 672.

15. This is the point of the legal discussion of the distinction between causation in fact and proximate causation. See, for example, the discussion in Chapter 7 of W.P. Keeton, *Prosser and Keeton on the Law of Torts*, 5th ed. St. Paul, MN: West Publishing, 1984.

16. Most recently in B.A. Brody, "Special Ethical Issues in the Management of PVS Patients," *Law Medicine and Health Care* 20; Spring-Summer 1992: 104–115.

17. For a defense of them, see my discussion in B.A. Brody, *Identity and Essence*. Princeton, NJ: Princeton University Press, 1980, pp. 65–70.

18. Kagan, *Limits of Morality*.

19. Kagan, *Limits of Morality*, pp. 101–111.

20. I am indebted for helpful comments to Tris Engelhardt, Andy Lustig, Larry McCullough, George Sher, and Larry Temkin.

Killing and Letting Die: Some Comments

JUDITH JARVIS THOMSON

Massachusetts Institute of Technology, Cambridge, Massachusetts

Baruch Brody's paper covers a lot of very interesting territory, but I think that the two things most important to him in his paper are first, his argument for the conclusion that "the distinction between killing and letting die is a clinically relevant and morally significant distinction...." (p. 96), and second, his discussion of the question what exactly that distinction consists in. I will concentrate primarily on the second.

Brody says he will discuss two ways in which it might be thought possible to distinguish between killing and letting die, but in fact he doesn't do this. What he invites us to consider are instead two ways in which it might be thought possible to distinguish between a *decision* to kill and a *decision* to let die. That's puzzling. For it wasn't the distinction between kinds of decision that was supposed to be clinically relevant and morally significant, but rather the distinction between the kinds of things those decisions are decisions to *do*.

Let's anyway begin with the first of the two ways. Brody says: suppose a decision made by a doctor is a necessary condition of the patient's dying earlier than he would otherwise die. Then, Brody goes on, the first way of making the distinction is this: "the decision constitutes a decision to kill if the earlier death of the patient is intended as an end, or as a means to attain an end, for which the decision is made, and constitutes a decision to let die if the earlier death of the patient is foreseen but not intended in either way." (p. 97)

Now a person's intentions are surely relevant to the question whether he decides to kill or to let die, but I think they are flatly irrelevant to the question whether in acting on the decision he actually does kill or let die. If I fire a gun out the window, and the bullet lodges in Alfred's head, and I thereby cause him to die, then my intentions in firing the gun may be thought relevant to the question whether I decided to kill Alfred; but my intentions are irrelevant to the question whether I actually did kill him—indeed, I did kill him no matter what my intentions were, whether I fired the gun to kill him or merely thought it would be fun to fire a gun out the window, not caring in the least whether I shot anyone. Similarly, if I can but do not save the life of someone I have no connection with, and who therefore dies, I do not kill him; I merely let him die, whatever my intentions are in refraining—I merely let him die whether I refrain from saving him in order that he die, or merely can't be bothered to save him.

What this means is that while an appeal to intentions may be helpful in settling whether a *decision* is a *decision* to kill or to let die, it is no help in settling whether a person does in fact kill or let die. An interesting question that arises is whether appeals to intention—and the doctrine of double effect from which all this issues— would loom as large in this literature as it does had the subject not been unwittingly changed, that is, from the distinction between killing and letting die to the distinction between deciding to kill and deciding to let die.

But it really is the distinction between killing and letting die that Brody wants to say is clinically relevant and morally significant. If that distinction is relevant and significant, then of course we will want people to take account of it in deciding what to do. We will want them not to decide to kill where killing would be impermissible, and we will think it all right for them to decide to let die where letting die would be permissible. But the prior question is whether killing or letting die would be permissible or impermissible, and prior to that is the question what the distinction between killing and letting die is itself supposed to consist in.

So let us turn to the second of the two accounts that Brody discusses. What he offers us is again an account of the distinction between decisions to kill and decisions to let die. Brody says: suppose a decision made by a doctor is a necessary condition of the patient's dying earlier than he would otherwise die. Then, he goes on, the second way of making the distinction is this: "the decision constitutes a decision to kill if it causes the earlier death of the patient and constitutes a decision to let die if it is no more than a necessary condition of the earlier death." (p. 97)

Now I think this is markedly less plausible as an account of the distinction between *deciding* to kill and *deciding* to let die: that distinction can't at all plausibly be thought to turn on whether one's decision does or does not in fact cause a death. But it does suggest the possibility of distinguishing between killing and letting die in terms of causality; and that idea seems more promising than the idea of distinguishing between killing and letting die in terms of intention.

How exactly are we to proceed? One possibility suggested by Brody's words comes out as follows. Suppose that Bert died at a certain time. Suppose also that Alfred's doing or refraining from doing something was a necessary condition of

Bert's death at that time. Then if in addition Alfred's doing or refraining from doing the thing positively caused Bert's death, then Alfred killed Bert; whereas if Alfred's doing or refraining from doing the thing was merely a necessary condition of Bert's death at that time, and did not positively cause it, then Alfred merely let Bert die.

Brody likes this proposal. He discusses two possible objections to it, but thinks they are not insuperable. I want to focus on his discussion of the first objection since it seems to me that something instructive emerges from it.

The first problem, he says, "is that [the proposal] presupposes the possibility of distinguishing causes from necessary conditions in such a way that normal cases of witholding/withdrawing care will turn out to be necessary conditions and not causes." (p. 99) The problem, he says, is not that of distinguishing between necessary conditions and causes; the problem is rather how to get it fixed that normal cases of witholding or withdrawing care are *not* causes of the death that then ensues.

That's interesting. Why should it get fixed that normal witholdings or withdrawings of care are not causes of the death that then ensues? Well, perhaps it seems intuitively right to think that normal witholdings or withdrawings of care are lettings die and not killings. Brody cites Shelley Kagan, who is certainly not alone in suggesting that "a normal case in which a physician disconnects a dying patient from a respirator" (p. 101) is a case in which the doctor does not kill the patient but merely lets the patient die. That means that normal witholdings or withdrawings of care had better turn out *not* to be causes of the death that then ensues if we are to accept Brody's causal account of the distinction between killing and letting die.

But let's have a closer look at that doctor who disconnects his dying patient from the respirator. Let's suppose he does this by pulling out the plug. Why isn't his pulling out the plug a cause of his patient's death?

Kagan invites us to compare the doctor with a stranger who wanders into the hospital, and pulls out the plug of another patient's respirator. Kagan says that's surely a killing, and not merely a letting die. But Kagan says: surely the one plug-pulling is no more a cause of the ensuing death than the other is.

Brody's reply is yes, the one plug-pulling is no more a cause of the ensuing death than the other is. Given Brody likes the causal account of the distinction between killing and letting die, he concludes that neither act is a killing, both acts are merely lettings die. But his conclusion that neither act is a killing strikes me as bizarre. If somebody is attached to a life-support system in a hospital, and I wander in and for my own purposes pull the plug, surely I do kill my victim. If a deep-sea diver is attached by a pipe to a breathing apparatus on board ship, and I'm a passenger and cut the pipe, surely I do kill the diver. If a window-washer is supported by a rope, and I untie it, surely I do kill him. It seems to me counter-intuitive in the extreme to deny these things.

What to do? One possibility of course is to reject Brody's causal account of the distinction between killing and letting die.

A second possibility is to say that both plug-pullings cause the ensuing deaths, and that both acts are therefore killings. I said that perhaps it seems intuitively right to think that normal witholdings or withdrawings of care are lettings die and not killings; but what is the source of that intuition? To the extent to which it issues from a desire to have *both* that the doctor's act is permissible, *and* that its permissibility is to be explained by appeal to the fact that it is not a killing but merely a letting die, then the intuition is suspect. For why does the permissibility of the doctor's act have to be explained in that way? I will return to this question later.

A third possibility is to say that the stranger's plug-pulling causes his victim's death whereas the doctor's plug-pulling does not cause his patient's death. How can that be the case given the fact that the one plug-pulling seems to have the same connection to a death that the other does? (Brody says the connection "is clearly the same". p. 101.) Well, but *is* the question whether a plug-pulling causes a death settled only by consideration of the events that follow the plug-pulling and issue in the death?

My own impression is that that is not all that matters. Let me mention just briefly two kinds of further considerations that are at least arguably relevant to the question whether one thing caused another.

In the first place, there is the question of who is under a duty to do what. If a train signalman is under a duty to flag the four o'clock train, and doesn't—perhaps he is eager for a crash, perhaps he is drunk, perhaps he simply couldn't care less— then we are inclined to want to say that his failing to flag the train causes the ensuing crash. By contrast, a bystander who could flag the next day's four o'clock, and doesn't cause the next day's crash. How so? The signalman was under a duty to flag his train, the bystander was not.

Second, there is the question who is, as it were, supplying the goods. If I am supplying life support for someone by pumping on a bicycle, and don't want to go on doing so, then arguably I do not cause the ensuing death if I simply stop pumping. If I'm happy to go on pumping, and you barge in and make me stop, then arguably you do cause the ensuing death.

If not the first, then anyway the second of these two kinds of consideration might be appealed to as ground for saying that while the stranger's plug-pulling does cause his victim's death, the doctor's does not. The doctor does not of course himself supply the current for the respirator he detaches his patient from; but he is agent for the hospital, which does.

There is much more that calls for examination here, and more generally as to which choice we should make among the three possibilities I mentioned. But I think that something instructive does emerge. Let's go back. Brody had argued in the first part of his paper that "the distinction between killing and letting die is a clinically relevant and morally significant distinction...." But we find ourselves in a philosophical mess and tangle when we try to become clear what that distinction consists in; and it should be stressed that we can't even begin on the task of working out why that distinction should be thought to matter from a moral point of view until we are clear what it consists in. Moral theorists need to worry about these matters; do *medical* people need to?

One of Brody's chief concerns was to have it turn out that normal witholdings and withdrawings of care are morally permissible. Does this *have* to be explained by getting it fixed that they are merely lettings die as opposed to killings? Consider again the doctor who disconnects his dying patient from the respirator. Why not explain why this is permissible by pointing to the array of facts that seem intuitively—and prephilosophically—to make it permissible, such as perhaps that we have been supplying that patient with something that is costly and in short supply, a something that no longer benefits him or his family, and that can be used instead to the benefit of others. We all certainly want rules laid down to guide medical practitioners in making decisions about the end of life; no one wants haphazard decisionmaking off the cuff. What I doubt is whether it is needed or even useful to try to view the wide variety of cases in the offing here through a grid marked off into killings and lettings die.

The Right to Refuse Treatment[1]

N. ANN DAVIS

University of Colorado, Boulder, Colorado

It is widely believed that patients are both morally and legally entitled to refuse life-saving medical treatment. But not all who endorse such rights believe that patients may receive support or assistance in ending their lives, even when it would involve "passively" (but deliberately) withholding or withdrawing lifesaving treatment rather than "actively" employing life-ending measures.[2] There are, it is believed, important differences between endorsing a patient's right to refuse lifesaving treatment (on the one hand) and allowing suicide, assisted suicide, or euthanasia (on the other).[3]

If many people assign moral significance to the distinction between honoring a refusal of treatment and assisting suicide or committing euthanasia, it seems reasonable to think that our laws and social policies should do the same. There are both moral and pragmatic reasons for thinking that social policies should be constrained by, and consistent with, widely held moral convictions.

But there are sometimes good reasons not to tailor our public policies to the cut of our common sense moral beliefs. On closer investigation, such beliefs may emerge as incoherent or insufficiently grounded; heaping the weight of social policy on such a tenuous foundation may thus be an invitation to sophistry, confusion, and abuse. I will argue that this is so in the present instance. If we choose to enact social policies that acknowledge a patient's right to refuse life-sustaining medical treatment, then we cannot narrowly constrain that right to exclude the permissibility of suicide or various forms of assisted suicide, including euthanasia.[4] On the other hand, if we are immovably committed to the rejection of all forms of medically assisted suicide and euthanasia, then we cannot continue to claim that patients have a strong right to refuse life-sustaining medical treatment. There is no viable *tertia via*.

My focus in this essay will be on one form of, or supposed rationale for, the restriction of the right to refuse treatment. The view that a patient's right to refuse lifesaving medical treatment is bounded by the state's entitlement (and perhaps, obligation) to prevent individuals from committing suicide, or to assist them in so doing.[5] I believe that this view is untenable, and that a consideration of why this is so can help illuminate our understanding of both the right to refuse treatment and the moral foundations on which it rests.

Part I of this essay contains a brief characterization of the right to refuse treatment. In Part II, I consider one attempt to restrict this right to refusals of treatment which are deemed nonsuicidal. In Part III, I present some reasons for rejecting this proposed restriction of the right to refuse treatment in favor of the broader construal of that right presented in Part I.

PART I: THE RIGHT TO REFUSE TREATMENT

Both our widely shared moral beliefs and our legal traditions acknowledge that patients have at least some sort of right to refuse lifesaving medical treatment. And, though it may be overridable in extreme circumstances, this right is generally thought to be a strong one. Provided they are competent, rational (i.e., able to perform the relevant means-end reasoning, and to understand the implications of their choices), and informed[6] about the nature and consequences of the proposed treatment and its alternatives, patients have the right to decline medical treatment even when the treatment appears to be beneficial, and the patient's reasons for rejecting it seem less than compelling to disinterested observers. Patients may reject lifesaving medical treatment even if—at the limit—the conditions obtain the following:

1. The treatment is thought to be essential to preserving the patient's life, and it is very likely that he or she would die without it. The patient's death would thus be a "foreseen consequence" of nontreatment, and the patient understands that this is so.[7]

2. The treatment is both efficacious and safe: it is likely that the patient's life would be prolonged by the treatment, and the risk of medical complications or side effects is low.

3. The treatment is restorative: if the patient were to have the treatment, he or she would not merely survive it, but survive it in a condition that would not be deemed medically unacceptable (i.e., the patient's projected post-treatment medical condition would not be one marked by unendurable pain, suffering, serious disfigurement, or a marked loss of dignity).

4. The treatment is neither prohibitively expensive nor highly technological.

5. It is reasonable to think that if the patient were to submit to the treatment (and perhaps, even if the patient were forced against his or her will to submit to it), he or she could go on to live a life that reasonable people would assess as a life worth living. Though there may be some risk that the patient would respond to forced treatment with distress and humiliation, disinterested observers believe that there is a significant possibility that these

would be surmountable, even if the attempt to restore the patient to a satisfactory life would involve a period of intensive psychotherapy or (nonvoluntary) hospitalization.

Finally–more controversially:

1. There are grounds for believing that the patient is declining the treatment not simply because he or she objects to that specific form of treatment as itself painful or demeaning–as might be the case in some sorts of chemotherapy–but because the patient believes that continuing to live in such circumstances would compromise important personal ideals or values. Either the patient follows an organized religion or personal creed that proscribes this form of treatment, or the patient simply thinks, for his or her own considered reasons, that undergoing the treatment would compromise his or her values in ways that would be unacceptable. There is thus good reason to resist the claim that the patient's decision is "simply a sign or result of clinical depression," and good reason to think that the patient has reflected on the moral or spiritual meaning of his or her choice, and chosen death.[8] The belief that we are entitled to repel others' interference–particularly when that interference takes the form of an invasion of our bodies–even when death is both foreseen and preventable is deeply held and widely shared. It is a reflection of belief in the importance of self-determination in the most personal dimensions of our lives, and of our understanding that the ability to exercise control over what others may do to our bodies is both a necessary condition of the success of most of our personal projects and the cornerstone of moral requirements that we respect both ourselves and other persons as rational agents. Belief in a person's right to refuse treatment is a part of moral common sense and the common law, and a tenet of many moral political and social theories. Thus, people often quote these noble sentiments:

> [n]o right is held more sacred, or is more carefully guarded by the common law, than the right of every individual to the possession and control of his own person, free from all restraint or interference of others, unless by clear and unquestionable authority of law.[9]

and "every human being of adult years and sound mind has a right to determine what shall be done with his own body."[10]

These sentiments eloquently express the conviction that recognition of the importance of bodily integrity and personal autonomy is essential. But beneath our widely shared agreement about the importance of these values lies significant disagreement about the proper interpretation of the notion of personal autonomy and its application to the question of refusing lifesaving medical treatment.

One source of disagreement concerns interpretation of the notions of competence, rationality, and the possession of adequate information. Though such disagreements can be substantive, there is often an element of circularity, or a "catch 22" flavor to them. People who want to preclude the permissibility of certain sorts of refusals of treatment often maintain that a person who refuses such treatment is *a fortiori* not rational, competent, and informed.[11] A second source of disagreement concerns the relative weighting of competing values, and the issue of what sorts of countervailing moral concerns can justify overriding a competent, rational, and informed patient's refusal of treatment. Even if a patient who refuses treatment under conditions (1) through (6) can be deemed competent, rational, and informed, still it might be thought that such a refusal could be justifiably overridden if honoring it would have significant untoward consequences for other people. Thus, many people believe that it may be justifiable to override a competent parent's informed refusal to prevent untoward consequences for the parent's minor children.

I will not discuss either of these issues in depth here. The "catch 22 tactic" is clearly problematical, since the very issue under discussion is precisely that of when we are morally obliged to honor a person's refusal of life-sustaining treatment, and excluding the possibility by definitional fiat does nothing to illuminate, or resolve, that issue. There are thus good reasons to insist that the notions of rationality and competence be defined in a way that allows people who disagree about the strength of the right to refuse treatment to identify the same patients as rational and competent. This will enable them both to clarify the nature of their disagreement and assess the merits of their competing solutions to it. The second issue, that of determining the correct weight to be attributed to the value of personal autonomy, cannot be adequately discussed anecdotally. Proposals about the proper weighting of values need to be considered in the context of assessing a moral theory that provides a more comprehensive account of the ordering of values, and a political theory that presents us with principles for balancing respect for the moral autonomy of individuals against the preservation and pursuit of public goods.

The issue that I will focus on here is one that relates specifically to the determination of the scope of the right to refuse lifesaving medical treatment. As I noted, it is often claimed that the obligation to respect individuals' rights of bodily integrity and personal autonomy does not include the obligation—or even the permission—to stand by and allow another to commit suicide; still less, it is alleged, does it include the permission to assist in a suicide or commit euthanasia. On this view, a physician has no obligation to honor a patient's refusal of treatment when that refusal is seen as suicidal, even if this means that the physician must override a patient's sincere moral convictions, and forcibly treat the patient against his or her will. I shall call this the *suicide constraint*.

Acceptance of the suicide constraint would significantly restrict the scope of a patient's right to refuse treatment. I shall argue that the ways it which it would restrict the scope of the right would, in addition, threaten its very foundation. I thus believe that the suicide constraint is untenable as a basis for social policy, and that it should be explicitly disavowed. Though we are loath to sanction what we may regard as a tragic loss of life, and we recoil from the prospect of appearing to welcome another's death, a careful consideration of the reasons for rejecting the suicide constraint should convince us that neither is a necessary consequence of that rejection. I shall briefly explain one rationale for adopting the suicide constraint and then go on to offer some reasons to thinking that we should reject it.

PART II: THE SUICIDE CONSTRAINT

Those who endorse the suicide constraint believe that the right to refuse treatment is not as strong or unqualified as the characterization in Part I suggests. Though few contemporary philosophers or jurists would argue for our recognition of an absolute prohibition of suicide, there is a long legal and moral tradition of rejecting suicide as a defensible personal option.[12] Moreover, even among people who would allow suicide under some conditions, there is strong resistance to the tolerance of assisted suicide, which is seen to involve some sort of endorsement of the patient's death, and is thus thought to blend insensibly into tolerance of euthanasia. Many people who profess to support some sort of right to refuse treatment would thus reject the view that we are obliged to assist (or even allow) another person to end his or her own life. They think this even when, as may often be the case in a medical setting, the form of assistance at issue is "merely passive," that is, it involves our refraining from interfering with another person's attempt to end his or her own life. Those who endorse this restricted view can cite legal and moral grounds for thinking that we are permitted, and perhaps even obliged, to restrain an individual whom we know to be deliberately pursuing a suicidal course. For example, in his concurring opinion in *Cruzan*,[13] Justice Antonin Scalia maintains that "the power of the State to prevent suicide is unquestionable" (4926), and that

> American law has always accorded the State the power to prevent, by force if necessary, suicide—including suicide by refusing to take appropriate measures necessary to preserve one's life. (4924)

Though Scalia holds that there are "reasonable and humane limits that ought not to be exceeded in requiring an individual to preserve his life" (4926), he also thinks that "starving oneself to death is no different from putting a gun to one's temple as far as the common-law definition of suicide is concerned" (4925).[14] This has obvious implications regarding the refusal of medical treatment.

> Insofar as balancing the relative interests of the State and the individual is concerned, there is nothing distinctive about accepting death through the refusal of "medical treatment" as opposed to accepting it through the refusal of food, or through the failure to shut off the engine and get out of the car after parking it in one's garage after work. (4926)

Justice Scalia thus construes the State's right to prevent a suicide as a strong right. One cannot hold that the State has the right to prevent a person from slashing his wrists, [but] it does not have the power to apply physical force to prevent him from doing so, nor the power, should he succeed, to apply, coercively if necessary, medical measures to stop the flow of blood (4925).

This reasoning would profoundly restrict the right to refuse medical treatment. If a patient's refusal of treatment is (tantamount to) suicide–which Scalia thinks it is if the "active" or "inactive" cause of the patient's death is a "conscious decision to 'pu[t] an end' to his own existence" (4925)–then provided it does not exceed "reasonable and humane limits" for us to do so, we may override rational patients' informed refusals and treat them against their will.[15]

How great a restriction is posed by the suicide constraint will presumably depend on what we take to be involved in someone's making a "conscious decision to pu[t] an end to his [or her] own existence," and on how we understand the admonition that we may not exceed "reasonable and humane limits" in our efforts to prevent such an individual from ending his or her life. But if Scalia's interpretation is correct, then our laws and social policies should be restricted by the suicide constraint. And if the prevailing social and legal interpretations of what constitutes a "conscious decision" to end one's life or the "reasonable and humane limits" that we cannot justifiably exceed in preventing an individual from pursuing a suicidal course of action are more restrictive than the interpretation that a suffering patient puts on either notion, then the suicide constraint may compel a rational, competent, and informed patient to submit to treatment in circumstances that he or she finds unconscionable.

PART III: REASONS FOR REJECTING THE SUICIDE CONSTRAINT

There are a number of grounds for rejecting the suicide constraint and construing the right to refuse medical treatment as a strong right, one that would allow a competent, rational, and informed patient to refuse treatment even when that refusal could be deemed suicidal, and a physician's compliance with it could be construed as an instance of assisted suicide. First of all, if acceptance of the suicide constraint is not to involve the wholesale–and implausible–rejection of the right to refuse treatment in every case in which the patient's death is thought to be a consequence of nontreatment, we must be able to determine which refusals of treatment are correctly deemed suicidal, and hence impermissible, and which are not. But this in turn involves the presupposition that we can determine whether, in Scalia's language, an individual has in fact done anything that can be construed as his or her having made a "conscious decision to put an end to his [or her] own existence." Though this may seem like a straightforward enough undertaking, closer examination should convince us that it is not, especially in cases involving the refusal of treatment. There are, in such cases, good reasons both for doubting whether we can accurately make such determinations, and good reasons for doubting whether we may even attempt to do so.

In section A, I sketch some reasons for being skeptical about any scheme that proposes that we determine whether a patient is suicidal by appealing to (what might be called) our common-sense views about motivation and intention. Such an approach is, I believe, fundamentally wrong-headed: peoples' intentions and motives are not accessible to us in any straightforward, nonequivocal way. In section B, I consider why we cannot gainfully respond to the worries raised in section A by trading reliance on our anecdotal assessments of a patient's motivations and intentions for appeals to the considered judgments of mental health professionals (e.g., psychologists, psychiatrists, or social workers). There are good reasons for questioning whether such individuals are able to make accurate and disinterested determinations of a patient's intentions and motivations in refusing treatment. Moreover, even if it were reasonable to believe that these individuals were more likely to be able to make accurate assessments of whether a patient should be deemed to be suicidal, there are good reasons for supposing that patients are not obliged either to submit themselves to this sort of scrutiny or to allow mental health professionals' assessments to be the final determinant of their fate. This will take us into a discussion of the connections between privacy and autonomy (section C), and a brief discussion of some of First Amendment-based objections to the suicide constraint (section D).

SECTION A: RELYING ON COMMON SENSE VIEWS ABOUT INTENTION AND MOTIVATION

Our beliefs about people's motives and intentions strongly color, if not uniquely determine, our assessments of their conduct. It is a dictum of moral common sense that the intentions and motivations with which a person acts are relevant not only to the moral assessment of the character of that person, but also to the determination of the permissibility (or rightness) of the person's performing that sort of action in the first place. There are more and less subtle versions of this view. Classic deontological moral theories attach proscriptions and permissions to action types, and assign agents' intentions a large role in determining whether their conduct is in fact conduct of the relevant kind, that is, conduct that falls under the relevant proscription or permission. Thus, lying is deemed to be proscribed, for example, but if lying is defined as "intentionally misrepresenting the truth (to one who has right to be provided with it)," then an agent who does not intentionally utter a falsehood to mislead someone who is entitled to be told the truth does not lie.[16] Unless there is some other proscription that governs more broadly deceptive behavior, the agent may escape the charge of wrongdoing by refraining from speaking at all, while, at the same time, deviously concealing important information.

This sort of reasoning can clearly be applied in the current context. If a rational, competent, and informed patient who refuses treatment is thought to have the intention to end his or her life, then the refusal may be deemed to be suicidal; as a suicidal act it would thus fall foul of the suicide constraint, and hence be impermissible. The patient's physician could thus claim to be justified in overriding the patient's informed refusal and imposing the unwanted medical treatment on him or her. On the other hand, when a patient's refusal is thought to involve "merely foreseeing," but not intending, death, the patient's refusal of treatment would not constitute the commission of suicide, and (other things being equal) it would thus not be an impermissible act. And so the suicide constraint could not be invoked, and the physician would be obliged to honor the patient's refusal of treatment.[17] Variants of this move have long been involved in discussions of the morality of suicide, assisted suicide, euthanasia, and other terminations of life, most notably abortion and self-defense.[18]

The view that the motivation and intention with which agents act bear strongly on the moral assessment their conduct, and perhaps the permissibility of their doing something in the first place, is widely shared. But there is little agreement on the details of the view. It is often unclear, most notably, just how agents' motives and intentions are supposed to bear on that moral assessment or on the determination of permissibility. Yet both the intellectual soundness and the practicability of such views clearly depend on the possibility of our being able to make fairly determinate, generally uncontroversial, claims about what someone's intentions and motivations are, and on the plausibility of the account that purports to explain why and how motivations and intentions affect the rightness of an agent's acts. Few secular philosophers would admit to being adherents of narrow deontological theories, and many would agree that there are problems both with attempting to arrive at a definitive determination of an agent's intentions and motivations, and with trying to provide a satisfactory account of how intention and motivation determine the moral permissibility (or rightness) of our acts. Yet—as both Scalia's characterization of suicide and the invocation of the suicide constraint clearly show—the belief persists that the intention and motivation with which agents act play a large role in determining the permissibility of their so acting. Clearly there is a problem here.

Appeals to common-sense views about intention are problematical in other ways as well. In our daily lives, we often treat the question of whether someone intended x (or did not intend x, or intended y instead) in acting as a species of relatively straightforward empirical question. If we do not know the answer to it in some instance, it is because we have inadequate or equivocal evidence. But—at least in theory—there is a determinate answer to the question of what someone intended, even if we may never be in a position to know what it is.

The tendency to treat the question of whether someone had a particular intention in acting as a species of empirical question has a number of sources. Though philosophers profess to eschew such a view as naively Cartesian, it is common for us to act as if intending (or wanting, or believing) something were like having a certain item of mental furniture in our own mental inventory. And this connects with another problematical aspects of our treatment of agents' mental and intentional states. We often act as if each of us possessed some sort of clear access, and consequent privilege with respect to, our motives and intentions. If someone is competent and rational, then he or she is able to provide definitive information about his or her mental states, hence his or her intentions and motivations in acting. It is easy to see how these beliefs fit together. If whether or not I intended something is an empirical question, and one about the contents of a private mental inventory that is directly accessible to me, then it seems plausible to believe that–provided I am sane, truthful, and attentive–I can know what it is that I intended, and why, when I undertook a certain deed, or made a certain decision. Since questions about my motives and intentions are questions about what I took myself to be doing (and thus what, in some sense, I *was* doing), they are ones that I myself am in the best position to answer. Others' doubts about my judgment are (*a fortiori*) doubts about my competence or truthfulness.

Along with this view goes the belief that other people's intentions are directly accessible to them, but not to us. At the limit, we may act is if we can know what another person intends or wants only if we can be provided with a report of his or her intentions, beliefs,' and desires; we therefore treat our achieving our correct understanding of other people's deeds as contingent on the others being attentive and truthful in describing their mental states. There are some correctives to this view; it is also a dictum of common sense that people's deeds speak louder than their words. There are thus some circumstances in which we are willing to discount people's own reports and attribute to them motives and intentions that they may well disavow. But even in such cases, we treat an agent's own report of his or her intentions and motivations as primary, and the substitution of a rival interpretation of the agent's deeds is accompanied by the sort of explanation that characterizes the person as in some way less than fully competent, or his or her own report as less than truthful. When people deny that they intended what we think it obvious they must have intended–because, based on our observations of human behavior, we can say that just about any normal person would have had that intention, or based on our careful long-term observation of this particular person, we think that he or she is concealing the truth–then we suppose that they are incompetent or deceptive. That is, they are either incapable of getting an accurate view of their own mental inventories, or misrepresenting what they observe to be there. (It is as if we believed that each of us had the mental equivalent of billiard balls present to our consciousness, and that each of our mental states were a thing of determined size and color, with clear markings that differentiated them from one another. We could thus be wrong in our reports of the content of our consciousness only by design or pathological inattention.)

Though we may be willing to supplement and perhaps even supersede people's reports of their intentions and motives with our own explanations of their behavior when it is people's "positive" actions (or commissions) are at issue, we are generally less comfortable in doing this when it is "negative" actions (or "indirect actions," or "omissions") that are the object of our concern. We know that the inference from "Jane did not do *x*" to any particular mental state of Jane's–for example, intention, desire, belief, or motivation–is a problematic one. We can observe that Jane did not feed the dog last night, but we cannot tell from mere observation why she did what she did, or what it was that she took herself to be doing. (She may have not fed the dog in order to spite her spouse; or spite the dog; or annoy the downstairs neighbors, who had to listen to the dog's pacing and whining for hours; or because she thought she was out of dog food; or because she looked closely at the dog, and began worrying that the dog might be sick or too fat; or believed that the food was spoiled, or some combination of these things). If–as is entirely possible–Jane never intended not to feed the dog, but simply forgot to do so, then nothing (particular) in her mental inventory may correspond to her "negative" action of not feeding the dog. Generalizations about others' mental states when we characterize then as *not* doing something are thus problematical.[19]

If we think that our mental states in (not) doing *x* are unknowable to other people (except insofar as we choose to report them), yet their beliefs about our intentions and motives are relevant to their assessment of whether our doing it is permissible, we may find ourselves in an extremely uncomfortable predicament. When we are in circumstances in which (it is believed) there is no possibility of independent verification of what our intentions were, and we want very much (not) to do a particular thing–for example, not to institute lifesaving procedures on a particular patient because we want to assist that patient in dying–we may be tempted to misrepresent our own mental states in a way that misleads both ourselves and other people into thinking that it is permissible for us (not) to do it. Thus, a physician who deliberately disconnects a suffering patient's respirator or feeding tube may vehemently deny that he or she intended the patient's death–for doing such a thing with that intention would be killing the patient (albeit justifiably)–and maintain that he or she merely foresaw that the death would be a consequence of (not) acting in the relevant way. This enables the physician to maintain both that disconnecting the life-sustaining respirator or feeding tube involved "merely allowing" the patient to die, and that the causation of death is to be traced not to the physician's agency, but to "natural causes."

One does not have to be very cynical to suppose that patients, too, can be taught this trick. Thus, patients who really prefer death to the institution of some form of lifesaving medical treatment may achieve their end by exaggerating the degree of their aversion to the proposed lifesaving treatment in order to prevent other people–and perhaps themselves–from reaching the conclusion that the patients' refusals of treatment are, in these circumstances, tantamount to suicide. If we assign special priority to agents' representations of their own intentions and motivations, it is clear that we are licensing deception, self-deception, and abuse: people's views about what it is permissible of them to do will determine their views about how they choose to describe their intentions and motivations, rather than the other way around. And it is reasonable to think that this will be so whether it is the assessment of patients' supposedly suicidal, or physicians' allegedly nonhomicidal motivations and intentions that is at issue.

Nor is it only people's conscious desires to mislead others (or themselves) about their own intentions that poses problems for reliance on our everyday views about how we can obtain and assess information about people's motives and intentions. If–as moral common sense and deontological views maintain–an agent's intentions can determine the permissibility (and justifiability) of the agent's actions, we may be tacitly underwriting a potentially pernicious form of bad faith or indirection, particularly if an agent's declaration of his or her intentions is the ineffable and privileged affair described. If intentions can play such a powerful role in determining permissibility, then we may be tempted to–silently–gerry-rig our descriptions of other people's intentions to ensure that they will be permitted to do the things we think, antecedently, they ought to be able to do. Again, though we profess to be basing our assessments of other people's actions on our beliefs about their motives and intentions, it may in fact be our antecedent (and undefended) views about what is and is not permissible that determine how we characterize agents' motives and intentions, and not vice versa.

Examples may be helpful here. In cases in which we think it would be reasonable for a patient not to continue with life, we are more likely to describe the physician who supplies the needed (active or passive) assistance as having "merely foreseen" the patient's death, or as merely allowing it to occur, and less likely to characterize him or her as having intended the death. Many people profess to believe that physicians who deliberately suspend nutrition and hydration for patients who are seriously ill can honestly claim that they do not intend their patients' death. This allows them to deny that the physicians' conduct constitutes euthanasia, even passive euthanasia; they can describe the physicians as merely (permissibly) discontinuing "extraordinary measures," foreseeing that the patients will then die of "natural causes."[20] But rather fewer people would be willing to accept this characterization of the conduct of a physician who withheld nutrition and hydration from a Down's Syndrome infant with a potentially fatal, but easily correctable, anatomical anomaly. Many people think that the physician must be viewed as intending the infant's death, and many would resist the classification of withholding (or suspending "artificial") nutrition and hydration as passive euthanasia, or indeed any sort of euthanasia; it is, rather, the deliberate killing of an infant with a handicap to serve other people's interests.

Though there are differences between the two cases, it is hard to believe that such differences can support the weight of entirely different categorizations of the two. Once again, it appears to be people's differential moral assessment of the desirability–and hence the permissibility–of ending the two lives that forms the basis for the differential claims about the intentions of the physicians, and not the reverse.[21] It is not hard to see how this would apply in the context of assessing physicians' obligations to honor patients' refusals of treatment. It may not be the patient's own intentions and motivations, but rather our views about the reasonableness or moral defensibility of this patient's dying, that determines whether we view the patient's decision as suicidal.

Though we may believe that there is a difference between refusals of medical treatment that can be characterized as suicidal and those that cannot, and that the difference lies in the intentions and motivations of the patient who is refusing treatment, we cannot effectively appeal to what I have been calling our common-sense views about intention and motivation to ground either theory or practice. I have explained some of the theoretical difficulties with the view, and offered some examples to show that the problems are not purely theoretical. It is clear, moreover, that the practical difficulties are neither subtle nor speculative. If patients who want to refuse lifesaving treatment know that the likelihood of their refusal being honored depends on how they represent their intentions and motivations, they will presumably have little incentive to engage in accurate reporting of their intentions and motives. A social policy that gives patients an incentive to mislead their doctors has very little to recommend it; one that gives patients incentive to misrepresent their true doubts and feelings at the end of life has even less.

SECTION B: SUBSTITUTING THE JUDGMENTS OF MENTAL HEALTH PROFESSIONALS FOR RELIANCE ON COMMON-SENSE ASSESSMENTS OF PATIENT'S INTENTIONS AND MOTIVES

One response to these problems is to continue to insist on the importance of agents' motives and intentions, but to substitute a better scheme for ascertaining what they are. Thus, we might ask that the patient undergo an examination by a trained and disinterested mental health professional, who is presumably able to ascertain the patient's real (deeper) motives and intentions. We could thus insist that the suicide constraint be understood to involve this sort of procedure. If, for example, an independent psychologist determines that the patient's intentions in refusing treatment are suicidal, then the suicide constraint applies, and the physician is justified in overriding the patient's refusal and treating the patient against his or her will.

Obviously, this proposed remedy has severe practical limitations; it is inapplicable when (as is quite often the case) the decision to honor or override a patient's refusal of treatment must be made quickly. But I shall ignore that complication here. There are other, more principled objections that apply even when there is sufficient time to implement this proposal.

The proposal overlooks both the notorious fallibility of professional assessments of patients' mental health or illness, and the risk of abuse, or bias-based misdiagnosis. Though classifications of mental health or illness are alleged to be criteria-based and objective, and mental health professionals present themselves as being both unbiased and disinterested, there are too many familiar counter-examples to accept either claim without demurring.[22] We should recall that homosexuality was classified as a mental disorder until 1973,[23] and that the norms that form the baseline for professionals' assessment of mental health are gender-biased in ways that have been both unacknowledged, and pervasive.[24] Though we should be cautious in generalizing from the demographic data regarding forced cesarean sections[25] there is reason to worry that white, male middle-class physicians may be less likely to understand or respect the views of patients who are nonwhite or nonmale, less educated, less affluent, or members of ethnic groups whose culture differs significantly from that of the dominant culture. This obviously bears both on the validity of determinations of whether a patient is rational, competent, and informed, and on the correctness of a professional's assessment of whether the patient is suicidal. When there is a large cultural divide between patient and providers, there is greater reason to worry that physicians and mental-health professionals may see a patient's decisions as foolish or irrational when they are more properly seen as different. The greater the cultural distance, the livelier is the worry that the practitioners who seek to override a patient's refusal of treatment may have an inaccurate understanding of their patients.

These worries are obviously more acute when there is no longstanding relationship between the patient and his or her providers. Though some patients who face potentially life-ending choices may have long-standing relationships with the physicians who are currently treating them, the increased geographical mobility of both patients and physicians and the vagaries and caprices of insurance requirements make this increasingly less likely. Often a physician does not know a patient well enough to have a clear-sighted view of who the patient is as a person, and the patient does not know the physician well enough to be comfortable in trusting him or her in anything but a technical, medical sense.[26] A patient who has had only a brief relationship with a physician may have no grounds for thinking that the physician really understands who the patient is, or how the patient's moral and psychological worldview is constructed; the same, of course, is true of the mental health professional assigned to determine the patient's intentions and motivations in refusing treatment. There may thus often be good reasons for patients to be skeptical about medical professionals' ability to make accurate determinations of their views, and good reasons for them to feel anger and resentment at being compelled to submit to such an investigation. It thus seems both cruel and arrogant to make respect for a patient's refusal of treatment contingent on assessments undertaken by these medical strangers. To the injury of being compelled to undergo treatment that the patient believes is morally objectionable is added the insult of having his or her moral views, or reasons for holding them, assessed by a stranger who one understands little about the patient's background, culture, moral outlook, or spiritual identity.

SECTION C: THE CONNECTION BETWEEN AUTONOMY AND PRIVACY

As I noted in Part II, the basis for our thinking that we should honor a person's right to refuse treatment lies in our shared belief in the importance of respect for the autonomy of the individual. Though there is disagreement about the precise scope and weight to be assigned to the right of bodily self-determination, it is clear that acknowledgment of this right tacitly involves recognition of some right of personal privacy.[27] Intuitively, if we may justifiably resist others' physical invasion of our bodies, then we may resist unwelcome attempts at invading our minds or selves, and do so for the same reason: either may do profound damage to us as persons.

The right of privacy seems especially strong in the context of assessing the suicide constraint. When someone has clearly gone out of his or her way to initiate a life-ending sequence of deeds—for example, climbed to a high place to jump, or initiated some other complex death-causing plan (like those described in books that outline fail-safe suicide procedures)—we may be able to determine whether the person is suicidal without engaging in detailed investigations of his or her intentions, desires, and ends. But determinations of whether a patient's refusal of treatment is suicidal are far more difficult. In such circumstances, there is no overt attempt to initiate a life-ending sequence of deeds, and there may be nothing that is easily identifiable as "a conscious decision to put an end to [one's] existence." We may, thus, not be able to make a determination about whether a patient's refusal of treatment is suicidal without subjecting the patient to a grueling investigation. This is problematical in itself; by what right do we compel patients to spend what may be their final hours on the planet in such an undertaking? And it is problematical in other ways as well. It is clear that the investigation of the patient's intentions, desires, and ends could itself be seen as the first step in an assault on his or her autonomy. If a patient who wishes to refuse treatment knows that his or her refusal will be honored only if the patient is deemed not to be suicidal, then the patient will know that giving the 'wrong' answers to clinicians' questions will result in being compelled to undergo treatment against his or her will. It is not hard to see why such patients would regard attempts to ascertain their intentions and so forth as illegitimate. It should be noted that it does not matter here whether it is a commonsense-style inquiry or a mental health professional's investigation that is employed to ascertain the patient's motives and intentions. Both are problematical, and for the same reasons.

Nor can it plausibly be claimed that a detailed investigation (whether by a mental health professional, or a physician who employs common-sense techniques of assessment) is needed to determine whether a patient is competent, rational, and informed. We can generally make determinations of rationality and competence without knowing fine details about an individual's personal life, or his or her values, ends, and intentions. Additional information may be helpful in a particular case, but it is not generally needed—still less is it always needed—to determine a patient's rationality and competence to make treatment decisions. It is thus reasonable for the patient to insist that detailed personal information is private information, and to maintain that he or she has the right not disclose it.

There is, thus, a dilemma here. Medical personnel may be unable to determine whether a patient's refusal of treatment is suicidal without acquiring detailed personal information from the patient, but their attempts to acquire such information may violate the patient's right of privacy. Those who endorse the suicide constraint may believe that the importance of preventing medical suicides is so great that it justifies invasive assaults on patients' privacy. But on the face of it, it is hard to see why this is so. How we are to overcome the difficulties of ascertaining whether a patient is suicidal, or how we are to justify our devoting significant amounts of energy to interviewing patients who do not want to be interviewed. The burden of proof thus lies on those who would invoke the suicide constraint to show us both that assessments undertaken against a patient's will can be, nevertheless, both accurate and fair, and why we should compel patients to surrender their right of privacy and endure invasive investigation of their most personal concerns at this critical juncture in their lives.

It is worth emphasizing that this reasoning does not presuppose the view that autonomy should be seen as the most important moral value in human interactions, or even in physician-patient relations. I have not argued that this is so; I have been arguing, rather, that attempts to circumscribe or limit the exercise of patient autonomy in refusals of treatment are problematical in both in practice and in principle. Moreover, one can argue that the recognition of the right of personal autonomy entails the recognition of significant rights of personal privacy and still allow that there are circumstances that would justify overriding a competent and rational patient's informed refusal of treatment. One might believe, for example, that paternalistic or moralistic (e.g., utilitarian) interventions are sometimes defensible. But it should be noted that the sort of worries raised in the preceding section give us some grounds for regarding such a claim as problematical in the current context of medical care in the United States.

SECTION D: FIRST AMENDMENT-BASED WORRIES

The last reason for rejecting the suicide constraint that I shall discuss may seem to some to be the most persuasive. The attempt to restrict the right to refuse treatment within the confines of the suicide constraint is clearly subject to some First Amendment objections. Presumably, those who would so circumscribe the right would distinguish between cases in which patients' grounds for refusal were that undergoing the treatment would be in conflict with the tenets of their religion, and those in which patients refused treatment "merely" because that they believed, for some complex package of personal and moral reasons, that their post-treatment life would not be worth living. If First Amendment objections to the establishment of religion are to have any substance, then we must be allowed to structure our lives in accordance with the dictates of our religion, even when the consequences of our doing so, are, by the lights of many other people, untoward, foolish, or morally objectionable. Provided our conduct does not directly harm other people, the choice of what religion to practice (or not practice), how to practice it, and how much to let it control our lives, is up to us. As cases involving the refusal of blood by Jehovah's Witnesses make painfully clear, such choices may have profound implications not only about how a person's life will be lived, but also on how it will end. And yet it is widely believed that a competent, rational, and informed Jehovah's Witness should be able to refuse a blood transfusion, even when doing so is clearly foreseen to have fatal consequences.[28]

But if this is so, then on what grounds could we deny the same sort of entitlement to individuals whose organized religions do not proscribe suicide, or to those who are not members of any organized religion, but practitioners of a "purely personal" religion? Why should not the rights of a principled atheist who believes that there is greater moral harm in submitting to certain sorts of "undignified" or "impure" procedures than in having life end, be accorded equal respect? We obviously cannot claim that the State accords Jehovah's Witnesses the freedom to refuse transfusions because that is a more reasonable outlook than the atheist's; this is favoring one religion over another–and over no other–which is a clear violation of the First Amendment.

To restrict the right to refuse treatment to those who oppose the treatment on religious grounds (or on some other grounds that the State declares morally reasonable) is to invite nonreligious individuals to misrepresent the grounds of their refusal of treatment. If atheist Jones seeks death in rejecting treatment x, it would obviously be prudent for her to represent herself as having a religious objection to x, for then she might have hopes of having it honored. If it is a violation of the First Amendment, (as well as a violation of rights of privacy) to insist that Jehovah's Witnesses submit their beliefs to other persons for rational or moral scrutiny, then it would appear to be a similar violation to insist that anyone else do so. Or if we do so insist, we should not be surprised to learn that many people will regard it as an invitation to misrepresent–or at least conceal–their true motivations.

CONCLUSION

It thus appears that the attempt to circumscribe the right to refuse treatment by appeal to the suicide constraint has little to recommend it. It is harder to determine whether a patient's refusal of treatment is suicidal than it may first appear to be; reflection on some of the problems with our common-sense views of intention and motivation suggests that determining whether a patient really intends to die, or why the patient is refusing treatment, is far more complex than Justice Scalia's invocation of the presence or absence of a "conscious decision" to end one's life might suggest.

Nor can we address these worries by prescribing that determinations of whether a patient is suicidal should be made by mental health professionals. There may often be good reasons to doubt the competence or fairness of such assessments, particularly when there is no longstanding relationship between patient and provider, or when there are significant cultural differences between them.

Finally–perhaps most fundamentally–insisting that patients submit to detailed scrutiny of their motivations, intentions, desires, and beliefs violates patients' rights to privacy, freedom of conscience, and the free exercise of religion, rights that are clearly closely related to, if not actual components of, the right of self-determination. Such an insistence is thus at odds with the moral foundation of the right to refuse treatment. We cannot exercise our rights of bodily self-determination in a meaningful way unless we can also decide how, when, and to whom we reveal personal information about our values, choices, and ends. And we cannot see ourselves as autonomous beings who are, as such, worthy of respect, if we know that our life-or-death medical decisions can be overruled by people who do not share our values, or acknowledge our right to live our lives–and, when need be, die our deaths–in accord with them.

NOTES

1. This is a revision of a paper prepared for the conference on Intending Death in
    Medicine in 1992. I received comments from other participants at the conference,
    and organizational suggestions from Tom Beauchamp. I am grateful to Sally
    Susnowitz for editorial advice.

2. Many philosophers dispute the claim that the modality of producing death is itself
    morally relevant, and thus question the widely held view that there are important
    moral differences between active and passive euthanasia. James Rachels' essay,
    "Active and Passive Euthanasia" in the *New England Journal of Medicine* 292,
    1975: 78–80, is perhaps the best-known short statement of such a claim. There is
    also a prior, taxonomic worry, that is, that we cannot distinguish between "active"
    and "passive" euthanasia in the sort of clear, principled, and neutral way. People
    clearly have different understandings of the logic of the distinction and of what it is
    that makes something an instance of passive euthanasia. In some contexts, it is a
    physician's nonmovement that is cited as the basis for the claim that there was no
    "active killing." In others it is the supposed causal genesis of the patient's death: for
    example, was it a death from the disease process (or "natural causes") or a death
    caused by "external" factors? Often, it is blatantly normative factors that determine
    people's assessment of how a case should be classified. Thus, some would claim that
    the suspension of nutrition and hydration constitutes a merely passive withholding
    or withdrawing of life support in some contexts—for example, those in which the
    patient is terminally ill, or in a coma—but that it would be active killing in oth-
    ers–for example, one in which food and water are withheld from an otherwise
    healthy deformed neonate. For a useful discussion of some of the difficulties
    involved in defining "euthanasia," see the Introduction of James Rachels,
    "Euthanasia," pp. 28–31, in Tom Regan, ed. *Matters of Life and Death* 1st ed.. New
    York, NY: Random House, 1980, pp. 28–66, and "Euthanasia" by Helga Kuhse, in
    Peter Singer, ed. *op. cit.*, pp. 294–302. I have discussed the problems associated with
    attempts to classify euthanasia as active or passive by appealing to our intuitions
    about what does and does not constitute a killing in "Euthanasia and the Three
    Strands of 'Killing'" (working paper available through the Center for Values &
    Social Policy, University of Colorado at Boulder).

3. It is hard to draw lines between assisted suicide and euthanasia with any precision.
    If, at your request, I stand by and watch you ingest what we both know is a lethal
    substance, and then pointedly refrain from pumping your stomach, or otherwise,
    forcibly preventing the successful metabolism of the poison, is this an instance of
    suicide (you took the poison), assisted suicide (I gave you emotional support, over-
    saw your dying, and [at your request] deliberately refrained from interfering), or
    passive euthanasia (I deliberately refrained from instituting "extraordinary mea-
    sures" precisely because I was motivated by humanitarian considerations and sup-
    ported your assessment that your life was too unbearable for you to endure)? For
    something to count as an instance of assisted suicide, must the assistance supplied
    be "active"–for example, I obtain the poison for you, or drive you to a location in

which you will face no interference with the execution of your plan–or is it sufficient that it is assistance sought by the person who is ending his or her life, and deliberately supplied by the (putative) assistant? Is it assisted suicide or euthanasia if, at the patient's request, a physician administers an overdose to a patient who is paralyzed, or too weak to ingest the substance on his or her own? If a physician observes this patient taking an overdose whose effects he or she could easily counteract, and deliberately does not take steps to do so? If the physician does nothing to stop it precisely because he or she supports the patient's decision to die in these circumstances? Obviously, one's answer to these questions depends on the technical details of one's definition of the relevant terms, and different definitional schemes will support very different understandings of both the terms themselves, and claims about the normative force of our descriptions of agents' conduct. It should also be noted that here—as in our assessments of the defensibility of deliberately allowing patients to die, and of the bounds of permissible overridings of patients' refusals of treatment—there is reason to think that our assessment of the permissibility of the relevant sorts of conduct strongly affects our decision about how to classify it. See note 2, and section IIIA.

4. If we are convinced by arguments to the effect that there is not a clear conceptual difference between active and passive euthanasia, or by arguments that allow that there is a clear conceptual difference, but that this provides no basis for concluding that there is a substantive normative difference between the two, then acceptance of a strong right to refuse treatment may provide us with some grounds for accepting active as well as passive euthanasia.

5. I mean this to be understood broadly, so that, for example, one could deny that the source of a physician's right to override a patient's refusal of lifesaving treatment was in some publicly recognized overarching moral obligation, not necessarily vested in the powers of the State per se.

6. This is what I shall mean by rational, competent, and informed throughout. It should be noted that this is a relatively weak standard, and that it is a decision-relative standard. A patient who is deemed rational, competent, and informed relative to one sort of decision might not be so relative to others. For helpful discussion of what it means to be rational, competent, and informed and the application of the notions to questions of informed consent, see the President's Commission for the Study of Ethical Problems in Medicine and Biomedical Behavioral Research, *Making Health Care Decisions: the Ethical and Legal Implications of Informed Consent in the Patient-Practitioner Relationship* (1982). For a discussion of what constitutes a rational suicide, see M. Pabst Battin, *Ethical Issues in Suicide.* Englewood Cliffs, NJ: Prentice-Hall, 1982, Chapter 4, pp. 131–159.

7. Both the distinction between intended and "merely foreseen" consequences and the assessment of the moral significance of relying on it have received much discussion by philosophers and legal theorists. Sometimes, the difference between intending a death and "merely foreseeing" one is thought to be a distinction between logically different kind of acts, for example, between direct and indirect killing (to which different proscriptions are held to apply); sometimes it is thought to be, or to reflect, important differences in the kind of agency involved in the production of some

result, or the sort of responsibility correctly attributed to the agent whose conduct has realized that result. See, for example, Jonathan Bennett, "Morality and Consequences," in S. McMurrin, ed. *The Tanner Lectures on Human Values*, vol. 2. Cambridge: Cambridge University Press, 1981, pp. 45–116, esp. lecture III; Philip E. Devine, *The Ethics of Homicide*. Ithaca, NY: Cornell University Press, 1978, Chapter 4, pp. 106–133; Nancy Davis (N. Ann Davis), "The Doctrine of Double Effect: Problems of Interpretation," *Pacific Philosophical Quarterly*, 1984, reprinted in Fischer and Ravizza, eds. *Ethics: Problems and Principles*. New York, NY: Harcourt Brace, 1992, pp. 199–212; and "Contemporary Deontology," in Peter Singer, ed. A Companion to Ethics. Oxford: Blackwell's, 1991, pp. 205–218; H.L.A. Hart, "Intention and Punishment," *The Oxford Review*, 1967; reprinted with modifications in H.L.A. Hart, Intention and Punishment. Oxford: Oxford University Press, 1968, pp. 113–135; John Mackie, Ethics: *Inventing Right and Wrong*. New York, NY: Penguin, 1977, Chapter 7; Judith Thomson, "Rights and Deaths," *Philosophy and Public Affairs*, 1973, reprinted in Fisher and Ravizza, *op. cit.*, pp. 189–199. The scare quotes are meant to remind us that the term "intended consequences" is a technical one, and one whose interpretation and significance are disputed.

8.   I would maintain that conditions (1) through (6) could characterize a young, otherwise healthy, Jehovah's Witness' refusal of a life-sustaining blood transfusion. I also believe that, in some such cases, the patient is properly characterized as intending his or her death, not as "merely foreseeing" it, and thus that the patient's refusal in such circumstances can properly be classified as suicidal. The issue is complicated; see note 6, and the discussion of the definition of suicide in Tom L. Beauchamp, "Suicide," in Tom Regan, ed. *op. cit.*, pp. 67–108, esp. pp. 68–78. The cost of denying that such a patient intends death are far-reaching, and potentially very damaging to our understanding of the notions of free action and responsibility. Many people, in many contexts, find themselves faced with the necessity of choosing between two unhappy options. If we insist that a patient who chooses death in preference to medical treatment does not intend his or her death, then we will have to say that the same is generally true of agents who are faced with a choice between two bad options. But there are good reasons to resist the suggestion that such agents do not in fact intend the option they finally choose in such circumstances.

9.   *Union Pacific R. Co. v. Botsford*, 141 U.S. 250, 251 (1891).

10.   *Schloendorff v. Society of New York Hospital*, 211 N.Y. 125, 129–30, 105 N.E. 92, 93 (1914).

11.   Discussions of suicide with students and clinicians exemplify this nicely. Students think that an otherwise physically healthy person who would allow him or herself to die must be irrational or incompetent, and clinicians tend to take the choice as itself indicative of the patient's being "clinically depressed," and therefore, not relevantly rational or competent.

12.   See Beauchamp, *op. cit.*, and Battin, *op. cit.*, Chapters 1 and 2.

13.   All page references from *Cruzan* are to *The United States Law Week* of 6 June 1990 (*58 LW*).

14.   This reasoning would presumably either undermine the attempt to assign different

legal status to passive and active euthanasia, or compel the categorization of the withholding of a patient's nutrition and hydration—which is, after all, starving the patient to death—as the deliberate termination of life.

15. It should be noted that Scalia's allowance that the relevant cause can be either "active" or "inactive" will allow for the inclusion of a very broad range of things as constituting a patient's death being caused by his or her "conscious decision" to die. For example, if there is a patient who would have changed his or her mind about refusing the medical treatment if she had seen the refusal as involving a decision to die, then it could be alleged that the decision to die was the "inactive cause" of her refusing treatment, and hence, that her refusal of the treatment was suicidal.

16. See for example, Charles Fried, *Right and Wrong*. Cambridge: Cambridge University Press, 1978, Chapters 1 and 3; Alan Donagan, *The Theory of Morality*. Chicago: University of Chicago Press, 1977, Chapter 3, section 3. This view of lying is criticized in Davis, "Contemporary Deontology," *op. cit.*

17. See notes 2 and 3.

18. Disagreements about the permissibility of withdrawing treatment exemplify this particularly well. Philosophers who have consequentialist sympathies usually prefer to define "killing" in mechanistic or causal terms—for example, "killing" = "causing death." Since there can clearly be justified causings of death, the adoption of this mechanistic conception of killing does not support, and is not consistent with, the view that killing is intrinsically wrongful. On the other hand, those who hold deontological views, or embrace traditional moral outlooks, usually define "killing" in more intentional terms, as for example, "the intentional termination of life" (in which "intentional" = "characterized by the killer's having intended the victim's death"). Killing is then held to be intrinsically wrong because it (by definition) involves intending another's death. If, as common sense views about intention appear to allow, a physician can knowingly disconnect a respirator without being thought thereby to intend the patient's death, then it can be claimed that a physician can disconnect a patient's respirator without thereby killing the patient, even when the patient's death is foreseen with certainty. The withdrawal of treatment may thus be deemed permissible when and because it does not violate the moral prohibition against killing. See notes 2 and 6.

19. It is important to remember that the division into "negative" and "positive" acts, events, or concepts is one that does not mirror anything in the external world, but is, rather, a division guided by our purposes, expectations, and explanatory needs.

20. I discuss some of the telling ambiguity in our notion of causation in "Euthanasia and the Three Strands of Killing," *loc. cit.* See also notes 2 and 6.

21. See Helga Kuhse and Peter Singer, *Should the Baby Live?* Oxford: Oxford University Press, 1985, Chapters 1 and 2 for a clear indication of how people's normative views about the value of an infant's life affect their categorization of the termination of that life.

22. See Thomas S. Szasz' classic paper, "The Myth of Mental Illness," *American Psychologist* 15; 1960: 113–118; Szasz, "Politics and Psychiatry: The Case of Mr. Ezra Pound," in R.C. Allen, E.Z. Ferster, and J.G. Rubin, eds. *Readings in Law and*

Psychiatry, 1968, pp. 388–395; William J. Curran, "The Hiss-Chambers Trial: Some Definitions of Psychopathic Personality," ibid, pp. 132–135; Phyllis Chesler, *Women and Madness*, 1972; D. L. Rosenhan, "On Being Sane in Insane Place," Science 179; 1973: 250–257.

23. This is the year that the DSM ceased to classify homosexuality as a disorder.

24. See, for example, Phyllis Chesler, *op. cit.*

25. See, for example, Lawrence J. Nelson and Nancy Milliken, "Compelled Medical Treatment of Pregnant Women," *Journal of the American Medical Association* 259; 1988: 1060–1066.

26. This provides one of the most important disanalogies between the Netherlands and the United States. See Carlos F. Gomez, *Regulating Death: Euthanasia and the Case of the Netherlands*. New York, NY: Free Press, 1991.

27. See Jeb Rubenfeld, "The Right to Privacy," *Harvard Law Review* 102; 1989: 737–807.

28. See Berton Roueche, "A Good, Safe Tan," *The New Yorker*; 1991: 69–74, for discussion of an unusual transfusion refusal case.

Borderline Cases of Morally Justified Taking Life in Medicine

DAN W. BROCK

Brown University, Providence, Rhode Island

The problem of borderline cases of justified taking life has received remarkably little attention. There are two broad issues. The first is what kinds of cases are on the borderline between morally justified and unjustified taking life, and for what reasons? In addressing this question it will be necessary to distinguish borderline cases from cases about which there is radical moral disagreement. It is also necessary to distinguish different kinds and sources of borderline cases. The second broad issue is whether there are any principled ways of handling borderline cases?

What are the different bases on which a particular action of taking life (I shall use "action" broadly in this paper to include omissions, unless otherwise indicated) might be held to be on the borderline of justification? I shall make a broad distinction between cases whose source of borderline justified status arises from moral factors and those which arise from empirical factors. It will be important also to distinguish cases whose borderline status arises within a single person's moral judgments from cases whose borderline status can only be understood by reference to the moral views of more than one person. In principle, and to a great extent in practice as well, a nearly unlimited number of properties can play a role in making particular instances of taking life in medicine borderline morally justified. In actual practice, several diverse factors may contribute to a particular case being borderline morally justified, but for initial analytic clarity it is useful to distinguish the different kinds. The two broad kinds of factors creating borderline cases are moral factors and empirical or descriptive factors, and I shall examine each in turn.

BORDERLINE JUSTIFIED TAKING LIFE IN MEDICINE BASED ON MORAL DISAGREEMENT

In some respects the most troubling and difficult kind of borderline case based on moral factors is when different people have relatively clear, precise, and determinate moral standards for dividing justified from unjustified cases, but do not agree about what the correct standard is. In practice, this is an extremely common and important source of disagreement, and I will call this the *moral disagreement* version. The disagreement can arise because different persons hold different basic views about what makes taking life morally wrong in paradigm cases in which it is morally wrong, including cases in which there need be no disagreement about whether a particular action taking life is wrong. For example, it is common in many discussions of moral theories to distinguish in very broad terms between goal-based, rights-based, and duty-based moral theories.[1]

In a goal-based theory, the evaluation of states of affairs as to varying degrees good or bad, valuable or disvaluable, is morally basic and actions are judged to be justified or unjustified to the extent that they maximize valuable states of affairs. Depending on the specific standard of value, one will have different goal-based theories. For example, if human happiness is the feature which makes states of affairs good, killing will be justified when doing so maximizes happiness for all affected by the action, including others besides the one killed. With critically ill or seriously impaired newborns, for example, some commentators have argued that burdens for other family members of sustaining the newborn's life can be sufficiently great to justify allowing it to die or to kill.[2]

In rights-based views, the basic moral principle for evaluating taking life will be a moral right not to be killed. One important function of rights generally is to limit the imposition on some people of particular burdens or harms that would violate their rights in order to secure greater benefits for others. Thus, in most versions of this view, taking the life of a newborn or a profoundly demented adult to prevent serious burdens to family members would usually not be justified because it entails a violation of the newborn's or adult's rights. However, when a patient consents to or otherwise requests that an action be taken that will end his or her life, in the rights view that can be understood as waiving the patient's right not to be killed and so as making taking the patient's life permissible.

In a moral theory in which the fundamental moral principle for evaluating taking life is a duty not to deliberately take innocent human life, for example Catholic moral theology, a very different line distinguishing justified from unjustified taking life is drawn. As with the rights view, preventing burdens to others will not justify deliberate killing. If the duty is not derived from a more basic right not to be killed (which would make it rights-, not duty-based) but is understood, for example, as owed to God, then the patient's consent to be killed need not thereby justify doing so. The patient cannot waive or extinguish a duty owed to God—only God could do that.

An informed, voluntary, and competent request of a patient to be killed will not, in this view, justify a physician or others doing so, but instead could be understood as a request, or even a temptation, to act wrongly or to do evil.

These structurally different views about the morality of taking life represent only very broad differences on this issue. Much more would need to be said to fill out the details of any of these three positions. I am now trying only to illustrate the moral disagreement version of borderline cases. More specific and detailed accounts of each will differ in a number of respects, including both the weight relative to other moral considerations given to the disvalue of taking life, the right not to be killed, or the duty not to kill, and the precise account of what actions are covered by the moral principle concerning killing (how killing is construed, when taking life is deliberate, and so forth). But either in these relatively general forms or construed with more detail and precision, these different views will put the line between justified and unjustified taking of life at very different places. This means that proponents of these three sorts of views will place some particular instances of taking life on different sides of the morally justified/unjustified division.

It is worth distinguishing two different kinds of moral disagreement, only one of which is best understood as generating genuine versions of borderline cases. One way to think of the full array of cases of taking life, with regard to their status as morally justified or unjustified, is as on a broad spectrum from the most unjustified or seriously wrong at one end to the most justified or right or best at the other. This spectrum is a continuum, even though we lack any single, precise metric for measuring and precisely quantifying justification. At one end are the most seriously unjustified or wrong cases; moving toward the midpoint, cases become progressively less unjustified or wrong; at the midpoint cases move from being barely unjustified or wrong to barely justified or right; continuing along the spectrum, cases become increasingly justified or right cases until the other extremity at which the most justified or right cases are located. Of course, the image of a spectrum of all things considered moral justification of this sort masks much complexity and diversity in the factors relevant to where, according to a particular moral view about taking life, a specific action should be placed on the spectrum. But it does permit highlighting two different kinds of moral disagreement, only one of which is a genuine version of borderline justification. That version occurs when two different moral positions place the division between justified and unjustified taking life at different points on the spectrum; as a result, particular action comes just on the justified side on one view, but just on the unjustified side on the other. This is represented in Fig. 2.

The case represented in Fig. 2 is a genuine borderline case of moral disagreement because each view places the action close to the point at which it demarcates justified from unjustified cases. Of course, moral disagreement can also exist where neither view places the action in question near the morally neutral point on their spectrum, as in Fig. 3.

There can be many sources of the difference about the neutrality point, as

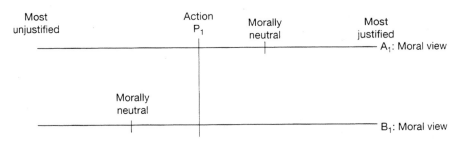

Figure 2

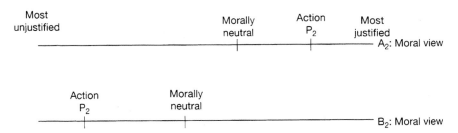

Figure 3

represented by Fig. 2; for example, moral views A_1 and B_1 might agree on what are the morally relevant features bearing on moral justification, but give those features different relative weight. It might be wondered why in Fig. 3 moral views A_2 and B_2 not only have a different point demarcating moral neutrality, but also place the same case of taking life at different points on the two spectrums. The reason is that the two views may hold different descriptive properties of taking life to be morally relevant to their evaluation and justification, and so the two continua pick out different empirical properties of the particular case of taking life as relevant to its justification. Thus, on view A_2 the particular case of taking life is strongly justified while on view B_2 the same action is strongly unjustified. In neither view is the case of taking life near that view's borderline of moral justification, and so for neither view is it an instance of a borderline morally justified taking of life.

Perhaps the most familiar example of this radical moral disagreement is strongly "pro-choice" and strongly "pro-life" views about abortion. In neither view is an elective abortion, for example in the twelfth week of pregnancy by a 16-year-old girl who decides she is too young to become a mother, close to that view's borderline between justified and unjustified actions. The example of abortion highlights the difficulty in reaching any accommodation or consensus about either what an individual should do or what public policy should permit in cases of radical moral disagreement. For many people, active euthanasia is another example of radical moral disagreement of this form.

The notion of a spectrum of justification with a single point demarcating the justified from the unjustified, as in Figs. 2 and 3, misrepresents the structure of many people's moral views in a way important to thinking about the problem of borderline justified cases of taking life. The problem is in the identification of a single point, with all actions falling either on one side or the other of it, and so as either morally justified or unjustified. For many people, instead of a single point of this sort, there is a significant range of cases in which either performing the action or not performing it is morally permissible. So long as two people place a particular action within the area of moral permissibility they can agree that individuals should be permitted to decide for themselves whether to do it, even if they disagree about whether they would themselves do it, whether it would be best for a particular individual (not necessarily themselves) to do it, or even whether on some views it would be wrong though still permissible to do it.[3] Figure 4 represents this kind of case, with points within the ranges of a_1 to a_2 and of b_1 to b_2 representing the ranges of morally permissible taking of life for individuals A_3 and B_3.

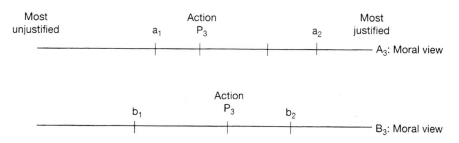

Figure 4

It is a feature of most versions of goal-based theories, and commonly noted about their best known variant utilitarianism, that they require individuals in all cases to do the action among possible alternatives that will produce the best consequences; doing anything else is wrong. As maximizing theories, they lack any category of morally permissible, but not required or best, actions, a feature which to many critics makes these maximizing theories too demanding. It is most rights-based theories that commonly contain significant classes of actions which are morally permissible but not required or obligatory. In particular, theories that give substantial weight to individual self-determination or autonomy, typically use rights to define significant areas of protected choices within which individuals are left free to choose as they wish.

For many people, there is a significant range of cases of taking one's own life that falls within this range of the morally permissible, though they might disagree about whether the choice was rational or, more important for my purposes here, morally justified. Patients sometimes ask their physicians to forgo life-sustaining treatment, or for assistance in suicide or voluntary active euthanasia, all in circumstances in which others, including family members or health-care personnel caring for the patient, believe the patient's choice is not justified. Nevertheless, these others may grant that the patient has a right, or is morally entitled, to make that bad or wrong choice, and so will not hinder and may even help in carrying out that choice. For the range of cases that most people agree are morally permissible to do or not to do, it will usually be possible to agree on a policy that leaves that choice to the individuals. This is precisely what public, professional, and legal policy in the United States now does for many life-sustaining treatment decisions.

An important related, though significantly different kind of case from the morally permissible but not required, is the case in which a person judges an action to be on balance morally justified (or unjustified), but nevertheless grants that reasonable people might disagree with this judgment. The individual's own standard clearly makes the action morally justified, but he or she recognizes that there is some aspect or part of that standard about which reasonable persons can and do disagree. This means there is an area on the individual's spectrum of moral justification within which he or she acknowledges others could reasonably put the morally neutral point at different places. For example, I have argued elsewhere that in determining a level of decisionmaking capacity adequate for competence in a particular borderline case of competence, it is necessary to balance two principal values—respecting the person's self-determination while protecting and promoting his or her well-being.[4] Different people can and do reasonably disagree about the relative weight to be accorded these two values, both in general and in particular cases, and so they will disagree about whether a patient's decision about treatment on a particular occasion should be judged competent, and therefore, respected. When involved parties can all agree that a particular case falls within a range in which reasonable people can disagree, one of at least two kinds of "solutions" to the disagreement should be possible. When the action taking life primarily affects the person whose life is taken, then the particular relative weighing of the different values and moral considerations of that affected person can be accepted; the rationale for this solution is pointedly suggested in the title of the film about a patient's desire to stop life-sustaining treatment, "Whose Life Is It Anyway?" When a policy must be adopted that will affect many people, it should be possible in this kind of case to obtain broad agreement to rely on fair, democratic procedures to arrive at a reasonable compromise or accommodation of these conflicting views.

BORDERLINE MORALLY JUSTIFIED TAKING LIFE IN MEDICINE BASED ON MORAL INDETERMINACY

The borderline cases I have considered until now under the heading of moral disagreement have involved relatively clear and determinate moral standards demarcating the justified from the unjustified, but disagreement between different people about what is the correct standard. Cases whose borderline status has a moral source are also created by what I will call *moral indeterminacy* in a particular individual's standard for demarcating the morally justified from the unjustified. One of the most familiar examples of this moral indeterminacy concerns the concept of a person as it functions in the abortion debate. Many people use the concept of a person as a moral concept, holding that it is persons who have rights not to be killed or whom it is seriously wrong to kill.[5] To many participants in that debate, it is clear that a normal adult human is a person, and clear as well that the biological entity which exists immediately following conception is not a person. However, their concept of person has some degree of indeterminacy, whatever the properties relevant to personhood, such that for a significant period during fetal development it is in turn indeterminate whether a particular fetus is a person. For a few people, it may be indeterminate even whether a newborn infant is a person. When this moral indeterminacy exists, whether an abortion during this period is wrong or a violation of the fetus' rights will be indeterminate and so a borderline case. This moral indeterminacy in the concept of a person also affects debates about the treatment of anencephalic newborns, persistent vegetative state patients, and profoundly demented patients.

The properties bearing on whether an entity is a person are multiple, and in some cases hold in different degrees as well; the indeterminacy in the concept comes from vagueness about which combinations of these properties, in which degrees, are necessary and sufficient for being a person.[6] There are other moral categories or standards that are like the concepts of "tall" or "short"–even applied to a specific category like humans, the concepts have what have been called *fuzzy edges* creating borderline cases in their application.

While some concepts employed in moral reasoning refer to "all or nothing" properties, such as being pregnant, others refer to properties that can obtain in different degrees, even when we lack a precise measure for those degrees, such as benefits and burdens, quality of life, and conflicts of interest. Matter-of-degree concepts are especially prone to generating borderline morally justified cases of taking life because when they are important to the moral evaluation of a case, it is often difficult or impossible to decide how a particular degree of the property in question affects the degree to which an instance of taking life is morally justified or unjustified.

A closely related, but nevertheless different kind of morally relevant concept that also is especially prone to generating cases of borderline moral justification in taking life is when the property referred to need not obtain in different degrees, but the moral value or importance of it varies in different degrees depending on the circumstances. For example, individual self-determination, understood as making decisions about one's life for oneself and according to one's own conception of the good, has different value depending on such factors as how central or peripheral a particular choice is in an individual's life plan, how adequate the individual's decisionmaking capacities are which are needed for the particular choice, and so forth.[7]

Some particular accounts of the nature of moral reasoning in practical ethics are also especially prone to generating borderline morally justified cases, or at the least to illuminate why such cases are common. I will cite only two examples. Albert Jonsen and Stephen Toulmin have argued that moral reasoning in medical ethics is properly understood as a form of casuistical reasoning.[8] Reasoning about a particular case involves fitting that case to moral paradigm cases, which are the locus of moral knowledge. In this account, moral reasoning is essentially analogical reasoning from the particular paradigm cases in which we have ethical knowledge. In most ethically difficult or problematic cases, the case at hand will only imperfectly fit a given paradigm case and/or there will be more than one paradigm case which it to some extent fits, making its ultimate assignment to a given paradigm a borderline case.

Henry Richardson has proposed a method he calls *specifying norms* for resolving ethical conflicts in concrete cases in which two or more conflicting norms seem to apply to the case at hand.[9] It will often be possible plausibly to resolve the conflict in different ways by specifying different norms, or by specifying a particular norm in different ways. Even after choosing a particular specification, our recognition of the alternative plausible specifications that we or others might have chosen instead should make us recognize the case as a borderline morally justified case.

Finally, I conclude this section on moral sources of borderline morally justified cases of taking life in medicine by simply providing an incomplete list of some of the main morally relevant considerations or questions which can generate moral disagreement or moral indeterminacy resulting in borderline cases. When these considerations can also be given different plausible interpretations, can hold in different degrees, or can have their moral value or importance vary in different circumstances, all of which are often possible, the likelihood of borderline cases only increases. A full analysis of why and when there are borderline morally justified cases of taking life in medicine would have to explore all of these possibilities for all of the considerations on the list, as well as many others not on it. One point of the list is simply to display why no such full analysis is possible here. Here then is the list, formulated so as to display how the moral consideration can generate borderline morally justified cases.

1. The elements of valid consent:
    a. When is the patient's choice to end life adequately informed?
    b. When is that choice sufficiently voluntary?
    c. When are the patient's decisionmaking capacities needed for the choice adequate for competence?
2. If the patient is incompetent:
    a. What is the standard for selecting the appropriate surrogate?
    b. What is the appropriate decisionmaking standard for the surrogate to employ, and when is a choice reasonably in accord with it?
    c. When, if ever, can an advance directive justify taking life?
    d. When an advance directive asking for taking life conflicts with the best interests of the incompetent patient, should it be followed?
3. When is taking life intentional, as opposed to foreseen, and what is its moral significance?

4. When is taking life killing, as opposed to allowing to die, and what is its moral significance?

5. Who or what is the cause of death, and what is its moral significance?

6. What religious views bear on justified taking of life, and what is their moral significance? In a particular case? For public policy?

7. When is the taking of life suicide, and when is suicide irrational or immoral?

8. Which, if any, taking of life is incompatible with the aims and norms of medicine, and what moral difference does it make if a physician plays a particular role in taking life?

9. Which, if any, slippery slope arguments against permitting particular taking of life in public or legal policy are sufficiently strong to warrant prohibiting that taking of life?

10. When, and to what extent, if ever, are the economic or other costs of not taking life relevant to the justification of doing so?

11. When is taking life permissible, though morally not justified or even wrong?

12. When should a patient's own assessment of the benefits and burdens of continued life be set aside?

13. What is the basic moral principle for evaluating taking life?

14. Does this basic principle prohibit taking the life of persons, and if so, what are the conditions of personhood? If the principle applies to some different class of beings, which class?

I emphasize that this list is not intended to be complete. Instead, its point is that uncertainty on the part of a single person, or disagreement between different people, about any of these questions can result in borderline morally justified cases of taking life. In fact, the full range of considerations and issues bearing on the morality of taking life can be the moral source of borderline cases, and so only a full analysis of all of those considerations and issues could fully explicate the moral sources of borderline cases.

BORDERLINE MORALLY JUSTIFIED TAKING OF LIFE IN MEDICINE BASED ON EMPIRICAL FACTORS

A second broad kind of borderline case of justified taking of life is when the moral standard distinguishing justified from unjustified cases is relatively clear, precise, and uncontroversial, but there is empirical disagreement or uncertainty about on which side of that dividing line a particular case falls. I will call this the case of *empirical indeterminacy*. Here are some examples of this sort of case. A patient suffering from mild or moderate dementia has requested that some form of life-sustaining treatment be stopped. A thorough evaluation of the patient's competence leaves the evaluators with a significant degree of ineliminable uncertainty about how well the patient has understood the alternatives before her. A second patient whose competence to refuse life-sustaining treatment has also been called into question is found to be suffering from some degree of clinical depression, but two evaluating psychiatrists disagree about the severity of the depression and to what extent it has affected the patient's decision. A third patient who has refused life-sustaining treatment is believed by some persons, but not by others, to be under subtle coercive pressures which raise doubts about the voluntariness of the choice. (A request for physician-assisted suicide or voluntary active euthanasia could be substituted in any of these examples leaving the same empirical uncertainties.) In each of these cases there need be no disagreement or indeterminacy about the precise content of the relevant standard (understanding of information, lack of depression, lack of coercion), only disagreement, generally arising from sometimes ineliminable limitations in the relevant evidence, about whether the case at hand meets that standard.

It will not always be easy to tell whether one has empirical or moral disagreement, or both, and in some cases what appears to be one may on closer analysis turn out to be the other. A disagreement about whether a particular action is killing or only allowing to die appears to be an empirical disagreement about what was done. There may turn out, however, to be no disagreement about what took place, only disagreement about whether to place it under what is for most people the more seriously wrong category of killing. This is a moral disagreement. To the extent that taking life in medicine is evaluated by what Bernard Williams calls *thick moral concepts*,[10] such as cruelty, which intertwine together descriptive and moral content, instead of thin moral concepts, such as obligatory or wrong, then moral and empirical disagreement often will be difficult if not impossible to disentangle fully.[11]

Just as moral disagreement or indeterminacy can arise for the full range of potentially morally relevant factors bearing on cases of taking life in medicine, so too empirical disagreement (two or more individuals have determinate but conflicting beliefs about a morally relevant empirical fact concerning a case of taking life) and empirical indeterminacy (one or more individuals is uncertain about, or does not know, a morally relevant empirical fact about a case of taking life) can arise concerning the full range of morally relevant empirical factors. Put somewhat differently, once we have resolved all the moral questions on the list, at the end of Section II, nearly all can arise again about any particular case in empirical form. Just to illustrate with the elements of valid consent:

1. Do the elements of valid consent obtain in this case?
   a. Is this patient's choice to end life adequately informed?
   b. Is this patient's choice to end life sufficiently voluntary?
   c. Are this patient's decisionmaking capacities adequate for competence to make this choice?

I shall not take the space here to spell out the empirical analogue to the rest of the moral issues on that list. Suffice it to say that at least in principle, but typically in practice as well, empirical or factual disagreement or uncertainty can occur about the extent to which any morally relevant empirical or descriptive property is present in a particular instance of taking life in medicine. This empirical disagreement or uncertainty can generate borderline morally justified cases of taking life in medicine in much the same manner as with moral disagreement or indeterminacy. In principle, if often not in practice, we might hope to be able to resolve empirical disagreement or uncertainty to an extent not always possible when the sources of borderline cases are moral, although the extent of difference between the moral and empirical cases on this point is philosophically controversial.

It is natural to think of borderline morally justified taking life in medicine, whether from moral or empirical sources, as resulting from interpersonal disagreement or uncertainty. But it is worth noting that there are both interpersonal and intrapersonal versions of most of these cases. To illustrate the intrapersonal case, one individual can find a particular case of taking life borderline because that individual's standard of moral justification for taking life results in some cases falling close to, and on either side of, the borderline separating morally justified from unjustified taking life. There also may be an area of moral indeterminacy in the individual's moral standards for evaluating taking life, where he or she is unable to decide whether some cases are justified or unjustified. These can sometimes be cases of intrapersonal disagreement, though perhaps only disagreement in a metaphorical sense, of an empirical or moral form when we find ourselves of "two minds" about a particular hard moral case, and so can see the plausibility of arguments in support of, but also against, that taking of life, or in support of conflicting accounts of the facts in the case. Similarly, there are also intrapersonal cases of empirical indeterminacy in which a single individual is uncertain about what the empirical properties of a particular case of taking life are which bear on its moral justification. Any of these forms of moral or empirical uncertainty or disagreement can generate "hard cases" in which a particular individual is uncertain or ambivalent about whether particular cases are morally justified.

PRINCIPLED BASES FOR HANDLING BORDERLINE MORALLY JUSTIFIED TAKING LIFE—A CRITIQUE OF THE BIAS TO LIFE

Is there a defensible principled approach to resolving or evaluating borderline cases of decisions to take human life in medicine? This question can arise for patients, surrogates, or physicians faced with a decision about taking life, but it is especially important for public, professional, or legal policy. In the law, one specific form in which the question arises concerns the procedural and substantive standards which must be satisfied when life support generally, or some subset of cases of life support that are viewed as borderline justified cases, is forgone. What form would a principled basis take for deciding borderline morally justified cases of taking life? What would make a general response to such cases a principled response? A case will be borderline when some feature or features of it of the sort discussed in the first two sections generate significant uncertainty or disagreement, for one or more persons, about whether the case falls on the justified or unjustified side of the moral border. If we assume there is, at least in principle for a given person's moral view, a correct answer to whether the particular action taking life is morally justified, the case will be borderline because the correct answer is uncertain or in dispute. In any decision about the case we risk one of two kinds of mistakes–deciding it is unjustified when it is not, or deciding it is not justified when it is.

One principled basis for dealing with borderline morally justified cases of taking life subject to these two kinds of potential mistakes would consist in showing that one of these two kinds of error or mistake is substantially worse morally than the other, so that, at least for some significant subset of the cases, we should err on the side of risking the less serious mistake. The most commonly asserted form of principled basis for such cases–what I will call the *bias in favor of life*–is of this form and I will critically evaluate it in some detail. A different kind of principled basis would consist in showing that neither one nor the other kind of mistake is, in principle, morally worse than the other, and so we must evaluate the seriousness and likelihood of each kind of mistake on a case by case basis. I shall defend this position, but want first to evaluate the position that in borderline morally justified taking of life we should err in favor of life.

A prominent use of the bias in favor of life is the burden of proof established by the state of Missouri's evidentiary standard for surrogates to forgo life support, which was reviewed and upheld by the U. S. Supreme Court in the Cruzan case.[12] Missouri requires "clear and convincing" evidence that the patient wished to forgo the particular treatment in question, in the circumstances the patient is now in, before a surrogate is permitted to forgo such treatment for an incompetent patient. The "clear and convincing" evidence standard is weaker than the "beyond a reasonable doubt" standard generally used in the criminal law and stricter than the "on the preponderance of the evidence" standard used in much of the civil law, but it was clearly understood by the state of Missouri and by the U. S. Supreme Court in reviewing it to be a relatively strict standard. As such, and because it applies to decisions to forgo, but not to employ or continue, life support, it in effect places a relatively high burden of proof on surrogates before life support for an incompetent patient can be forgone. What would justify placing this high burden of proof on surrogates that an incompetent patient wished to forgo a particular form of life support in specific circumstances?

Some would argue that just because life itself is at stake, we should always err on the side of protecting or preserving life when there is any significant doubt about the person's wishes or what is in the person's interests. There are usually two important components to this argument, although they are not often distinguished by its proponents. The first, which I shall call the *supreme importance* or *value of human life*, asserts the very high value or importance of one's own life to individuals–continued life is typically valued both in itself and as a necessary condition for pursuing and achieving virtually everything else people value in life. The second component, which I shall call the *irreversibility claim*, asserts the irreversibility of the decision to take life, whereas a decision to preserve life can be later reversed if found to be mistaken or if circumstances change. Many decisions in medicine, for example to try a specific treatment in the hope that it will prove to be of benefit to a patient, can be reversed and the treatment discontinued if it fails to provide the hoped for benefits. Similarly, decisions not to pursue a particular treatment that is not necessary to sustain the patient's life can also be reversed later and the treatment then instituted. Because of this reversibility, many choices either to pursue or not to pursue a particular treatment course can justifiably be made in conditions of substantial uncertainty about what the consequences of the decision and treatment will be. As the U. S. Supreme Court put it in Cruzan, an erroneous decision to end life cannot be corrected, whereas "an erroneous decision not to terminate results in a maintenance of the status quo, with at least the potential that a wrong decision will eventually be corrected or its impact mitigated by an event such as an advancement in medical science or the patient's unexpected death."[13] A similar line of reasoning underlies the emergency exception to the requirement of informed consent, and the practice of treating a patient without consent in circumstances in which delaying treatment until informed consent can be obtained will likely result in substantial and irreversible harm to the patient.[14] Do these two component claims justify a strong bias in favor of supporting life and placing a high burden of proof on any decisions to take life?

In assessing this defense of the bias in favor of preserving life, it is important not to be misled by the U. S. Supreme Court's decision and argument in Cruzan. The issue before the Court in Cruzan was not whether the decision of the Missouri Supreme Court in Cruzan was sound or wise public policy, or otherwise morally justified, but only the much more narrowly circumscribed issue of whether Missouri's policy was constitutionally permissible. In upholding the state of Missouri in Cruzan, the U. S. Supreme Court held only that the state's position did not violate the U. S. Constitution. My question here is quite different—is a strong bias in favor of life morally justified for individual decision makers, and is it sound public policy? We will need to examine the two components of the defense of the bias in favor of life separately. I have called the first component the *supreme importance of human life* in order to mark the unique position of a person's life as necessary to the pursuit of virtually all else of value to him or her. (The "virtually" qualification is necessary because people value or care about things that do not require their continued existence or experience—for example, a parent who wants his child to have a happy and productive life after the parent has died, or a person's concern that a unique environment such as a wetland be preserved for future generations.) It is undeniable that life has this instrumental value as necessary for our pursuing the various aims and activities that give value and meaning to our lives. Thus, the value of preserving people's lives normally derives both from life's intrinsic value—the value or desire people have for life itself—and from its instrumental value. In these respects, continued life does normally have supreme value for people—it has whatever intrinsic value sheer continued existence itself has, and has instrumental value by piggybacking on the value of the aims and activities that fill a life.

Life does not always have this intrinsic value, however. There are circumstances in which individuals do not value continued existence for itself, and are not able to fill their lives with experiences and activities that make their lives on balance of value and so a benefit or good to them. The condition of persistent vegetative state (PVS) is the best example for many people of circumstances in which they do not value continued life for its own sake and apart from the experience in that life. A patient in PVS has irreversibly lost all capacity for any conscious experience. Many people say they would not want their life maintained in PVS, which calls into question whether most people do in fact value continued life itself, apart from any experience in that life.[15]

Not only may life itself not be judged of value or a good, at least by some people in some circumstances, but people's experience can also come to be on balance a disvalue or bad for them. This is perhaps shown most clearly by the firm consensus that competent patients are entitled or have a moral right to refuse life-sustaining treatment. One ground of that consensus is the very high value placed in our society on individual self-determination or autonomy. This ground, of course, establishes little about whether the patient's life is no longer of value or a good to him or her. The value of self-determination could justify others respecting, in the sense of honoring, the patient's choice even if the patient is mistaken in no longer valuing his or her life. But consider the typical judgment of a patient who decides to forgo life support: the best life possible for me with life-sustaining treatment is sufficiently bad that it is worse than no further life at all. Continued life is no longer a good, but has now become on balance a burden, for the patient. Especially when patients are near death no matter what is done, are suffering or in untreatable pain, or no longer find their lives meaningful or satisfying, others do not view their decisions to forgo life-sustaining treatment as *always* mistaken, irrational, or unreasonable. (Though, of course, sometimes they are this, for example, in cases in which the patient's decisionmaking is affected by clinical depression.)[16] Continued life in such circumstances for many patients no longer has the supreme value necessary to support the bias for life.

Moreover, for public policy purposes, we can reliably identify at least some circumstances in which a large majority of people do not assign this supreme value to preserving life. For example, being in a persistent vegetative state, being in great pain and/or suffering (these are different and should not be equated[17]) while dying from some forms of cancer, coronary, or pulmonary disease, or being very severely cognitively impaired from stroke or advanced dementia. Of course, some people still value continued life in these circumstances, but most probably do not. We need to develop better data on the states that most people consider worse than death or such as to make life no longer of significant value. But it is clear that over a substantial range of conditions, the claim of the supreme value of life is not plausible.

The second component of the support for the bias in favor of life is that decisions to take life are irreversible, while decisions to support life are reversible, either by the later death of the patient despite treatment or by later taking life if doing so

becomes clearly justified. This irreversibility claim is problematic as well. The underlying idea of the irreversibility claim is that in an unclear or borderline choice in
which either alternative may be mistaken, if one choice will not allow us to correct
or reverse it should we later decide it was mistaken, while the other choice can be corrected should it later prove to have been mistaken, we should opt for the latter alternative. This amounts to a form of cautious conservatism or humility in the face of
uncertainty–recognizing that we may be wrong, we proceed in a manner that allows
flexibility and changing course if it turns out that we are. A decision to take life is
obviously irreversible in a strong sense–once the person is dead, that outcome cannot
be even partially corrected or reversed. The bias to life tells us in borderline cases of
justified taking life to prefer the reversible alternative of supporting life so as to limit
the potential harm or wrong should our choice prove to be mistaken. Why is this line
of reasoning unsound?

The fundamental difficulty is that the comparison the irreversibility claim sup-
poses between the alternatives of taking life and preserving life is misleading in its
characterization of each alternative. Consider first the alternative of preserving life.
The typical grounds for taking a patient's life being borderline morally justified will
be that preserving that life seems plausibly, although not conclusively, in conflict with
the patient's best interests and/or wishes. Treatment, and the life which it sustains,
will typically be burdensome and involve suffering for the patient, or provide little or
no benefit, as when the patient is in a persistent vegetative state.

Moreover, the greater moral importance we justifiably accord to individual self-
determination, the more serious the wrong we do people in preserving their lives
when they do not or would not have wanted that done. While reversing at a later time
the decision to sustain the patient's life can put an *end* to the earlier harm and/or
wrong done by sustaining the patient's life when that should not have been done, this
will not remove or undo the harm and/or wrong that has already occurred. Consider
the analogy with a person wrongly convicted of a crime whose innocence is discovered only after a long imprisonment; on release, it is common to note how those lost
years of the person's life can never be given back to him. The same is true of a
patient's unwanted and burdensome existence when life is wrongly or mistakenly
continued–these harms, this wrong, can never be removed. The general point then is
that acting on the bias to life is not without moral risk of serious harm or wrong to
the patient, a harm or wrong which cannot be removed or undone later by the patient's
death or by reversing the earlier decision to sustain life. In this respect, the harm or
wrong from a mistaken decision to sustain life is irreversible as well.

What of the alternative of taking life? Surely the irreversibility claim is correct
that once this is done we cannot correct the error if we later decide that the earlier
decision to end life was mistaken. This point is made against capital punishment–if
we find later that an innocent person has been wrongly convicted and executed, no
correction of the mistake is possible. In neither case can we restore life to the person
if we later decide that the life was wrongly taken. To this extent, the irreversibility

claim is correct. But this irreversibility of the decision to terminate life should only seem to us a serious enough harm or wrong to warrant the bias in favor of life if we also accept the claim of the supreme value or importance of life, which I have argued is usually false in borderline morally justified cases of taking life. To see this, suppose you are deciding whether to go to the movies or to take a bike ride with your child. This is the last local performance of the movie. Since its reviews were mediocre and its audiences small, it is virtually certain you will never again have the chance to see it, so a decision now not to see it is irreversible. On the other hand, you regularly take bike rides with your child and will have many future opportunities to do so again. The irreversibility of your decision not to see the movie counts little if at all in favor of choosing to go to it, despite the possibility you may later decide it was a mistake not to, when the desirability of going to the movie now appears no greater than the alternative of taking the bike ride. So it is only if a possible loss is irreversible *and* of great value in comparison with a competing good that we should adopt a policy of not risking the loss of that value.

Now a person's life under normal circumstances is of great value and so does warrant a bias to life to limit the risk of its loss, but in the borderline justified cases of taking life at issue here, the very conditions that make the cases borderline make the life that would be preserved not of disproportionate value in comparison with the value to the person of ending his or her life. Thus, no bias to life is justified that seeks always to avoid the possible mistake of ending life when it should not be ended. Instead, the probability and relative seriousness of each mistake—ending a life that should be continued or continuing a life that should be ended—must be weighed on a case-by-case basis. No general bias to life, nor high burden of proof for decisions to end life, is warranted in cases of borderline morally justified taking of life in medicine.

The case-by-case assessment of the alternatives of ending life or continuing life will have both empirical and evaluative components, each of which will be potentially controversial. The empirical components include what the consequences will be of the alternatives of continuing life (in many cases there will be more than one alternative that involves continuing life, for example, by pursing different alternative life-sustaining treatments) and ending life (here too, there may be alternative ways in which this may be done, for example, by forgoing life-sustaining treatment, by physician-assisted suicide, or by voluntary active euthanasia), together with the probabilities of the various significant components of these alternative outcomes. While sometimes there will be empirical disagreement about whether a particular outcome is even possible, disagreement more commonly will be about the probability of different outcomes. The evaluative disagreement will be about the relative positive or negative value of different features of these alternative choices. In part because there is a wide range of reasonable disagreement about these evaluations, the moral importance of individual self-determination in the choice to continue or end life warrants acknowledging broad authority of competent persons to make this choice according to their own values. When surrogates must decide for incompetent individuals, more substantive and procedural safeguards are appropriate. The correct principled basis for making decisions about borderline morally justified cases of taking life is the assessment of the benefits and burdens of alternatives from the patient's perspective. No general bias in favor of life is warranted.

Before concluding, I want to complete my critique of the bias in favor of life by briefly considering two other arguments sometimes offered in its support. If there is a moral right not to be killed and a moral duty or obligation not to take innocent human life, then perhaps the moral importance of ensuring this right or duty is not violated is sufficient to warrant the bias to preserving life. Rights, after all, are moral protections of sufficient importance to require our taking great efforts to respect them. At bottom, this suggestion has the same difficulties as the arguments in support of the bias in favor of life that I have just considered. If the alternative of preserving life so as not to risk violating this right or duty was itself without significant moral risk or cost, then this line of support for the bias in favor of life might be persuasive. But the very same circumstances which typically make taking life borderline morally justi-fied also make the alternative of preserving life carry the risk of violating important moral rights or duties. What rights or duties? First, a right of self-determination, which in some form is given fundamental importance in most moral thought, as well as the law, and which grounds the right to refuse unwanted life-sustaining treatment. Second, the duty of physicians, long acknowledged to be a central aim of medicine, to relieve the pain and suffering present in many cases of borderline morally justified taking of life. Neither alternative of preserving or ending life is without serious moral risk or cost. Important moral rights or duties may be violated whichever alterna-tive–taking or preserving life–is chosen, and so respect for patient's rights does not support a general bias in favor of life.

Finally, the last argument in support of the bias in favor of life appeals to a puta-tive state interest in protecting life. Appeal to this state interest is common in legal cases about life-sustaining treatment. In the words of the U. S. Supreme Court in Cruzan, "Missouri has a general interest in the protection and preservation of human life."[18] Apart from whether this is a sound legal claim, which is not my concern here, is there any moral basis for such a state interest. No attempt at a full answer to this question is possible here, but the general outlines of what I take to be the correct answer can be given.

Modern democratic societies have long since given up the idea that citizens belong in some property-like sense to the state. Nevertheless, the state does have a crucial role in preventing morally wrongful taking of life, wrongs which are com-monly considered to be among the most serious of moral wrongs. Wrongful taking of life is at its core a moral wrong to the person whose life is taken, not to the state. Because the state's moral interest in preserving life is grounded in its role in pre-venting this wrong to people, that interest is derivative from and dependent on the wrongfulness to the victim of taking his or her life. In normal circumstances, the state's interest in preserving a particular individual's life does not exceed that individual's own interest in having his or her life preserved. Any independent state interest in preserving life, apart from the interest of the individual whose life it is, is ungrounded and unnecessary. This state interest, however, is typically asserted *against* the wishes or interests of the person who wants to die, in order to justify preventing his or her doing so. When an individual no longer has an interest in or desire for continued life, there is no significant residual state interest in preserving life to be opposed to the individual's interest.

This is not to say that the state cannot have a legitimate role in establishing and supporting procedures to ensure that competent patient's choices to end their lives are fully informed and voluntary, and that surrogates' choices for incompetent patients are properly guided by the patient's wishes or interests. But this role requires no appeal to any independent state interest in preserving human life beyond the interests of individuals in their own lives. Nor is there any place in a society that views individuals as in a deep sense free, self-determined persons for the assertion of what would amount to an ownership interest in the lives of its citizens, which could justify forcing life on them when that life has become burdensome and unwanted by them. If the state had a legitimate and weighty interest in preserving human life per se, without regard to whether that life was a good to or wanted by the person whose life it is, then that interest would stand against any decision that would shorten life, including patients' clearly competent and reasonable choices to forgo life-sustaining treatments. Courts that have considered the putative state interest in preserving life in cases of forgoing life-sustaining treatment have consistently, and in my view rightly, held the patient's self-determination interest to be more weighty and controlling.[19]

NOTES

1. This particular taxonomy of moral views was first stated by Ronald Dworkin, Taking Rights Seriously. Cambridge, MA: Harvard University Press, 1977, Chapter 6. I have applied it to killing in "Moral Rights and Permissible Killing," in John Ladd ed. *Ethical Issues Relating to Life and Death*. Oxford: Oxford University Press, 1979, and reprinted in my *Life and Death: Philosophical Essays in Biomedical Ethics*. Cambridge: Cambridge University Press, 1993.

2. Peter Singer and Helga Kuhse, *Should the Baby Live: The Problem of Handicapped Infants*. Oxford: Oxford University Press, 1985.

3. See, for example, Jeremy Waldron, "A Right to Do Wrong," *Ethics* 92; 1981: 21.

4. Allen E. Buchanan and Dan W. Brock, *Deciding For Others: The Ethics of Surrogate Decision Making*. Cambridge: Cambridge University Press, 1989.

5. Michael Tooley, *Abortion and Infanticide*. Oxford: Oxford University Press, 1983.

6. Mary Anne Warren, "On the Moral and Legal Status of Abortion," *The Monist* 57; 1973.

7. Buchanan and Brock, *Deciding for Others*, pp. 36–40.

8. Albert R. Jonsen and Stephen Toulmin, *The Abuse of Casuistry*. Berkeley, CA: University of California Press, 1988.

9. Henry S. Richardson, "Specifying Norms as a Way to Resolve Concrete Ethical Problems," *Philosophy & Public Affairs* 19; Fall 1990: 279–310.

10. Bernard Williams, *Ethics and the Limits of Philosophy*. Cambridge, MA: Harvard University Press, 1985.

11. For one such use of a thick moral concept, see Susan Braithwaite and David Thomasma, "New Guidelines on Forgoing Life-sustaining Treatment in Incompetent Patients: An Anti-Cruelty Policy," *Annals of Internal Medicine* 104; 1986: 711–715.

12. *Cruzan v. Director, Mo. Dep't of Health*, 110 S. Ct. 2841 (1990).

13. *Cruzan v. Director*.

14. Alan Meisel, "The 'Exceptions' to the Informed Consent Doctrine: Striking a Balance Between Competing Values in Medical Decision Making," *Wisconsin Law Review*, 1979: 413–488.

15. P. Painton and E. Taylor, "Love or Let Die," *Time*, 19 March 1990: 62–71; Boston Globe/Harvard University Poll, *Boston Globe*, 3 November 1991.

16. Robert Misbin, "Physicians Aid in Dying," *New England Journal of Medicine* 325; 1991: 1304–1307.

17. Eric Cassell, *The Nature of Suffering and the Goals of Medicine*. New York: Oxford University Press, 1991.

18. *Cruzan v. Director*.

19. See the discussion of state interests in several places in Robert F. Weir, *Abating Treatment with Critically Ill Patients: Ethical and Legal Limits to Medical Prolongation of Life*. New York: Oxford University Press, 1989.

The Physician's Role in Killing and the Intentional Withdrawal of Treatment

RONALD E. CRANFORD

Hennepin County Medical Center, Minneapolis, Minnesota

PRIMARY GOALS OF MEDICINE

A logical starting point for a discussion of the physician's role in letting die and killing is a consideration of the primary values and goals of medicine. According to the Hastings Center, four central values derive "from the moral traditions of medicine and nursing and from the ethical, religious, and legal traditions of our society." These values are the well-being of the patient (best interests), the patient's autonomy (right to self-determination), the integrity of the health care professional, and justice or equity.[1] The President's Commission asserts that the primary basis for medical treatment of patients is the prospect that "each individual's interest (specifically, the interest in well-being) will be promoted. Thus, treatment ordinarily aims to benefit a patient through preserving life, relieving pain and suffering, protecting against disability, and returning maximally effective functioning."[2]

But what values, goals, or objectives are appropriate when treatments are not effective for their intended purposes? When none of these goals are served, and the patient is experiencing extreme suffering for which there is no effective treatment, should the physician just stand by and let nature take its course, or can assisted suicide or euthanasia be justified in these circumstances?

FOUR CATEGORIES OF MORALLY DISTINGUISHABLE ACTIONS

From a clinical and ethical perspective, there are four categories of morally distinguishable actions: (1) letting die (by forgoing treatment); (2) palliative care; (3) physician-assisted suicide; and (4) euthanasia. These categories are broad and there may be significant gray areas between them in some circumstances. Nevertheless, there are enough meaningful distinctions to warrant the establishment of these categories.

Letting die by forgoing treatment (where the underlying primary cause of death is the pathologic condition) is extremely common. Negotiated death probably occurs in well over one million of the 2.2 million deaths that occur each year in the United States. In my own clinical practice, over 90 percent of deaths are negotiated to some extent, usually by withholding or withdrawing various forms of treatment (most commonly, cardiopulmonary resuscitation).

LETTING DIE VERSUS KILLING

There are major differences—clinically and morally—between letting die by forgoing treatment and killing (e.g., euthanasia, physician-assisted suicide). In most circumstances, the clinical distinctions between physician-assisted suicide and euthanasia are clear, but (because both are acts of killing) the moral distinctions are less obvious.

Even though physician-assisted suicide and euthanasia are both forms of killing, physician-assisted suicide appears to be less objectionable to most physicians in the United States—but for the wrong reason: there is less legal liability. The most common means of assisting suicide is for the physician to help the patient stockpile medications and to advise the patient concerning the means of administration and the effective (lethal) dose. This means of assisting suicide makes it extremely difficult for legal authorities to determine that the physician was involved. Though many American physicians may believe that there are major moral distinctions between physician-assisted suicide and active euthanasia, both are in fact forms of killing, or at least assistance in bringing about death.

In contrast, Dutch physicians strongly believe that active euthanasia is preferable to physician-assisted suicide. They feel a stronger moral commitment to their patients. Euthanasia in the Netherlands occurs in the context of a close patient-physician relationship; often the patient and physician (and family) have known each other for years. Dutch physicians believe they should be present at the time of death, when the patient needs them most, to ensure that the patient's wishes are properly carried out. Hence, Dutch physicians prefer active euthanasia because of their concern and commitment to their patients, whereas American physicians seem to prefer physician-assisted suicide because of their concern about legal liability.

EXAMPLES OF JUSTIFIABLE KILLING

Acts of killing (physician-assisted suicide and euthanasia) can be justified on an individual basis when the physician's moral obligation to relieve suffering and respect patient autonomy outweighs the duty to preserve life, when the *only* way to relieve suffering is not simply by letting die, but by killing.

In the debate on letting die (stopping treatment), and also in the incipient controversy over euthanasia, some have emphasized what they perceive to be important distinctions between the "terminally ill" and "chronically ill." "Terminally ill" is used to mean that death will occur in a relatively short time (days, weeks, or months), with or without continued treatment. For example, patients with wide-spread metastatic cancer in its final stages may be terminally ill because death will result soon even with continued medical treatment. Or some would consider a terminal illness to include patients in a persistent vegetative state who would die soon if medical treatment, that is, artificial nutrition and hydration, were stopped—even though in this latter case the patient could live for years with continued medical treatment.

Patients may be "chronically ill" when they have a devastating neurological or medical condition which seriously compromises quality of life, but they are not directly dependent on life-support systems for survival. The Hastings Center defines this condition as "an illness or disabling condition that is severe and irreversible." Unfortunately, there is no consensus on any of these terms and definitions.

The distinction between terminally and chronically ill may be morally relevant in some cases, but it is not always clear-cut. Furthermore, the distinctions are usually used to focus less on what is best for the patient and more on what is believed to be best for society. A major justification for cases of physician-assisted suicide and active euthanasia may be in the chronically ill patient (one with prolonged disability and great suffering, but no end in sight) because the patient is not dependent on life-support systems. Although the release from suffering (by killing) may be most important for the individual, it may be most threatening to society. Why should it make any difference to the individual patient whether death is imminent, provided the suffering is intolerable? The patient wants control over his or her existence, and the patient wants the physician to honor his or her values. Thus, in many situations a stronger case can be made for killing in instances of the chronically ill than in the terminally ill.

What are the most compelling cases in which it can be argued that physician-assisted suicide or active euthanasia are permissible? From a patient's standpoint, three conditions must be met, and these conditions are sufficient to justify the action. (1) The patient's suffering is extreme, and *all* other alternatives to relieve suffering have failed; the only way to relieve suffering is by killing. (2) The suffering is so extreme that it outweighs any positive aspects of the patient's well-being and autonomy. (3) The patient has decisionmaking capacity, and it is clear exactly what the patient wants (valid informed consent). The patient need not be terminally ill (in the traditional sense) nor imminently dying; however, if the patient is terminally ill and thus dependent on life-support systems, it is much simpler and less controversial to simply stop medical treatment, provide aggressive palliative care, and let the patient die. Aggressive palliative care should include giving the patient enough sedatives or hypnotics to induce coma if necessary.

In the Netherlands, four conditions must be met prior to active euthanasia: (1) the patient must be competent, (2) the patient must request euthanasia consistently and repeatedly over a reasonable length of time, (3) euthanasia must be performed by a physician in consultation with another physician, and (4) the patient must be suffering intolerably and have no alternative for relieving the suffering. The fourth condition allows for active euthanasia in patients other than those with a terminal condition. Dutch physicians emphasize that the suffering may be physical or psychological; in fact, more often than not, the justification for active euthanasia is psychological rather than physical.

In the Remmelink Commission Report, 187 cases of euthanasia and suicide were studied in depth through interviews with physicians.[3] It was found that patients' requests were based on loss of dignity (57%), pain (46%), unworthy dying (46%), being dependent on others (33%), or tiredness of life (23%). In only 10 of the 187 cases was physical pain the only reason. It is not clear exactly how many patients were considered "terminally ill" as traditionally defined. It was estimated that 2.9 percent of all deaths in the Netherlands were secondary to "euthanasia and related MDEL (medical decisions concerning the end of life)." Of this 2.9 percent, 1.8 percent were cases of voluntary euthanasia, where all four strict criteria for euthanasia were met. Assisted suicide (a physician intentionally prescribes or supplies lethal drugs, but the patient administers them) accounted for 0.3 percent of the deaths. Another 0.8 percent were "life termination by administering lethal drugs without an explicit and persistent request from the patient."

Sixty-eight percent of the cases studied were cancer patients; a variety of diseases accounted for the remaining 32 percent. Only 2 percent were diseases of the nervous system, and 15 percent were "others." In cases in which euthanasia was performed without all of the strict criteria being met, the study comments that "in most cases the amount of time by which, according to the physician, life had been shortened was a few hours or days only." In euthanasia, life was shortened by at least 1 week in 70 percent of all cases, and by more than 6 months in another 8 percent.

In which specific cases, then, is active euthanasia plausibly justified? Cancers of the head, neck, and mouth comprise one group of related cases. These patients may have a radical neck dissection with extreme surgical disfigurement of the face and neck, profound anorexia and weight loss, dry mouth, severe pain, and discomfort, yet not be dependent on life-support systems to the extent that stopping treatment would allow the patient to die. These patients can live for months or years in an agonizing condition under which death may be preferable to life.

AIDS patients represent another case in which, at some point, active euthanasia could possibly be justified. In the last few months of life, the patient may be competent, aware, and capable of great suffering. During this time of multiple medical and infectious disease complications, patients are often weak and cachectic with profound weight loss. They may also have other major complications such as intractable diarrhea coupled with extremely painful perirectal ulcers. Pulmonary problems can lead to profound dyspnea. At this point, the disease is invariably fatal, but the patient may live for months in agony and indignity while awaiting the final, fatal complication.

Another example is the patient with a severe neurologic disability, where the suffering and loss of dignity and control may extend over a protracted period, even though the patient may not yet be dependent on life-support systems, such as a respirator or a feeding tube. A patient with extremely severe multiple sclerosis may have a severe speech disability, double vision, weakness, incoordination, extremely painful muscle spasms, and weight loss. Quality of life is minimal (depending on the patient's value systems), and suffering and indignity is maximal, yet the patient may live for years.

But a major argument for active euthanasia in individual circumstances can be turned into a major argument against it when it is proposed as a social policy. Patients want control in many individual circumstances, but this control may establish a precedent that allows the abuse of active euthanasia in other situations.

PHYSICAL AND PSYCHOLOGICAL SUFFERING

In a clinical sense, suffering should be viewed in its broadest perspective, as both a physical and a psychological phenomenon. Eric Cassell defines suffering as "the state of severe distress associated with events that threaten the intactness of person." He notes that "the relief of suffering is considered one of the primary ends of medicine by patients and the general public, but not by the medical profession." He further states that "patients and their friends and families do not divide up suffering into its physical and nonphysical sources the way doctors do, who are primarily concerned with the physical."[4]

A patient may have terrible suffering, yet be free of pain or physical distress. As Cassell explains: "Someone devoid of physical pain, perhaps even devoid of 'symptoms' can suffer. People can suffer from what they have lost of themselves in relation to the world of objects, events, and relationships. Such suffering occurs because of our intactness as persons, our coherence, and integrity, and comes not only from the intactness of the body but from the wholeness of the web of relationships with self and others."[5]

To illustrate this form of suffering, Cassell discusses a patient of his, a 35-year-old sculptor with widespread cancer of the breast who has undergone aggressive medical treatment. She is house-bound and bed-ridden. Her face is changed by steroids. One breast is twisted and scarred. She also has been masculinized by her hormonal treatment. She has almost no hair. Much of her suffering is psychological, not physical, and the degree of importance attached to such losses is largely determined by cultural values and the personal meaning to the individual.

Cassell goes on to say, "we all recognize certain injuries that almost invariably cause suffering: the death or suffering of loved ones, powerlessness, helplessness, hopelessness, torture, the loss of a life's work, deep betrayal, physical agony, isolation, homelessness, memory failure, and unremitting fear."[6] One could also add the awareness of the loss of one's own personality, as in the early stages of Alzheimer's disease. Janet Adkins, Dr. Kevorkian's first euthanasia patient, exemplifies this latter phenomenon.

Nearly everyone (except American physicians) seems to agree that American physicians are doing a terrible job of understanding and treating suffering in their patients, and that this is one of the major driving forces behind the movement towards euthanasia. Stevenson and colleagues note that "it is ironic that condemnation of euthanasia is almost universal, but treatment strategies that *virtually insure unnecessary suffering* are generally accepted" (emphasis added).[7] Richard Selzer praises Cassell's book on suffering and comments, "Eric Cassell has hurled a bold challenge at the current practice of medicine whose *narrow vision of human suffering* is often a major cause of it" (emphasis added).[8]

A federal advisory panel, citing several dozen reports, concluded: "50 to 60 percent of patients with cancer pain lived the last part of their lives with unrelieved severe pain" and called for better use of "current knowledge and technology to control pain, stronger educational programs in pain management for health-care professionals, expanded research to develop new drugs and nondrug therapies, and use of reviews in hospitals to make sure that doctors are treating pain effectively."[9] One panelist, Dr. Emanuel M. Papper estimated that perhaps 8 million Americans per year undergo surgical operations in parts of their bodies where pain occurs if they move. Of these, perhaps 40 to 60 percent, or 3 million to 5 million Americans, are given too little medication for pain after surgery. Thus, there seems to be a monumental undertreatment of pain in the nondying setting as well.

PATIENT-PHYSICIAN RELATIONSHIP

In most other industrial countries, a close patient-physician relationship extending over a period of years is common; a physician often knows the patient's (and family's) needs, goals, and personal values quite well. In the United States, just the opposite circumstance prevails. Even the American Medical Association laments the infrequency of the close patient-physician relationship in this country.

Determining whether a patient will benefit from euthanasia requires an intimate understanding of the patient's concerns, values and pressures that may be prompting the euthanasia request. In the Netherlands, where euthanasia seems to be *fairly successful*, physicians who provide euthanasia generally have a *life-long relationship* with the patient which enables the physician to have access to this vital information. In the U.S., however, physicians *rarely* have the depth of knowledge about their patients that would be necessary for an appropriate evaluation of the patient's request for euthanasia (emphasis added).[10]

Many physicians and ethicists argue that physician-assisted suicide and active euthanasia will seriously undermine the trust and confidence of patients in American physicians. But this view is tempered by two considerations. First, many American patients already lack a great deal of confidence and trust in their physicians. They simply do not believe that their physicians possess sufficient compassion, courage, and common sense to let them die in the most humane way possible. Indeed, this is one of the major driving forces behind the interest in euthanasia in the United States. Second, not only may this argument be false, but just the opposite may be true. If more physicians were willing to be with their patients at the time of dying and do whatever may be necessary to minimize suffering and indignity (even if this rarely involved acts of killing), then there may be more, rather than less, trust and confidence in American physicians. In the Netherlands, euthanasia most commonly occurs in the context of a close patient-physician relationship; in the United States, in any context, a close patient-physician relationship is the exception rather than the norm. The Remmelink Commission notes: "Only in the face of unbearable suffering and with no alternatives would they [Dutch physicians] be prepared to take such action. Many respondents mentioned that an *emotional bond* is required for euthanasia and this may be one reason why euthanasia was more common in general practice where doctor and patient have often known each other for years and the doctor has shared part of the patient's suffering" (emphasis added).[11]

Surveys in the United States consistently find that over half of the American public favors controlling their own lives at the end, by having either themselves or physicians end their lives. Exactly what is meant by "ending a life" or "aid in dying" is unclear. But those physicians and ethicists opposing assisted suicide and euthanasia need to reconcile their theoretical, unsubstantiated views with the attitudes currently held by the American population.

Those who argue most strongly against killing are often those who are also most opposed to withdrawing artificial nutrition and hydration, and to patient and family control over medical treatment decisions. In other words, those most opposed to killing are also opposed to important elements in the humane care of the dying— a contradictory and self-defeating ethical position, like being against both abortion and contraception. For example, conservatives in our society who vigorously denounce suicide and euthanasia also take the view that artificial nutrition and hydration are not medical treatments and that the withdrawal of these medical means of nutrition and hydration is more like euthanasia than letting die by stopping treatment.

In an editorial calling for an open discussion of assisted suicide and euthanasia, Drs. Christine Cassel and Diane Meier criticize those physicians taking an absolute position in which they are opposed not only to acts of killing, but even to a discussion of acts of killing.

The fear and anxiety that many people feel when contemplating chronic and terminal debilitating illnesses is rooted, at least in part, in the fear that their suffering will be prolonged by medical technology and that they will have little or no control over its application. In this context, the medical profession's repeated and firm rejection of any participation by physicians in assisted suicide begins to appear self-serving in its emphasis on a professional scrupulosity that seems blind to the expressed needs of the patients.

The public appears to be losing faith in doctors, at least partly because of our paternalistic and sometimes cruel insistence on life at any cost.

The medical profession in the United States has reflected our society's unwillingness to accept death as part of life and to face it with some humility. Perhaps the public is now ahead of the medical profession in this regard, as patients increasingly seek the assistance of physicians in their time of need, when dying with dignity becomes more important than prolonging life. The rigid view that physicians should never assist in suicide denies the complexity of the personal meanings life can have in favor of a single-minded devotion to its maximal duration.

The refusal of physicians to deal with their patients at the level of the personal meaning of life and death is a reflection of how sterile and technological our profession has become.[12]

KILLING AS A GRASSROOTS PHENOMENON

A major driving factor behind the American grassroots movement towards assisted suicide and euthanasia is the public's fear of losing control and dignity, and undergoing a prolonged period of meaningless suffering and disability. As Wanzer and his colleagues have pointed out:

One of the most pervasive causes of anxiety among patients, their families and the public is the perception that physicians' efforts toward the relief of pain are sadly deficient. Because of this perceived professional deficiency, people fear that needless suffering will be allowed to occur as patients are dying. To a large extent, we believe such fears are justified.[13]

This lack of control feared by the American populace is strongly related to the lack of a close patient-physician relationship and a perception by the American public that they are not cared for by compassionate physicians who have the patient's best interests as the highest priority.

The enormous popularity of Derek Humphry's book *Final Exit*, which has now sold over one half million copies, reflects a massive failure on the part of the American medical profession to develop a humane care of the dying policy. As

Matthew Conolly and others have noted, "There is evidence to suggest that most requests for euthanasia or assisted suicide would be eliminated if patients were guaranteed that their pain and suffering will be eased, and their dignity and self-sufficiency promoted."[14]

ONLY PHYSICIANS AS KILLERS

If acts of killing are justifiable in individual cases, or are to become part of a broadly accepted medical or social policy, it is my opinion that the most logical people to perform these actions would be physicians. To perform acts of killing humanely and properly, a physician (or someone else) should be knowledgeable and experienced in at least five major areas.

1. The medical condition of the patient. Is the patient suffering from an incurable and irreversible disease? Does the patient have multiple medical complications, some of which may be more treatable than others? What will happen if medical treatment is discontinued? Will the patient probably die soon, or will stopping treatment merely accentuate the suffering? Is the patient suffering from a "terminal illness," "imminently dying," or suffering from a prolonged and severe disability (chronic illness)?

2. Decisionmaking capacity. Is the patient capable of making decisions for him- or herself? Does the patient fully understand what he or she is asking for? Have all of the requirements for informed consent been satisfied? Is the patient suffering from a "treatable" depression? Is the wish of the patient consistent with his or her own personal value system?

Drs. Conwell and Caine call attention to the fact that the impact of psychiatric illness on rational decisionmaking is notably lacking from the right-to-die debate.[15] They point out that only physicians, and sometimes only psychiatrists, have the expertise and training necessary to competently assess the mental state of an individual patient. Who can best determine when a "treatable component" of depression is present, or when depression is so severe that it makes the patient "irrational"? Psychiatrists are better equipped than most physicians to determine whether the decision to commit suicide is colored by mental illness. Even primary care physicians often fail to recognize treatable depression in their patients, particularly among the elderly.

> The distinction between the depressed mood or sadness that develops as a natural response to serious illness and the clinical depressive syndrome for which treatment is warranted is a subtle one that should be made by a physician.[16]

3. Suffering. How severe is the suffering? Is the suffering psychological, physical, or a combination of both? Does the patient have such extreme suffering for which all other alternatives to relieve it have been exhausted? Is the suffering sufficiently severe that a physician in good conscience can honor a patient's request for an act of killing?

4. Means of killing. What is the most effective and humane way for the patient to kill him- or herself, or for the physician to kill the patient? Does the physician have the experience

and knowledge needed to administer lethal doses of medication? Does the physician know the side effects of the medications, and the most effective ways to circumvent those side effects? What is the most effective way of killing a patient consistent with the patient's lifestyle and value system, and compatible with the ethical integrity of the physician? Who should be the agent of death: someone with whom the patient has closely bonded, or a complete stranger trained in the art and science of euthanasia?

5. Determination of death. Who will actually pronounce the patient dead? Who has the necessary training and experience to know when patients are dead? Who will sign the death certificate?

If knowledge of all five of these areas is necessary for a humane and proper act of killing, then who could be trained to perform these functions besides physicians? Are we going to train an elite corps of executioners used only for the administration of a lethal medicine and not for the other four functions? If acts of killing were permissible, either individually or socially, then would physicians be willing to assist in assessing these other necessary conditions? It is unrealistic to expect that our society can delegate all these functions to persons other than physicians.

If we believe that acts of killing now occur usually in the context of a close patient-physician relationship, as in the Netherlands, then where can a patient turn to find someone caring and sensitive enough to perform this morally problematic and psychologically difficult act? Where can the patient find someone who can be trusted to help the patient carry out his or her wishes, someone who will not be unduly worried about economic or legal considerations? If we are looking for a caring, sensitive individual whose overwhelming consideration is patient care, then physicians may not be the best group to serve these needs. What other group could serve these purposes: Nurses? Hospice workers? Paramedics? Technicians appointed and trained by the government? Veterinarians? (After all veterinarians love their animals enough that they never allow them to suffer needlessly.)

In the Netherlands, assisted suicide and euthanasia can only be performed by physicians. The Dutch Medical Association has taken a strong stand in support of this view and called for a specific box on the death certificate to allow the physician to indicate that death occurred by assisted suicide or euthanasia. When a physician experienced and knowledgeable in euthanasia performs this action, unconsciousness occurs within 10 to 15 seconds, and death within 10 to 15 minutes (intravenous administration of a short-acting barbiturate inducing coma, followed by a muscle paralyzing agent, causing respiratory paralysis and death).

To take an absolute position that doctors must never kill without an extensive discussion of the pros and cons of this position is simply to deny the complexity and reality of real-life situations, as well as the feelings of the American public. Why is there such a disparity between what patients want and what physicians are willing to give? Advances in medicine and public health have created greater longevity and other circumstances where the potential for the prolongation of meaningless suffering is far greater than ever. Directly as a result of recent advances in medical treatment, medicine itself has created situations in which suffering, loss of control, and lack of dignity are common in clinical practice. Physicians create dilemmas, then step back and say they can do nothing about them. As Martha Angell notes,

> The principal argument in favor of euthanasia is that it is more humane than forcing a patient to continue a life of unmitigated suffering. According to this view, there is no moral difference under some circumstances between euthanasia and withholding life-sustaining treatment. In both situations, the purpose is a merciful death, and the only practical difference is that withholding life-sustaining treatment entails more suffering because it takes longer. Furthermore, it requires an element of happenstance, such as the development of pneumonia for which there is treatment that could be withheld.[17]

No goal in medicine is absolute, including preserving life, or not killing. In some circumstances, minimizing patient suffering and enhancing patient autonomy may substantially outweigh the physician's moral obligation not to kill. To deny this as possibility, either in individual cases or as a social policy, is to seriously underestimate the complexity of modern society and the ability of medicine to prolong life and meaningless suffering when no hope for recovery exists.

POTENTIAL FOR ABUSE

The major concern I have about physician-assisted suicide and active euthanasia in this country is the potential for abuse, on both the physician's and the patient's part. If American physicians presently lack the moral fiber to let patients die well (by forgoing treatment and minimizing suffering), how can we expect them to have the courage to help their patients commit suicide or even kill their patients well?

Most arguments against killing apply equally to letting die and stopping treatment. Letting die where death is intended (for example, stopping a feeding tube in Nancy Cruzan) is already extremely common. The critical issue is not intending death, but whether the primary cause of death is the underlying disease process or the inherently lethal action of the physician.

Letting die can only be done when a patient is dependent on life support; stopping treatment will then allow nature to take its course, with the fatal pathology killing the patient. However, suicide and euthanasia (where the lethal action is independent of the patient's medical condition) can occur at any time, no matter how well or ill the patient is, and in any physical location—home, nursing home, or hospital. Presumably, there would be less oversight and procedural safeguards for acts of killing than for letting die; thus killing could give rise to more abuse.

Even if there are individual cases where killing may be justified, the more morally relevant question is: are such cases frequent enough—now or in the future—to justify reconsidering the strong medical and social prohibitions against killing by physicians? If we assume that American physicians would become much more caring and compassionate toward hopelessly ill patients and develop far more sensitive and enlightened attitudes toward the treatment of suffering (an unlikely possibility, but a laudable goal), then would cases of justifiable killing be so rare as to preclude any changes in social policy?

If killing were allowed for competent patients, would there be social or other pressures to kill incompetent persons? In my view, there probably would be more pressure to extend killing to the incompetent as well as the competent—if intolerable suffering were used as the threshold medical criteria for killing. The Dutch have maintained that euthanasia occurs only in a voluntary setting. But that reasoning is circular since by definition euthanasia can only occur in patients who are competent. If medical killing occurs outside the competent patient in the Netherlands, it is no longer called euthanasia. The Remmelink Commission found that a significant number of deaths occurred in the category of "euthanasia without strict criteria being met" (0.8% of all deaths as opposed to 1.8% of all deaths for euthanasia under strict criteria).[18]

CONCLUSION

In summary, I think we should do everything possible to emphasize the humane care of the dying — that is, follow an enlightened, compassionate policy of letting die by forgoing treatment and using aggressive palliative care. If this were done in the United States, and I frankly have serious reservations whether it is possible, then many of the motivating factors underlying the grassroots movement towards killing would be considerably diminished to the point where individual acts of killing could be justified, but one could take a justifiable position against any public policy sanctioned killing. Killing by physicians or anyone else is radically different, medically and morally, from letting die. The potential for abuse is far greater. Many do not trust American physicians to do the right thing. Particularly disturbing is the relative rarity of a close patient-physician relationship in the United States as compared to other countries.

Therefore, I believe that acts of physician-assisted suicide and euthanasia are morally justifiable in some extreme circumstances. At the present time, however, I do not favor legalization of physician-assisted suicide or euthanasia because I think there needs to be a great deal more discussion and more experience in these areas before we embark on a path of a formal public policy endorsing these actions. Lastly, even though I have extreme reservations about the capability of American medicine to act humanely in both the areas of letting die and killing, I still feel that only physicians should be given this power.

NOTES

1. *Guidelines on the termination of life-sustaining treatment and the care of the dying.* The Hastings Center, New York: Briarcliff Manor, 1987, pp. 18–20.

2. *Deciding to forego life-sustaining treatment.* The President's Commission for the Study of Ethical Problems in Medicine and Biomedical and Behavioral Research. U.S. Government Printing Office, Washington, DC, April, 1983: 81.

3. P.J. van der Maas, J.J.M. Van Delden, L. Pijnenborg, C.W.N. Looman, "Euthanasia and Other Medical Decisions Concerning the End of Life," *The Lancet* 338;1991:669–674.

4. E.J. Cassell, *The Nature of Suffering and the Goals of Medicine.* New York: Oxford University Press, 1991, pp. 32–33.

5. Ibid., p. 40.

6. Ibid., p. 44.

7. D.K. Stevenson, W.E. Benitz, W.D. Rhine, et al. "Point-Counterpoint: Physicians' Refusal of Requested Treatment," *Journal Perinatology* 10;1990:408–409.

8. Cassell, back cover.

9. P.M. Boffey, "Experts Say Many in Pain Get Too Little Medication," *New York Times* 1986, May 22:11.

10. Council on Ethical and Judicial Affairs of the American Medical Association, "Report B, Decisions Near the End of Life." Chicago, IL: American Medical Association. 1989: 13.

11. van der Maas, p. 673.

12. C.K. Cassel, D.E. Meier, "Morals and Moralism in the Debate Over Euthanasia and Assisted Suicide," *New England Journal of Medicine* 323;1990:750–752.

13. S.H. Wanzer, D.D. Federman, S.J. Adelstein, et al. "The Physician's Responsibility Towards Hopelessly Ill Patients: A Second Look," *New England Journal of Medicine* 320;1989:844–849.

14. M.E. Conolly, "Alternative to Euthanasia: Pain Management," *Issues in Law & Medicine* 4;1989:497–507.

15. Y. Conwell, E.D. Caine, "Rational Suicide and the Right-to-Die: Reality and Myth," *New England Journal of Medicine* 325;1991:1100–1102.

16. Ibid., p. 1101.

17. M. Angell, "Euthanasia," *New England Journal of Medicine* 319; 1988: 1348–1350.

18. van der Maas, p. 671.

The Place of Intention in the Moral Assessment of Assisted Suicide and Active Euthanasia

EDMUND D. PELLEGRINO

Georgetown University, Washington, D.C.

A moral event consists of at least four elements: an action, the circumstances under which it is taken, the consequences of the act, and its intention. Contemporary moral philosophy has tended to emphasize one or the other of these elements. Thus, consequentialists focus on the outcome of the act, that is, its balance of harms and goods. Situation ethicists focus on the circumstances surrounding the act, and deontologists focus primarily on the intention of the act itself, and on its intrinsic or intuitive rightness or wrongness. For virtue theorists, the moral agent takes center stage.

Any complete description or judgment of a moral event requires consideration of each component and of the relationships of the components to each other. Most ethical theories make these connections informally and indirectly. Consequentialists, for example, are concerned that moral agents choose acts with the best balance of harms and benefits; deontologists want agents to choose the right act; and virtue theorists want people to be habitually disposed to act well in all moral circumstances. Situationists want agents to have good intentions so far as circumstances dictate. Implicitly, whatever theory one may espouse, there will be some appeal to right intention. No moral theory would urge wrong intentions.

In this essay, I want to examine the place of intention in assessing the moral status of assisted suicide, active euthanasia, and letting an incurably ill patient die of his illness. I will argue that in those acts intention makes a morally significant difference. This paper thus falls into three parts: In Part I, I shall outline the meanings of the concepts of intention and intentionality; in Part II, I will discuss the relationship between intention and the Beneficence, Autonomy, and Trust Models of medical ethics; and, in Part III, I will attempt to relate the other components of the moral event to intention as these relationships are exemplified in a spectrum of clinical cases.

THE CONCEPTS OF INTENTION AND INTENTIONALITY

Intention and Intentionality

The concept of intention had its first serious development in medieval scholastic philosophy which was concerned with intentional existence. By this was meant the way the mind of conscious subjects is related to an object in the mind—whether that object was the essence of a physical being or some object of thought in the mind itself, that is, some metaphysical, logical, or linguistic object. In knowledge, for example, the scholastics saw some kind of union in the original sense of the term between the mind and the object and tried to unravel the nature of this union.[1] This notion of intention was given modern impetus in the philosophical psychology of Franz Brentano in the nineteenth century. Through him, it had influence on phenomenologist, existentialist, and linguistic philosophers in the twentieth century.[2]

In this essay, I shall use the terms *intention* and *intentionality* in their ordinary language sense as the reason, purpose, or end for which, and to which, moral acts are directed. This is not to deny the importance of their more fundamental metaphysical meanings nor their relevance in moral psychology for understanding intention even in its more common usage. Indeed, as I shall posit, there is in intent a kind of union between the agent and the act which links the agent with the moral quality of the act. Even in the ordinary sense, intention has not played much of a role in contemporary moral philosophy, although in recent years, its importance has been reaffirmed by Gewirth,[3] Mackie,[4] Fried,[5] and others. Its complexity and its place in any theory of human action have been carefully analyzed by Donagan[6] and Anscombe.[7]

On the other hand, intention has been a crucial element in Catholic moral theology, including the moral philosophy and psychology of St. Thomas Aquinas. Aquinas asserts that the species of a moral act is determined by what is intended.[8] But there is debate about whether rightness and wrongness have their origin in the act itself, for example, lying, or in what was intended by the act.[9] The view I shall espouse is that intention takes its moral tone from the act to which it is directed, but that a full explication of the moral event and, therefore, of its rightness or goodness, requires consideration not only of what is intended, why it is intended, and what is sought by the intention, but also of the relationship of intention to circumstances, motivation, and the intrinsic morality of the act intended. Full justification for this construal cannot be provided in this paper but its relevance for moral judgments may become clearer in the examination of a spectrum of clinical situations in Part III.

Intention should be distinguished from desire and motivation. Desire is a wish for something to be brought about. But wishing does not "make it so." We must *intend* to make it so, and this means choosing to take an action and choosing the means by which to achieve what we want to bring about by that action. Motivation concerns the reasons for which we might desire a certain end or object. Motivation, in itself, might be good or bad, for example, love, hate, fear, envy, or altruism. Motivation may initiate desire for a particular end, but it does not constitute intention until the will is fixed on the object. As Donagan points out, to intend an action is to choose it by fixing the will on the end and the means after deliberating about their relationship to each other. Clearly, intention is not simply the answer to the question, "Why did you do that?" as posed by Fried.[10] His question is more related to motivation than intention.

Desire and intention are not the same. To desire something is to apprehend it as attractive, as something good or apparently good. But intention takes desire a further step. It is a conscious movement of the will to take the means to reach the end. We may desire something which we do not intend—because we make no move to attain it. Thus, we might find the death of a suffering patient desirable as a means of relief of suffering, but this does not entail intending the patient's death by any action on our part. Contrariwise, we may intend something we do not desire—entering battle, risking an operation or firing someone to cut the operating expenses of a business.

The quality of a moral act for Aquinas depends on the interplay of three things—what is done, why it is done, and the circumstances.[11] Intention has a bearing on moral quality because it is concerned with why we perform an act. Aquinas uses the example of almsgiving. On the face of it, giving alms is a good act with a good end—helping the poor. But if we give alms simply to enhance our reputation or—to use a contemporary example—to avoid income taxes, then what could be good becomes morally suspect or wrong.

Contrary to what Abelard taught and some ethicists still maintain, good intentions, by themselves, are not sufficient to make an act morally good.[12] Certain actions are wrong as a species, like adultery, killing the innocent, suicide, and lying.[13] Otherwise, good or morally indifferent acts may also be wrong under certain circumstances, for example, shouting "Fire!" as a joke in a crowded theater, doing so to warn others, or doing so to hear the sound of one's own voice in an empty desert. Moreover, if the intention is bad, it can make a good act bad. The circumstances can do the same. But, no circumstance or good intention can make a bad act good.

Aquinas's view steers a middle course between Kant's primary emphasis, which is on conformity of the will to the moral law, and Mill's contention that moral quality rests primarily in the consequences of the act, that is, in whether it produces more good than harm. Aquinas thus reconciles the interior and exterior dimensions of moral acts in a subtle way important to any understanding of the moral psychology of intentionality.[14]

Intentionality has its major applicability in the case of voluntary actions and their results, that is, freely willed acts, some of the effects of which we foresee and some of which we do not. We are not morally responsible for acts we do not foresee, provided what we intend is good in itself, in its ends, and in its circumstances. However, there are also effects we do not intend and which, in that sense, are "accidental." These are possible or probable outcomes which may be wrong or harmful. The moral quality of accidental effects depends on the degree to which we foresee their probability or avoidability. The more certain, the more probable, and the more avoidable the accidental effect, the more carefully must the moral quality of the act be assessed. We are responsible for the whole moral event but culpable only for those parts of it which we intend. The full import and implications of these complex interrelationships cannot be explored further here. Suffice it to say that moral assessments depend on the way the agent's intention, the nature of the act, its circumstances, and its consequences are related to each other.

How Intentionality Makes a Difference

One may accept the operation of intention as a fact of moral psychology yet ask what moral difference it makes. Whether we intend to kill the patient by active euthanasia or "let her die" by omission of life-sustaining treatment, the effect is the same: the patient dies.

The answer lies in the original notion of intentionality as involving a certain union between the mind and person of the agent and some object in the world or the mind. To unite our persons with an act that is morally wrong has a deleterious effect on the agent himself or herself. In the remainder of this paper, I hope to show that euthanasia and assisted suicide are violations of beneficence, autonomy, and trust and, therefore, of the healing relationship. For physicians to intend these violations is to unite one's person with distortions of the healing relationship. Further identification of one's person with an act of killing weakens the intuitive human inhibition against killing even if that killing were to be in self-defense of a just war.

Repeatedly intending the death of patients by assisting them to end their lives or ending their lives for them has its impact on the physician's character, that is, on the habitual disposition to act in certain ways in moral matters. It is to act against the virtues of medicine itself.[15] When what is ordinarily a vice becomes a virtue in one case, it is logically and emotionally easier to violate the inhibition in the next instance. Whatever rationalization we may use to justify killing, there is a residuum of guilt which is difficult to eradicate. In an attempt to assuage that guilt, the act is repeated to convince ourselves how harmless it really is. Vice, like virtue, is learned by repetition. There is a psychological slippery slope in the intentional life of moral agents as there is in the realm of logic and action. Wrong intentions have inevitable effects on the character of the moral agent. If enough moral agents in a society have wrong intentions about killing in the medical context the attitudes of the whole profession and society will be affected with a disvaluation of human life itself.

Two Assumptions

So far as active euthanasia and assisted suicide go, the account I have just given of the place of intention in moral choice makes two crucial assumptions, both of which are intensely debated today. I refer to the traditional proscription against homicide and suicide and the principle of double effect.

First is the assumption that there are certain acts of a kind that cannot be made morally right by a "good" intention. Such is the case with killing of others and self. Under certain circumstances, these acts may be justified—that is, for reasons of self-preservation, saving the lives of others, or in a defensive war. But even in these circumstances, the death of the aggressor must not be what is sought, but rather the preservation of the lives of self or others. Moreover, to the extent it is practicable, the minimum of force must be used to attain the end. If killing can be avoided, it must be avoided.

With variations in content and style of argument, historically, this has been the moral intuition of a wide range of philosophical and religious belief systems.[16] Notable departures, like Hume's position on suicide, stand out as exceptions to what, until recently, might be properly termed a *common morality* that condemned intentional killing of self as well as others. Today, however, the very idea of certain acts being of a kind that is intrinsically wrong is seriously challenged. This is the position of the protagonists of euthanasia and suicide who depend on intent and circumstances to justify the act of killing. But they also argue that autonomy should be respected. In this, they redefine the species of intrinsically wrong acts from the act of killing, to the act of violation of autonomy. Thus, they extend the concept of autonomy to include absolute mastery over the time and manner of one's own death. On this view, the traditional "state interest" in preserving life becomes an intrusion on the right of privacy.[17] Others go further and redefine life itself. They distinguish between biological life, which has no claim on others, and a biographical life which does have such a claim, but not an absolute claim.[18] Still others speak even of an obligation to take life as a matter of justice in cases in which life is overly burdensome and the patient cannot consent.

Against these views, most opponents of euthanasia and assisted suicide hold to the traditional view that intentional homicide and suicide are intrinsically wrong because human life is a basic good of human persons, humans are stewards but not absolute matters of their lives, and the taking of life is a matter of societal concern not a matter of simple personal choice. Clearly, between the antagonists and protagonists, there is a vast difference in philosophical and theological perspectives on the origin and meaning of human life. The resulting opposition of viewpoints is of the "incommensurable" kind, often unresolvable by moral discourse.[19]

The second assumption is that the principle of double effect, labeled by some as the "doctrine" of double effect, is a viable instrument for analyzing the morality of acts which have results that are both good and bad, right and wrong. On this principle, one may undertake acts in which morally good and bad effects are foreseeable if four conditions are observed: (1) the directly intended object must not be intrinsically wrong, (2) the agent's intention must be to achieve the morally good and not the morally bad effect, (3) the morally good effects must equal or exceed the bad, and (4) the good effect must not result from the bad. In items (1) and (2), intentionality plays a central role.[20] Some such principle as double effect is essential in the analysis of human acts if we wish to hold that intention is an important but not the sole determinant of their moral quality. The kind of act and the circumstances are also important and the double effect concept takes these into account in a principled way.

To be sure, no such principle as double effect is needed if we argue that the principle of autonomy is absolute and that it extends to the control of every aspect of our own lives. On this view, active euthanasia and assisted suicide at the request of the patient are *ipso facto* justifiable; death is foreseen, intended, and justifiable. Nor is the principle of double effect needed if we classify some human lives as "biological remnants" or as so diminished as to have no "worth."[21]

On this view, intentional killing, then, is not homicide at all, but simply ending suffering, ceasing to value something without value, or relieving society of a burden. Of course, if the act of killing is thus defined as a beneficent rather than a maleficent act, there is no "double effect" to worry about. But, as I hope to show next, even when the intention is "good" (i.e., to relieve suffering), killing the patient at his request may not be the beneficent act its protagonists take it to be.

INTENDING TO KILL: A DISTORTION OF THE HEALING RELATIONSHIP

Distortions of Beneficence

The strongest arguments in favor of euthanasia and assisted suicide are based in appeals to two basic principles of contemporary medical ethics—beneficence and respect for autonomy. Would a beneficence model of the healing relationship permit and/or oblige the physician to engage in intending death or at least provide a warrant for doing so? Would intending death enhance or distort the ends and purposes of the healing relationship?

Protagonists of intentional death argue when the patient is suffering intolerably, is ready to meet death, and able to give consent, that it is compassionate, merciful, and beneficent to kill the patient or assist in killing. Not to do so would be to act maleficently, to violate the dignity and autonomy of the suffering person, and to inflict harm on another human—in effect, to abandon the patient in time of greatest need. Since the doctor has the requisite knowledge to make death easy and painless, it is not only cruel but immoral not to accede to the patient's request.[22-24]

On this view, it violates the morality of medicine (which calls us to relieve pain and suffering) to refuse the patient's requests for "assistance in dying." Some would carry the argument further into the realm of justice. They would make euthanasia a moral obligation. Not to "assist" an incompetent patient is to act discriminatorily, for it deprives the comatose, the retarded, and infants of the "benefit" of an early death. When the patient's intention cannot be expressed, the obligation, in justice, is to provide involuntary or nonvoluntary access to the same benefit of death accessible to the competent patient.[25] The Dutch Pediatric Society is already moving in this direction in the case of badly handicapped infants.[26]

On this view, ending the life of the patient could be construed as a social obligation of the profession resulting from its possession of knowledge that the patient
both needs and is entitled to, and for which the physician is licensed. A weaker view
would use the same arguments but would not impose an ethical obligation on the
physician. It would, however, provide a warrant for legalization of euthanasia and
assisted suicide which would empower those physicians who see no moral harm in
killing, or helping to kill, patients who requested it.

No one who has practiced clinical medicine for any time, who has nursed or in
any other way tried to help fatally ill and suffering patients, can be unmoved by the
appeal to compassion and benefence. Indeed, such insensitivity to human suffering
would disqualify one as a humane, or even a competent, practitioner. But feeling
compassion and empathy are not sufficient reason for approving the intention of
death. On the model of intentionality I have suggested, this would be clearly a case
of the false notion that a "good" intention makes an act which is *wrong in kind* morally right.

It will not do to argue that one is not intending to kill but only to relieve suffering. This is a misuse of the principle of double effect which has as one of its key
requirements for legitimate use the proviso that the morally permissible intention and
act (relief of pain) should not be caused by a directly intended, morally impermissible act (killing the patient). Obviously, if one denies that killing is a morally wrong
act, then one will not worry much about intention or double effects.

The beneficence model of care certainly includes provisions for a good death,
but it is not clear that a good death includes the option of killing the patient. It is not
at all certain that euthanasia is a beneficent act, even if it is motivated by compassion
at least on the surface. It seems a peculiar kind of beneficence that extinguishes the
beneficiary. Many times one suspects that the beneficiary is not the patient at all, but
either the family which is thereby relieved of an emotional or fiscal burden, or the
doctor or nurses who are relieved of a time- and emotion-consuming, frustrating
patient, or society and the institution which are relieved of persons who consume
inordinate amounts of resources in personnel and material.

Moreover, the patient's own intention or decision to die may be less motivated
by intolerable suffering than by a conscious or unconscious attempt to act benefi-
cently towards family, doctor, or society. The "benefit" sought may be relief of guilt
for being the "cause" of distress and trouble to others or the wish to die "nobly." In
this regard, it is interesting that the Remmelink study shows that only 10 of the 187
cases of patients studied who asked for active euthanasia in Holland did so for relief
of pain alone, while 46 percent mentioned pain in combination with loss of dignity,
unworthy dying, dependence, or surfeit with life.[27]

What, then, is beneficent about active killing when there are other, less noxious
ways of helping the patient, that is, by caring for, rather than by killing? Pain, now,
with few exceptions can be properly controlled. Much of the suffering that accompa-
nies pain is the fear that it will worsen, that relief or medication will not arrive on

time, or that the medication will blunt consciousness. But these fears can, for the most part, be dealt with by newer, more selective, and improved methods of pain control. Devices for self-administration of analgesics can give the patient control over one's own pain. This relieves one very important source of anxiety and dependence. Even more important, is the sensitive management of anxiety, guilt, and depression that act synergistically with physiological causes of pain to make the pain intolerable.[28]

At this juncture, those who see euthanasia as beneficent may reply that, in fact, physicians do not manage pain optimally, that they are not educated to do so, and that they ignore contemporary methods of analgesia. It follows that we cannot realistically expect or trust physicians to control pain and this justifies killing the patient out of compassion. In this way, we make the victim of medical ineptitude a victim twice over. In fact, legitimating euthanasia in any form would relieve physicians of the time, effort, and care required to control both pain and suffering. The moral mandate is not to extinguish the life of the patient because doctors are inept at pain control but to better educate physicians in modern methods of analgesia. If properly employed, hospice services and the techniques of comprehensive palliative care should ameliorate or remove not only pain, but the emotional, psychological, and spiritual factors that constitute to suffering and make a hastened death desirable. In comprehensive palliative care, pain relief is coupled with diagnosis and specific treatment of the causes of the patient's despondency: concern about the costs of continuing care, the rejection and isolation of the sick—especially the chronically ill—in the presence of our culture of youth and "health," the loss of job and identity, the death of friends with the same disease, loss of zest for life, reactive depression, drug side effects, or insensitive treatment by health-care providers.

Some might argue that even if we are personally opposed to euthanasia and assisted suicide, we would do harm in another way if we did not permit it as an option. We would, in effect, be driving patients into the hands of practitioners like Jack Kevorkian and others who would provide what the patient wants, but without legal restraints. Is it not preferable to make it possible for patients to seek euthanasia at the hands of "regular" licensed practitioners or specialists in euthanasia in a legally controlled system? Is it not wrong to force patients into the hands of covert practitioners when their own physicians are in a better position to administer a "good" death by lethal injection?

This is a familiar argument used in many contexts today—that is, what is illegal or morally forbidden but desired by many should be "regularized" to keep it within respectable bounds. Examples of this kind of thinking include legalization of drug use, prostitution, commercialization of organ procurement, and so forth. This argument misses the fact that the more decorous and regulated injection of a lethal dose of morphine or potassium chloride to bring about death in a hospital or one's own bedroom by one's family practitioner is not morally different from Kevorkian's crude methodology. The intention is the same—to kill or to help the patient kill oneself. Efficiency in the killing does not eradicate the unethical nature of the act. To Kevorkian's credit, he does not sugar-coat the reality even though he has been criticized for his brashness which embarrasses many of the more decorous protagonists of euthanasia in the medical profession.

Furthermore, the intensity of the debate over what constitutes "dignity" notwithstanding, it remains problematic whether there is more dignity in an engineered exit than in awaiting the end of one's life. Perhaps it is to escape from finitude the final encounter with the inner self so starkly presented by death that ultimately motivates euthanasia. One may seriously question if the escape via euthanasia is more or less human, more or less "dignified," than its alternative. Most of the deaths I have witnessed have not been Promethean struggles. Most patients still die quietly, sometimes at home, often with family and friends around them. To be sure, the picture of a prolonged, painful, tube-ridden existence is also an unfortunate reality. It ought to be, and can be, avoided much more frequently than it is. However, the scenario of "undignified" death is not as universal, unavoidable, or "undignified" as the more articulate proponents of euthanasia would have us believe.

Beneficence does not require "doing everything" until the last flicker of life has disappeared. It does not include the specter so many patients fear of tubes, respirators, repeated resuscitation efforts, high-risk, last-ditch, high-cost, desperation treatments or other forms of medical futility. Regardless of good intentions, those efforts are maleficent, not beneficent. The physician's ethical obligation is to provide treatments that are demonstrably effective and/or beneficial in terms of values appreciated and selected by the patient. There must also be some reasonable relationship between the risks and burdens, and the effects and benefits, of each intervention.

On this view, effectiveness is defined as any intervention that has been demonstrated to favorably alter the natural history of a disease or symptom, for example, appropriate antibiotics for bacteria or morphine for pain relief. Effectiveness is an objective criterion, determinable by clinical observation and appropriate clinical trials. Clearly, we do not have enough studies of this type. But their relevance to morally sound ethical decisionmaking imposes an obligation on society to support outcome and effectiveness studies and on the profession to obtain such data.

Benefit, on the other hand, is a subjective standard that lies in the patient's assessment of whether the probable or projected outcome of a treatment is "worthwhile" in his or her value system. It is here that the patient's quality of life determination enters the decision. A patient may see an effective treatment as not "worthwhile" in terms of life-plan, threshold for pain and discomfort, preferences for risk-taking, disfigurement, and so forth. For example, some patients may reject radical, painful, and expensive surgical procedures and thus fail to gain a few more years of life, while others may seize on such opportunities to prolong their lives. On the other hand, a measure noneffective for the underlying disease or resuscitation for terminal malignancy may be beneficial to a patient who wants to live a little longer to see family or witness some event of importance—the birth of a child, a graduation, and so on. Here, effectiveness is measured in terms of a benefit perceived by the patient and not an alteration in the natural history of the disease.

Burdens are difficult to define and, at least for competent patients, would be included in the calculation of benefits. They can be physical, fiscal, or emotional; they may bear on the patient, her family, or the health-care providers. In every case, effectiveness and benefits are weighed against burdens. This is a highly individualized calculus for which no general formula is adequate. The outcome of the benefit-effectiveness-burden calculation will eventuate in a "quality of life" decision by the patient—not the physician. It is impossible for any person to assess the quality of another's life. When the assessor is the physician, the danger of imposing one's values are all too obvious.

Arguments based on euthanasia as a way to preserve the patient's dignity in dying are grounded in a misconception about dignity.[29] Patients do not lose their dignity as humans simply because they are suffering, in pain, perhaps disfigured by illness, incontinent, or comatose. A patient's dignity resides in his or her humanity. It cannot be lost, even through the ravages of disease. When proponents of euthanasia speak of loss of dignity, they are speaking more for their own reactions to seeing, living with, or treating terminally ill patients.

When patients speak of their fear of a loss of "dignity," for the most part, they are speaking of the way they appear to, or are regarded by, others—by physicians, nurses, other patients, and even their families. This type of "dignity" is the fabrication of the observer, not a quality of the person observed.[30] What patients want to avoid is being pitied, being seen as pathetic objects, as "unfortunates," or objects of fear and dread. The patient's fear is fear of how one looks in the eyes of the "other" world—of the healthy, the occupied, the busy, the physically unencumbered. The well all too often shun the grievously ill person because they know they, too, may someday be like that person. Well people do not wish to be continuously reminded of their own finitude and susceptibility to illness. They may wish, consciously or subconsciously, for the death of the long-in-dying person. To deal with these subconscious desires to be rid of the incurably ill person, the well may accede to the request for death via euthanasia for their own sakes as much as the patient's.

For patients, this is not death with "dignity"; it is more like death as a remedy for the shame they feel, or are made to feel. Shame is a potent cause of suffering. It is far more humane to treat that cause by treating the patient with true dignity. Acceding to the patient's request to die is not helping to restore his dignity. It is a confirmation of the loss of worth he has suffered in the eyes of those who behold him as an object of pity.

Distortion of Autonomy

Protagonists of euthanasia and assisted suicide argue that assisting the patient to die is a beneficent act since it respects the principle of autonomy. On this view, those who refuse to comply with the autonomous request of a competent patient are in violation of respect for persons. On this view, they are acting cruelly and in violation of a fundamental human right. Dr. Jack Kevorkian, in his usual blunt way, says, "The ultimate value is autonomy."[31]

Such absolutization of autonomy has two serious moral limitations that make any form of euthanasia or assisted suicide a maleficent rather than a beneficent act. For one thing, the mere assertion of a request cannot, of itself, bind another person within, or outside, the physician-patient relationship.[32] When a demand becomes a command, it can violate another person's autonomy. Even more problematic is whether a person desperate enough to ask to be killed or assisted in killing oneself can act autonomously. In the end, the person who opts for euthanasia uses his or her autonomy to give up autonomy. The person chooses to eradicate the basis on which autonomy is possible—consciousness and rationality. The patient gives up all control over all further experiences and options which cannot be foreseen and which could be of importance in terms of one's own value system. John Stuart Mill, a most vigorous proponent of personal liberty, nonetheless argued that one could not in the name of freedom sell one's self into unfreedom, that is, into slavery.[33]

The more the temporal distance between the expected death and the decision to be killed or to kill oneself, the more freedom one gives up. For example, Dr. Kevorkian's patient, Mrs. Adkins, presumably feared the ravages of Alzheimer's disease. She chose death when she had between months and probably years to live. Her suffering was largely the suffering of anticipation. By her decision, Mrs. Adkins gave up her freedom to make a series of future choices whose nature and meaning to her she could not predict.[34] Similar situations occur with the patient who is diagnosed as having early and treatable cancer of the prostrate, or multiple sclerosis, or the genetic predisposition to Huntington's disease. How large a segment of future life options, of human personal and communal experience are we free to eradicate without contradicting the idea of autonomy itself?

At the other extreme, when death is imminent, the empirical questions of autonomy are equally problematic. The person who is fatally ill is a person, often in pain, anxious, and rejected by those who are healthy, afflicted with a sense of guilt and unworthiness, perceiving oneself as a social, economic, and emotional burden to others. Can a person in this state satisfy the criteria for autonomous choice?[35] How well could these patients safeguard their autonomy if euthanasia were legalized? Chronically ill and dying patients are extremely sensitive to even the most subtle suggestions of unworthiness by their medical attendants, family, and friends. Any sign— verbal or nonverbal—that reinforces guilt or shame will be picked up as a subtle suggestion to take the "noble" way out.

The degree to which pain, guilt, and unworthiness may compromise autonomy is evident in the fact that when these are removed or ameliorated, patients do not ask to be killed.[36] Even if euthanasia were legalized, a first obligation under both principles of beneficence and autonomy would be to diagnose, ameliorate, or remove those causes of the patient's despondency and suffering that lead to a request for euthanasia in the first place. This is more humane and more protective of human dignity than the intentional facilitation of the demise of the patient by euthanasia or assisted suicide.

Distortion of Trust

Trust plays an inescapable role in whatever model of physician-patient relationship one chooses.[37] Even the contractual models which try to reduce trust by explicit contractual agreement cannot avoid trust. After all, the performance of contracts is still dependent on the trustworthiness of the contracting parties as each interprets and implements the agreement from moment to moment.

Trust is ineradicable in the patient-physician relationship. The sick person is forced to trust the physician because he or she lacks the knowledge requisite for one's own healing and because he or she is vulnerable and cannot be well without the physician's help. This state of affairs is further accentuated by the fact that a physician elicits trust when he or she offers to help. In that offer, there is the promise of competence and a promise not to take advantage of the patient's vulnerability and exploitability as a result of being ill and needing help. The patient trusts the physician to do what is in the patient's best interests as it is indicated by the diagnosis, prognosis, and therapeutic possibilities. When patients know that euthanasia is a legitimate choice and that some physicians may see killing as healing, they know they are vulnerable to violations of trust.

The grosser violations include unreported euthanasia, involuntary or nonvoluntary euthanasia of the aged, the infant, the comatose, and/or the retarded. These possibilities are not to be discounted since there is evidence that they do occur in Holland today.[38] In fact, some ethicists frankly regard such active euthanasia as tantamount to a moral obligation since the physician is the only one who has the power to relieve the patient of his "suffering" in an effective and "gentle" way.[39]

A much more common danger at present is the possibility that the physician's values and acceptance of euthanasia may unconsciously shape how vigorously one treats the patient or presents the possibility of assisted suicide. How is the patient to know when his or her doctor is persuading or even subtly coercing to choose death? The doctor's motives may be unconsciously to advance his or her own beliefs that euthanasia is a social good to gain relief from the frustrating difficulties of caring for the patient, of distress with the quality of life the patient is forced to lead, or promote a desire to conserve society's resources, and so forth. How will a patient ever be sure of the true motive for his or her doctor's recommendation? When is the doctor depreciating the value of available methods of pain relief or comprehensive palliative care because he or she believes the really "good" death is a planned death?

We are assured by some that we can depend on "good" doctors not to act this way. But since an increasing number of doctors are coming to consider death to be in the patient's interest under some circumstances, the definition of a good doctor is debatable. Reliance on the character of the physician is an insufficient safeguard against shaping the patient's decision to suit the doctor's values especially with the incompetent patient.

The power of physicians to shape their patients' choices is well known to every experienced clinician. Physicians can get a patient to agree to almost any decision they want by the way they present the alternatives. This applies to objective data, to say nothing of the subjective imponderables that enter into a decision to request euthanasia or assisted suicide. When does pain become "intolerable," when is the suffering "unbearable"? How competent is the patient? These are all judgments made by the physician. None are measurable in absolute terms. All may be influenced by the physician's attitude on euthanasia or emotional and physical frustrations in treating a difficult patient. How realistic is patient autonomy in such circumstances? How effective can the criteria proposed to prevent abuses of legalized euthanasia really be?

Assisted Suicide: Is There a Moral Difference Between Quill and Kevorkian?

What I have attempted to show is the way in which intentional killing, if accepted into the body of medical ethics, would distort the ethics and purposes of the healing relationship in at least three of its dimensions—beneficence, protection of autonomy, and fidelity to trust. One may justifiably ask: Is the ethical situation different if the physician intends only to advise the patient on how to attain the goal of a "good" death by assisting the patient to kill? Is not the causal and intentional relationship of the physician to the death of the patient essentially different?

I do not believe a convincing case can be made for a moral difference between the two. This is a classical instance of a distinction without a difference in kind. The intentional end sought in either case is the death of the patient: in active euthanasia, the physician is the immediate cause; in assisted suicide, the physician is the necessary cooperating cause, a moral accomplice without whom the patient could not kill himself or herself. In assisted suicide, the doctor fully shares the patient's intention to end his or her life. The doctor provides the lethal medication, advises on the proper dose, on how it should be taken to be most effective, and on what to do if the dose is regurgitated. The physician's cooperation is necessary if the act is to be carried out at all. The physician shares equal responsibility with the patient just as he or she would in active euthanasia.

This moral complicity is obvious in the cases reported by Dr. Timothy Quill and Dr. Jack Kevorkian. In both cases, the physician provided the means fully knowing the patient would use them and encouraging the patients to do so when they felt the time was right. Kevorkian's "death machine" was operated by the patient but designed and provided by Kevorkian. Quill's patient took the sedatives he prescribed. To be sure, Quill's account of his assistance in the death of a young woman with leukemia elicits more sympathy because the length and intensity of his professional relationship with her. Kevorkian's cases, in contrast, are remarkable for the brevity of the relationships, the absence of any serious attempt to provide palliative medical or psychiatric assistance, and the brusqueness with which the decisions are made and carried out. Kevorkian is the technician of death; Quill, its artist.

Quill's *modus operandi* is gentler and more deliberate, but this does not change the nature of the action in any essential way. Indeed, in some ways, Quill's approach is more dangerous to patient beneficence and autonomy because it compromises the patient more subtly and is conducted under the intention of "treatment." But when does the intention to treat become synonymous with the intent to assist in, or actively accelerate, death? Kevorkian's patients at least approach him with the intention already in their minds to commit suicide and to gain access to his machine. He is, after all, a pathologist, and his patients do not start out thinking he might be able to treat their illnesses. Quill's patients presumably come to him as a physician primarily, not as a minister of death. This may well change now that Quill has attained so much notoriety through his public zeal for assisted suicide.

In assisted suicide and active euthanasia, the physician's intention is ostensibly to relieve suffering and to respect the patient's autonomy and "dignity." These ends are, in themselves, commendable, and the intention to bring them about is also commendable. But the means to attain these ends must also be intended since moral choice entails fixing the will both on the end and on the means used to achieve it. As I have tried to show, killing is not a beneficent act and, therefore, to intend it as a means is malevolent.

KILLING AND LETTING DIE: SOME CLINICAL SITUATIONS

The questions of intending death span a broad spectrum of moral problems ranging from involuntary and nonvoluntary euthanasia, on the one hand, to withdrawing all treatment in total brain death, on the other. Even at the extremes, there is no universal agreement so that there will be unresolved moral issues at every point along the continuum.

At one end of the spectrum is the intentional death of patients who cannot give consent (nonvoluntary euthanasia), or who are able to give consent but are not asked to do so (involuntary euthanasia). Most of the protagonists of legalized euthanasia at present would limit their ministrations to patients with the capacity for valid consent. But some ethicists consider these limitations as illogical impediments to extensions of the beneficent ends of medicine.[40] They speak of certain patients—the severely retarded, handicapped, senile, demented, those in permanent vegetative states—as "biologic remnants," as beings who are biologically alive, but do not have biographical or human lives and, thus, are not entitled to the moral respect owed to those who live more fully human lives. Nonvoluntary euthanasia of infants, requiring only the consent of parents and the family physician, is already a recommended practice in the Netherlands.[41]

At the other extreme of the spectrum is the discontinuation of all life support in patients who are totally brain dead. To be sure, some still raise ethical objections to this practice, but it can be defended on grounds of the "internal morality" of medicine and clinical judgment which requires physicians and patients to recognize the limits of medicine. To continue medical interventions when, on the best clinical prognostic knowledge, there is no possibility of recovery, is to contravene the ethical injunction against using ineffective, nonbeneficial treatments. It also imposes unjustifiable burdens not on the patient, but on the family, the health-care team, and society's resources. The absolute certainty of the outcome entails an obligation not to treat under such circumstances but to provide pain relief and comfort only.

Within this spectrum are the incurably ill, nonterminal, fully competent patients like Ms. Bouvia and Ms. Requena. In the Bouvia case,[42] a nonterminal, fully competent young woman suffering from cerebral palsy and painful arthritis requested a hospital to provide pain relief while she intentionally starved herself to death. The hospital and her medical attendant refused to cooperate in this form of "assisted suicide." Here, the patient's autonomy is pitted against the refusal on moral grounds by the patient's medical attendants and institution to cooperate.

Those who would absolutize autonomy and deny the moral restriction on suicide, like the concurring Judge Compton, have argued that Ms. Bouvia had a moral and legal right to her intention to end her life and that it was reprehensible for her medical attendants not to comply.[43] Against this view, I would argue that Ms. Bouvia's intention was morally wrong, even if we sympathize with her plight. Her autonomy does not empower her to impose her morally wrong intention on her doctors or the institution. Even if her doctors disagreed with her, their cooperation would be necessary for her to achieve her wrong intention. They would have to share her intention, and this would make them her moral accomplices.

A somewhat related, but also dissimilar case, is that of Beverly Requena, a woman with amyotrophic lateral sclerosis, also competent and nonterminal in any strict sense.[44] This patient anticipated correctly that, sooner or later, she would not be able to swallow. She requested not to be fed by artificial means when that time came. Unlike Bouvia, whose intent was clearly to end her life by her own will, Ms. Requena's intent was to forego a treatment she found intolerable. Her intention might well have been to hasten death since an inability to swallow is a part of the natural history of her disease. The question here is less whether she might justifiably refuse tube feeding—or a respirator—but whether her attendants had an obligation to cooperate.

There are many patients who are obviously hopelessly ill but are not "terminal" in the sense that death is foreseeable in a matter of hours, days, weeks, or months, and whose great sufferings arouse our compassion. One thinks here of patients with severely disfiguring head and neck malignancies, extensive burns, wide-spread bone metastases, painful malignancies of stomach or liver, and so forth. Such patients understandably may well desire their own deaths as the only way out of their misery. The moral status of the patient's intention in asking for discontinuance of treatment is not something the physician can ascertain with any certitude. Even if he or she could, it would be rash under such circumstances to judge another person's moral intent. Rather, the question is how best to fulfill our obligation in medical ethics to assist the patient with a good death, but one which does not include intentional killing or assisted suicide.

There is a clear obligation to use all those measures included in comprehensive palliative care—discernment, removal, or amelioration of the reasons for the patient's request for death, optimal use of pain medication and psychosocial, spiritual support of those in attendance. Here the question often arises: May one use doses of analgesics which might depress respiration fatally? If one does, is this not tantamount to intending the patient's death and, therefore, not different from active voluntary euthanasia?

On the view of intentionality outlined earlier, if pain relief is the intended, benevolent purpose, then whatever dose is sufficient to relieve pain is morally defensible. Analgesics, like other potent medications, may result in unintended, but statistically significant, chances of serious and even lethal side effects. These are accidental, not intended, effects. In these situations, the patient may even hope for the lethal side effect, but the physician's intention is clearly not that side effect. There is a morally significant difference between giving titrated doses of potent analgesics to achieve the best possible pain relief and the deliberate intravenous injection of 2000 mg of morphine to a nontolerant patient with the intent to kill the patient as the means of ending suffering. Here the intent is to kill, and the cause of death is unquestionably the dose of morphine. We do not hesitate to do risky surgery, or use potent chemotherapeutic antineoplastic drugs when they might benefit the patient. Neither should we hesitate to treat pain and suffering because of possible noxious side effects.

I am obviously invoking here the principle of double effect which covers this and the many other clinical situations in which some things which should never be done (intentional killing) and some things that should be done (relief of pain, saving life) are intermingled so that both might occur as the result of a clinical decision. On this principle, such an action is morally defensible if the harms are not intended but are side effects (or are accidental), if there are sufficiently weighty moral reasons for taking the foreseen risks, and if the good effect is not the result of a morally wrong action and intention. This is not the place to define or defend this moral principle and its current status in moral philosophy.[45] Suffice it to say that a morally valid concept of intention is crucial if this principle is to be applied properly.

In general terms, withholding and withdrawing are morally defensible if: (1) The patient is fully competent or is represented by a morally valid surrogate or valid advance directive, and (2) the intervention, itself, meets certain moral criteria, that is; (a) the patient has a serious disease which may terminate in death with reasonable certitude in a foreseeable period of time; (b) the relations of effectiveness, benefit, and burden is disproportionate, that is, treatment is futile both from the medical point of view and that of the patient; (c) "quality of life" is used as a criterion as judged by the competent patient or valid surrogate, not the physician; (d) economics, likewise, as a criterion is judged by the patient or surrogate, not the physician; (e) age is not a criterion by itself; (f) HIV infection, social status, merit, and so forth, are not criteria; (g) some system for resolution of conflicts is in place which protects the moral values of all participants and provides mechanisms of decision if irreconcilable differences persist. I have detailed my reasons for each of these criteria elsewhere.[46]

One does not intend the death of the patient when withholding or withdrawing life sustaining treatment under the conditions just outlined. The physician might even find the patient's death a desirable outcome. But desire is not equivalent either to intention nor to choice. Rather, in these situations, the physician's intention can sincerely be to refrain from or withdraw treatment that is futile and, thus, not indicated. This is not the same as the intention which leads the physician to inject a lethal dose of morphine to end the life of the patient summarily. Marginal, futile, or unwanted treatment constitutes harmful intervention which the physician is obligated to remove. Removal is the primary intention. This is a morally required act since futile treatment does not promote the patient's well-being. The patient dies as a result because the futile treatment prolonged life without benefitting the patient. The patient dies not by the doctor's hand but by progression of the natural history of the disease.

The most difficult situations involve vegetative states in which the patient is kept alive by artificial feeding and hydration for prolonged periods. In such states, patients are unaware of self or environment although brain stem and hypothalamic autonomic functions are preserved. Such patients are not dead but they quickly die if life-support measures are withdrawn. Vegetative states become "persistent" when they last beyond a given period of time defined in terms of the type and cause of brain damage.[47] All vegetative states, therefore, are not persistent and consideration of withdrawal of life support can be considered only when the criteria for persistence are fulfilled.

The decision makers in these situations are the morally valid surrogate (informed, competent, and without conflict of interest) and the physicians and nurses attending the patient. If the criteria outlined in the preceding text are met, withdrawal of life support may be considered when the vegetative state is unquestionably permanent. If this is done, the question of intention will arise. Are we not intending death since it will occur by our act of omission of treatment?

On the view I have been taking, to intend death would be morally inadmissible. To remove futile treatment would be admissible, even though the probability of death can be foreseen. To foresee an event is not the same as intending to cause that event. The close union of the agent with the act depends on the active, willful choice of the death of the patient and of the means which will bring about that intention. This union is missing in events we foresee as possible or probable but do not actively intend.

SUMMARY

Intention and intentionality are integral elements in the assessment of moral events. They have received insufficient attention in contemporary biomedical ethics except perhaps in virtue-based systems. Yet, considerations of intention are implicit in any theory of ethics.

Intentions cannot be assessed in isolation from the other components of moral events. They must be related to the nature of the act in question, the circumstances under which it is performed, and its consequences. These interrelationships are of particular importance in assessing the moral status of active euthanasia and physician-assisted suicide and in ethical decisions surrounding withholding and withdrawing life-support measures.

NOTES

1. L. Sweeney, *A Metaphysics of Authentic Existentialism*. Englewood Cliffs, NJ: Prentice-Hall, 1965, p. 165.

2. F. C. Brentano, *Psychology from an Empiricist Standpoint*, trans. A. C. Rancurello, D. B. Terrell, and L. L. McAlister. London: Routledge and Kegan Paul, 1973.

3. A. Gewirth, *Reason and Morality*. Chicago: University of Chicago Press, 1978.

4. J. L. Mackie, *Ethics: Inventing Right and Wrong*. London: Penguin, 1987.

5. C. Fried, *Right and Wrong*. Cambridge, MA: Harvard University Press, 1978.

6. A. Donagan, *Choice, the Essential Element in Human Action*. Oxford: Blackwell, 1987.

7. G. E. M. Anscombe, *Intention*. Oxford: Blackwell, 1966.

8. St. Thomas Aquinas, *Summa Theologiae*, II-II, q.64, a7c.

9. J. F. Keenan, *Goodness and Rightness in Thomas Aquinas' Summa Theologiae*. Washington, DC: Georgetown University Press, 1992.

10. C. Fried, *Right and Wrong*.

11. St. Thomas Aquinas, *Summa Theologiae*, I-IIae, q.18, 2–11; V, q.83, a1c; I-Iiae, q.8–9; I-Iiae, q.6, a4a; q.15, a3; q.12, a21; q.20, a1c.

12. P. Abailard, *Abailard's Ethics*, trans. J. Ramsay McCallum. Merrick, NY: Merrick Publishing Company, 1976.

13. Aristotle, "Nicomachean Ethics" 1107a10–12 in *The Basic Works of Aristotle*, trans. Richard McKeon. New York: Random House, 1968.

14. St. Thomas Aquinas, *Summa Theologiae*, I-Iiae, q.18, 2–11; V, q.83, a1c; I-Iiae, q.8–9; I-Iiae, q.6, a4a; q.15, a3; q.12, a21; q.20, a1c.

15. E. D. Pellegrino and D. C. Thomasma, *The Virtues in Medicine*. New York: Oxford University Press, 1993.

16. F. Eahman, *Health and Medicine in the Islamic Tradition*. New York: Crossroads Press, New York, 1987, pp. 100–101, 125; H. Arkes, et al., "Always to Care, Never to Kill," *Wall Street Journal*, November 27, 1991; Sacred Congregation for the Doctrine of the Faith, *Declaration of Euthanasia*, June 26, 1980; P. Harvey, *An Introduction to Buddhism*. London: Cambridge University Press, 1990, pp. 202–203; B. Brody, ed. *Suicide and Euthanasia*. Dordrecht: Kluwer Academic Publishers, 1989.

17. H. T. Engelhardt, Jr., "Death by Free Choice: Modern Variations on an Antique Theme," in B. Brody, ed. *Suicide and Euthanasia*. Dordrecht: Kluwer Academic Publishers, 1989, pp. 251–279.

18. J. Rachels, *The End of Life: Euthanasia and Morality*. New York: Oxford University Press, 1986, pp. 24–27.

19. A. MacIntyre, *Three Rival Versions of Moral Inquiry*. Notre Dame, Indiana: University of Notre Dame Press, 1990, pp. 4–6.

20. B. M. Ashley and K. D. O'Rourke, *Health Care Ethics: A Theological Analysis*. St.

Louis, MO: Catholic Health Assn., 1989, p. 185.

21. J. Lachs, "Active Euthanasia," *Journal of Clinical Ethics* 1(2) 1990: 113–115; J. H. Van Den Berg, *Medical Power and Medical Ethics.* New York: W. W. Norton, 1978.

22. J. H. Van Den Berg, *Medical Power and Medical Ethics.* New York: W. W. Norton, 1978.

23. T. E. Quill, "Doctor, I Want to Die, Will You Help Me?" *Journal of the American Medical Association* 270(7); 1993: 870–873.

24. C. K. Cassell and D. E. Meier, "Morals and Moralism in the Debate Over Euthanasia and Assisted Suicide," *New England Journal of Medicine* 323; 1990: 750–752.

25. J. Lachs, "Active Euthanasia."

26. E. Van Leeuwen and G. K. Kimsma, "Acting or Letting Go: Medical Decision Making in Neonatology in the Netherlands," *Cambridge Quarterly of Health Care Ethics* 2(3) 1993: 265–269.

27. Commission on the Study of Medical Practice Concerning Euthanasia, "Medical Decisions Concerning the End of Life." The Hague: Staatsuitgeverij, 1991. See also P. J. van der Maas, J. J. M. van Delden, et al. "Euthanasia and other Medical Decisions Concerning the End of Life." *Lancet* 338(1991): 669–674.

28. S. Saxon, *Pain Management Techniques for Older Adults.* Springfield, IL.: Charles C. Thomas, 1991.

29. T. Quill, *Death and Dignity: Making Choices and Taking Charge.* New York: W. W. Norton, 1992.

30. D. P. Sulmasy, "Death and Human Dignity," *Linacre Quarterly* 61(4); 1994: 27–36.

31. J. Kevorkian, "The Goodness of a Planned Death: An Interview with Jack Kevorkian," *Free Inquiry*, Fall 1991: 14–18.

32. E. D. Pellegrino, "Patient and Physician's Autonomy: Conflicting Rights and Obligations in the Physician-Patient Relationship," *Health Law and Policy* 10;1994: 47–68.

33. J. S. Mill, *On Liberty*, A. Castell ed. New York: Appleton-Century-Crofts, 1947, p. 104.

34. "Janet Adkins' Suicide: Reexamining the Spectrum of Issues it Has Raised." *Issues* 5(4) July-August, 1990: 1–7.

35. Y. Conwell and E. Caine, "Rational Suicide and the Right to Die," *New England Journal of Medicine* 325; Oct. 10, 1991: 100–1103.

36. N. Coyle, "The Last Weeks of Life," *American Journal of Nursing* 1990: 75–78.

37. E. D. Pellegrino, "Trust and Distrust in Professional Ethics," in E. D. Pellegrino, et al. eds. *Ethics, Trust and the Professions.* Washington, DC: Georgetown University Press, 1991, pp. 69–92.

38. R. Fenigson, "A Case Against Dutch Euthanasia," *Hastings Center Report* 19(1); 1989: 522–530; R. Fenigson, "Euthanasia in the Netherlands," *Issues in Law and Medicine* 6(3); 1990: 229–245.

39. J. H. Van Den Berg, "Medical Power" and C. van der Meer, "Euthanasia: A Definition and Ethical Conditions," *Journal of Palliative Care* 4(1–2); 1988: 103–6.

40. J. H. Van Den Berg, *Medical Power and Medical Ethics*. New York: W. W. Norton, 1978.

41. H. Dupuis, "Interview with Heleen Dupuis: Actively Ending the Life of a Severely Handicapped New Born, A Dutch Ethicist's Perspective," *Cambridge Quarterly of Health Care Ethics* 2(3), 1993: 275–280.

42. *Bouvia v. Superior Court*, 179 Cal App 3d 1127, 225 Cal Rptr 279 (Ct App).

43. Cf. Judge Compton's concurring opinion in Bouvia.

44. *In re Requena*, 517 A2d 886 N.J. (Super Ch 1986), 517 A2d 869 (N.J. Super Ct App Div 1986).

45. J. Boyle, "The Roman Catholic Tradition and Bioethics," *Bioethics Yearbook Volume I, 1988–1990: Theological Developments in Bioethics*. Boston: Kluwer Academic Publishers, 1991, pp. 14–18; J. Boyle, "Sanctity of Life and Suicide: Tensions and Development Within the Common Morality," in B. Brody, ed. *Suicide and Euthanasia*. Dordrecht: Kluwer Academic Publishers, 1989, pp. 221–249; J. Boyle, "Who is Entitled to Double Effect?" *Journal of Medicine and Philosophy*, 16(5); 1991: 475–495; O. N. Grise, *Catholic Identity in Health Care: Principles and Practice*. Braintree, MA: The Pope John Center, 1987; H. G. Kramer, *The Indirect Voluntary, or Voluntarium in Causa* (Dissertation). Washington, DC: Catholic University of America Press, 1935.

46. E. D. Pellegrino, "Doctors Must Not Kill," in R. Misbin, ed. *Euthanasia: The Good of the Patient, the Good of Society*. Frederick, MD: University Publishing Group, 1992, pp. 27–41.

47. The Multi-Society Task Force on PVS, "Medical Aspects of the Persistent Vegetative State," *New England Journal of Medicine* 330: 1994; 1499–1508 and 1572–1579.

Management at the End of Life: A Dialogue About Intending Death

*JOHN M. FREEMAN, AND †EDMUND D. PELLEGRINO

*The Johns Hopkins University, School of Medicine, Baltimore, Maryland; and †Georgetown University, Washington, District of Columbia

TREATMENT OF INDIVIDUALS NEAR THE END OF LIFE

Many patients remain fearful of the quality of their medical care at the end of life. They are fearful that loss of control over decisions could lead to unnecessary physical pain and psychological suffering, to loss of dignity, and to prolongation of life when medical treatments are futile. This fear of loss of control and the accompanying indignity and financial cost appear to be a motivating factor in the euthanasia movement.

Modification of much of the current management of patients at the end of life is needed. Physicians must become far more attuned to the patient's physiological pain and make better use of contemporary pain management. They also must acquire far greater understanding of the specific reasons for a patient's psychological suffering. If physicians paid due attention to optimum palliation of both pain and suffering, they might reduce or eliminate patient requests for the physician's assistance in suicide or in bringing about death.

As we discussed our disagreement on some important principles, we found that we were in substantial agreement on potential guidelines for treating individuals near the end of life. Such guidelines might include the following:

1. Patient *always* should be managed with compassion, in a merciful and beneficent fashion;
2. Decisions about treatment and life support must be made by and with the patients or in consultation with their valid surrogates and should always be patient centered; and
3. Treatment and life support *always* must be effective or potentially effective and be of net potential benefit to the patient.

These criteria also apply to decisions about withholding and withdrawing treatment and life support. Such decisions require a complex evaluation of the interrelationships between effectiveness, burdens, and benefits. Our definition of an effective treatment is one that demonstrably either changes the course of the disease or ameliorates a symptom the patient finds disabling or burdensome. Burdens should be defined by the patient and are the sum of the physical, psychological, social, and economic stresses consequent to the course of action. Benefits should be the patient's estimate of both the short- and long-term "good" to be gained by the treatment and may include such events as being alive for the birth of a grandchild or for a holiday or anniversary.

A careful balancing of the interrelationships between effectiveness, benefit, and burden should be possible for the experienced clinician in consultation with the patient and/or surrogates, and such balancing is preferable to the use of any one of the three factors to the exclusion of the others.

4. Physician input to such individual decisions must not be based on considerations such as age, disease, social merit, or ability to pay.
5. Whenever possible, the patient's wishes concerning life-sustaining treatment should be obtained in advance of a clinical crisis through execution of a living will or durable power of attorney for health care.
6. There should be frequent reevaluation of the facts of the case, including the prognosis, as well as the benefits and burdens of previously made decisions. These reevaluations are of particular importance whenever significant new courses of action are contemplated.
7. Whenever there is reasonable doubt, the presumption should be in favor of continued life support, since this closes no options and permits continued reevaluation.
8. When the patient desires the withholding or withdrawing of life support, every effort must be made to avoid or alleviate pain and suffering, even if these efforts may unintentionally shorten the individual's life.
9. When conflicts arise between patients, family members, physicians, or other members of the medical team, mechanisms for conflict resolution *always* should be made available. These may include ethics committees, ethics consultations, consultations with colleagues, and pastoral counseling. Recourse to the courts is a last resort.

SOME FUNDAMENTAL ETHICAL DISAGREEMENTS

Despite careful attention to these issues, patients may, on occasion, request a physician's assistance in committing suicide or ask for the physician's active involvement in ending life. During our dialogue, we found that although we had seemingly irreconcilable moral and philosophical differences concerning such requests, with one of us feeling that assisted suicide is *always* wrong and the other disagreeing, our ultimate actions as physicians *might* be similar. These similarities and differences are revealed in the following case. A patient with severe amyotrophic lateral sclerosis who is receiving respiratory support requests her physician's help in ending her suffering by disconnecting the respirator. She asks that her death be as quick and painless as possible. Both of us might disconnect the respirator and provide morphine to the patient, but we would do so with different justifications.

One of us (J.M.F.), although philosophically equating this withdrawal of life support to the "killing" of the patient, after assessing that the patient was competent and that the request was not unreasonable, might agree to disconnect the respirator purely on the basis of the patient's right to self-determination. He also might alleviate anticipated suffering with administration of morphine, despite (or because of) its effect of possibly hastening the patient's death.

The other author (E.D.P.), unalterably opposed to killing or even assisting in suicide, might carefully reevaluate, together with the patient, the benefits and burdens of her condition and find that the respirator was ineffective in altering the course of the disease, was disproportionately burdensome, or was medically futile. Since efficacy of treatment and relief of burden are central to patient care, this second physician also might disconnect the respirator, thus allowing the patient to die. He might use morphine to prevent the patient's suffering but would never countenance intending death of that patient.

Many believe that this distinction between "killing" and "letting die" is of great philosophical and moral importance. Those who, like Dr. Pellegrino, operate on the principle that intentional and deliberate taking of a patient's life is morally unacceptable under *all* circumstances might articulate their position in the following way: A "good" death cannot include active euthanasia or assisted suicide. Both are equally proscribed by the widely held social, ethical, and religious injunctions against killing the innocent. To relax this proscription, even for reasons of compassion, is always wrong for both the physician and patient. Intentional killing is intrinsically a wrong act; it violates the moral purpose of the medical relationship, and it invites serious abuses that cannot be contained by legal constraints. Moreover, to permit intentional death is to abnegate the physician's moral obligation to provide comprehensive palliative care for the pain and psychological causes that drive patients to such desperation that they ask to be killed. Intending a patient's death is not beneficent, respectful of self-determination, or consistent with human dignity.

Those of us who do not accept these assumptions and principles might articulate their reasoning in the following fashion: Euthanasia (which means a good death) and assisted suicide can help to prevent the prolonged physical and psychological suffering that, on occasion, may accompany letting someone die. Although killing is proscribed by the Ten Commandments and the Hippocratic Oath, relief of suffering is not. Actively assisting death may not be, in some situations, ethically different from letting someone die. Once the concession is made that death *can* be a good, then the challenge is defining *when* death is a kindness, *when* it would be more compassionate and merciful than continued existence, and *how* the beneficent physician can assist the patient in achieving this goal. That physician would neither kill nor intend death but rather intend the relief of suffering in whatever fashion is most respectful of the patient's right to caring and compassionate self-determination. Consultation or outside review could ensure beneficent compassion and appropriate intent.

THE NECESSITY OF DIALOGUE

Despite these sharp differences in ethical justification, we were struck by our agreement on what ought to be done in certain specific clinical instances. Clearly, conscientious clinicians, equally motivated by beneficence and compassion, may take identical or similar actions in their care of patients at the end of life, even though they may hold divergent moral principles. However, just as clearly, when patients are not near the end of life or are in a terminal state but death is not imminent, philosophically irreconcilable positions could result in vastly different clinical decisions.

We appreciate the fact that despite our agreements in concrete cases, our principles remain irreconcilable. However, understanding the similarities, differences, and distinctions in our positions is critical to the continuing dialogue about what constitutes morally responsible care of patients at the end of life. In a democratic, morally heterogeneous society like ours, we cannot work together effectively in our common enterprise of helping the sick without such a dialogue, which involves physicians, patients, and society.[1]

REFERENCE

1. PELLEGRINO, E.D., "Withholding and Withdrawing Treatments: Ethics at the Bedside." *Clinical Neurosurgery* 35:1989: 164–184.

Should Some Morally Acceptable Actions of Killing and Letting Die Be Legally Prohibited and Punished?

ALEXANDER MORGAN CAPRON

University of Southern California, Los Angeles, California

The answer implicit in the question that frames this paper's topic suggests one of those classic disjunctions between law and morality—or, to the cynic, between law and common sense—that has led some to think the law an ass or worse. Why in the world, they wonder, should we seek to prohibit—much less to punish—actions that are morally licit?

Of course, one could avoid this difficulty by answering "No" to the question instead. This view would probably be based on a general linkage of legal and moral standards: as morality sets a high standard for right conduct, actions that are morally acceptable ought to be lawful. Even were I inclined in this direction (which I am not), I would reject this alternative because the denial of a necessary connection between moral acceptability and legality is productive of more interesting analysis. Moreover, it is also more likely to reflect the state of the law; that is, certain acts of killing and letting die are likely to remain illegal even if (or long after) they come to be seen as morally acceptable.

The proposition examined here is less familiar than its opposite—that some morally unacceptable actions should not be illegal. Indeed, the latter proposition is not only commonplace but is commonly accepted without creating the sense that the law is foolish. Several basic arguments have been adduced in support of this proposition, both general (that criminal laws always need an independent, utilitarian basis beyond morality) and specific (that "moral unacceptability" is invalid as a basis for law when it is nothing more than the majority's—or a dominant minority's—religiously based rejection of certain conduct). Putting these aside, many sensible reasons exist for not making illegal all acts that violate even commonly accepted moral standards. For one, attempting to enforce such laws may require official intrusion into private spheres (*cf. Griswold v. Connecticut*); for another, the harm caused (especially when it is more to onlookers' sensibilities than to their person or property) may be too small to warrant the expenditure of police, prosecutorial, and judicial resources needed to enforce the law, especially when compared with the benefits from other uses of those resources. Furthermore, laws tend to deter more conduct than they aim to prohibit, so it is often wise not to draw the line of illegality all the way to the edge of immorality, lest acceptable (and perhaps even valuable) conduct be suppressed as well.

Yet all these reasons for not "legislating morality" (as it is sometimes termed) only make the proposition under scrutiny in this paper—that some morally accepted actions should be legally prohibited and punished—seem that much less defensible. If it is unwise, dangerous, or worse to outlaw some *morally unacceptable* actions, how can it make sense to prohibit or punish actions that are *morally acceptable?*

Part of the answer rests, I believe, in an important distinction between prohibition and punishment, the first topic I will explore here. Another part turns on the specific context—killing and letting die. In this context, the harmful consequences of errors and of eroding standards are so great that under-deterrence may well be a greater danger than over-deterrence. Further, the moral values implicated in killing and letting die—not only the sanctity of human life but also personal, voluntary choice—are so widely held and nonparochial that any objection to the "legislation of morality" (in the sense of imposing restrictions based on religion or mere propriety) seems wide of the mark. Indeed, in this paper I will assume that we are not dealing with situations in which those who object to the legal standard differ with those who support it in how they view the moral acceptability of the conduct in question. Instead, I will assume that those who are going to be governed by the legal standard are in agreement that the actions in question are, at the least, not morally unacceptable.

To explore these latter points, I will examine two specific situations in which good reasons exist for prohibiting some morally accepted actions: decisions to forgo life-sustaining treatment in patients who lack natural or appointed guardians, and active, physician-administered euthanasia of patients at their own request.

PROHIBITION AND PUNISHMENT

Suggesting that morally licit conduct be criminalized conveys two thoughts: that the conduct should be declared illegal and that those who engage in it should be penalized. Though obviously linked—as they are in the title to this paper, "Legally Prohibited and Penalized"—these are distinct concepts. The first is a general rule, the second, a specific application, usually grounded in individualized fact-finding.

Prohibition. The conclusion that certain actions should be prohibited states a general rule because it takes as its subject all people in the group to which the prohibition applies and because some of the conduct it appears to encompass may be excluded through exceptions, justifications, and the like. If an interdiction succeeds, the actions in question will be extinguished in that group; even without complete success, a prohibition expresses the intention that these actions not occur.

Of course, the criminal law typically consists of more than a mere statement that certain actions are wrong. Prohibition is usually linked to punishment: in most conceptions of the criminal law, the general rule includes a threat that violations will lead to some sort of penalty. Yet the two are not the same. Prohibition without the exacting of punishment is not an incoherent concept.1 If the threat of punishment is credible, the mere existence of the prohibition can have many valuable consequences, such as deterring potentially harmful conduct. Furthermore, the mere articulation of a prohibition serves to set or reenforce standards for the community.

Do these functions of prohibition even absent punishment—articulating standards and deterring conduct—make sense in the context of morally acceptable conduct? Why should we set a community standard that condemns such conduct or that deters it? If the term "conduct" here refers to an entire category of actions, all of which are morally acceptable, then there are only two reasons for outlawing it. First, the conduct—whatever its moral acceptability—must be curtailed to reach social goals. This is true, for example, of many forms of regulation. (Although it is conceivable that some legal prohibitions on killing and letting die might be grounded in such regulatory, amoral grounds, that seems unlikely, and I will not explore that alternative further here.)

The second, and more interesting, reason is that the conduct in question cannot readily be distinguished from other conduct that is not morally acceptable. Hence, it is argued, this morally acceptable conduct must be prohibited lest those who engage in it feel themselves justified in also engaging in the morally unacceptable conduct or lest those who apply the laws fail to act against the morally unacceptable conduct because it seems to them no different than the conduct that is permitted. This was, I believe, part of the reasoning that for years led many physicians (and even some judges) to treat the forgoing of life-sustaining treatment as a form of suicide or homicide (and hence illegal) not because forgoing treatment was immoral in itself but because they thought no distinction could be made out between such "passive euthanasia" and "active euthanasia," which they were certain was wrong and had to be forestalled.

If the term *conduct* means an individual action, the meaning of the basic proposition alters and so does the rationale for holding that a particular morally acceptable act might be "legally prohibited." Since I have argued that prohibitions should be understood to be general rules, linking a prohibition with a specific act turns our attention to the individualized judgment associated with the imposition of punishment.

Punishment. As suggested earlier, prohibitions relate to general rules, while punishments relate to specific instances—penalizing a particular actor. We may assume that such imposition requires that a prosecutor (and perhaps a grand jury) has decided to bring the case before a duly constituted tribunal which in turn has determined (perhaps through a jury trial) that the person to be punished has violated the terms of a valid criminal prohibition.

The underlying question here is whether it makes sense ever to punish someone for engaging in morally acceptable conduct. One response might be that in the case of certain "regulatory" crimes which arise from conduct that carries very little moral baggage at all, there is nothing inappropriate about punishing someone for actions that are morally acceptable even though society has good reasons to use the threat of punishment to deter them. (As mentioned earlier, I pass over this possibility as not germane to our topic.)

A second response looks to the criminal law's intricate rules that cover questions such as whether people can be convicted for doing something they think is illegal but that turns out not to be (for example, because of a change in a statute). The issue addressed in this essay is not so narrowly technical. Instead, it is whether it is morally right for a law to inflict punishment on someone for engaging in a specific instance of conduct that is morally acceptable. The answer to this question turns, I believe, not only on the nature and severity of the punishment but on how the action is classified as morally acceptable, namely, in terms of its process or its outcome or both. As I argue more fully below, while criminal prohibitions on morally acceptable actions of killing and letting die can be justified by the other social goals that are served by the existence of the prohibitions, I would find it difficult to justify exacting any significant punishment for morally acceptable instances of killing or letting die. One hallmark of a just and well functioning system of criminal law is the barriers it erects between the existence of prohibitions and the imposition of punishment on individuals whose violation of those prohibitions involved actions that were morally acceptable.

LETTING DIE

Most people in this country now generally accept that it is not immoral to allow certain patients to die by the withholding or withdrawal of life-sustaining medical interventions. The law, both decisional and statutory, also embodies this conclusion.

Indeed, in 1976 when California adopted the first statute aimed at reassuring people (particularly the physicians involved) about the legality of honoring a now-incompetent patient's advance instructions to forgo treatment, it signalled the inherent acceptability of the conduct by entitling the law "The Natural Death Act."

What realm remains, then, for legal prohibition or punishment? Certainly, there are instances that go beyond the scope of moral acceptability; for instance, withdrawing curative treatment from an incompetent patient who has not expressed the wish to forgo treatment under the circumstances. It is appropriate for the law to continue to prohibit such actions and to punish them, both criminally and by permitting damages to be collected in a civil suit. Equally obvious, however, is that such a situation does not illustrate this paper's proposition, that a prohibition against certain actions that allow patients to die would be justified even if their dying were morally acceptable.

To test this proposition, we must dig deeper into the concept of "morally acceptable actions." In the context of letting die, it seems to me that ethical analysis usually focuses on the rightness of the actions (it is ethical to dispense with interventions that are wasteful and that burden more than benefit the patient) and of the outcome (it is ethical to release the patient from further suffering and even to allow the patient to die). The law has not neglected such factors, but it tends to emphasize the legitimacy of the actors as much as the action. The relevant statutes aim primarily at providing authority for particular people to act; by implication, any legal prohibitions that existed before the statute would remain as to conduct not encompassed by the statute, although such prohibitions would be of the most general sort (against negligent or intentional homicide or aiding suicide), since "euthanasia" (passive or active) is not a separate criminal category in American law.

Does this lead to cases of noncongruence between moral and legal acceptability? The law in most states now explicitly recognizes that when a person has expressed the wish not to have treatment continued under certain circumstances, that wish can be honored by others without fear of legal liability. Many jurisdictions make such "advance directives" effective at the time that patients are "terminally ill" (meaning that without treatment their illness or injury would be fatal in a short time) or "permanently unconscious" (meaning that they are unlikely ever to become sentient again). These are circumstances in which most people would probably agree that allowing death would be ethical, particularly if the patient's condition is painful.

In some jurisdictions, however, the advance directive statutes explicitly exclude withdrawal of food and fluids even if provided by tube. Assuming that such limitations have not been held irrelevant (because they merely limit the statute and not actions taken to effectuate a person's existing, common-law right to have any medical intervention withdrawn), are they improper? Legal objections are likely to be framed in terms of violating a constitutional right (the "liberty" interest that the *Cruzan* Court recognized people have to decline even life-sustaining treatment), but we can frame our question more broadly: Is this a circumstance in which a legal prohibition is not justified because withdrawal of artificial feeding and fluids is morally acceptable? Framing the question in this way excludes the assertion that a majority of people would support this limitation (vis-à-vis food and fluids) as morally acceptable. If we accept instead that most people would find the limitation unacceptable, then limiting the steps that can be taken in executing a patient's advance directive does not seem justifiable to me, provided that the patient while competent made his or her views clear.

If we shift our focus, as the law often does, from the action to the actor, we can easily imagine categories of prohibitions and instances of punishment that would be justified even when conduct is morally acceptable, especially in terms of its outcome. For example, by permitting next-of-kin to decide to cease life-sustaining treatment for an incompetent patient, the law has lifted a prohibition on one person taking an action that leads to the death of another. This means, in effect, that prohibition against withdrawal of treatment still exists as to strangers or others not authorized by a statute (or judicial decision) to take such action. Such prohibition is justified for several reasons. First, actors outside the permissible categories are unlikely to be predictably attached to the welfare of the patients whose death they bring about; second, such actors are unlikely to know enough about the patient to act in the fashion that the patient would have wanted; and third, there is no limit to the number of people (perhaps with conflicting ideas about what should happen when) who might attempt to fulfill such a role for a patient, whereas each patient has a limited number of "next-of-kin" (a common-law concept which is narrowed even further by the family-consent laws recently adopted in a number of states under which a rank order of surrogate decision makers is specified).

What about imposing punishment on a "stranger" who lets a patient die in circumstances where death is "morally acceptable" in an outcome sense? (In other words, had death occurred without human intervention, it would have been universally regarded as a blessing for the patient.) Do the reasons that favor the general prohibition justify imposing some punishment on the actor? Yes, because actions consist both in what is done and in who does it. While the discontinuation of treatment is in this instance assumed to be a benefit to the patient, the actor was not authorized to bring about that result. If a person forges my name to a check and then uses the proceeds to buy me a winning lottery ticket, he has still committed forgery. That the actor achieved a beneficial result in our hypothetical example may be adventitious (given his or her lack of identification with or knowledge of the patient); the actor may be just one of many people, each with his or her own idea of the point at which life support should be withdrawn and each with equal (that is, equally nonexistent) authority to act on that personal idea. In order to avoid unrelieved suffering of incompetent patients who have not appointed a proxy and who have no next-of-kin, it would be advisable for the law to have a means that would permit a stranger to be authorized (such as by being appointed the patient's guardian) to act, with appropriate advice (such as from attending and consulting physicians and perhaps with review by an institutional ethics committee). Where a stranger has acted without such authority, however, punishment is appropriate, though it might be mitigated by such factors as the appropriateness of the action (the degree of suffering that the patient would otherwise have experienced), the grounds the defendant had to believe that the action would serve the patient's best interests, the dearth of other available actors, and the absence of conflicting motives on the part of the defendant.

Thus, while there is little controversy about the moral acceptability of allowing patients to die under a variety of circumstances, this example makes clear that there are still good reasons to maintain legal prohibitions on some of these acts and to punish actors who violate these prohibitions even when their acts are of an acceptable type (*e.g.*, discontinued artificial ventilation on an unconscious patient with incurable, metastisized cancer) and produce an acceptable result (*e.g.*, relieve pain).

KILLING

Were it true that acts that cause death are morally equivalent to omissions that cause death, the preceeding would exhaust the subject and I could just say "ditto" for killing to all the points just made about letting die. But there are profound cultural, historical, medical, and legal difference that more than obliterate any formal similarity between the two.

Indeed, the most controversial area of the law on death and dying today concerns active euthanasia, physician aid-in-dying, assisted suicide, and related forms of killing for the sake of mercy. The morality of such actions is hotly debated: the American Medical Association continues to hold that it is unethical for physicians to kill, but a group of physicians who examined death and dying closely concluded in a 1989 *New England Journal of Medicine* article that active euthanasia is not always morally unacceptable; a physician's unashamed description in that same journal in 1991 of the assistance he gave a long-time patient in obtaining the means to take her own life when she was dying of cancer elicited at least as much praise as criticism; and polls show physician ambivalence (70 percent of the physicians polled by the San Francisco Medical Society believe incurable, terminally ill patients should have the option to request active euthanasia, but only 45 percent would carry out such a request). Similarly, the correct legal treatment of this category of killings is increasingly at issue: polls repeatedly show that a majority of Americans say that physician aid-in-dying should be legalized, but an initiative to do exactly that failed to qualify for the ballot in California in 1988 and another was defeated by an 8-point margin by Washington voters last November.

Because of these uncertainties, in discussing active euthanasia one cannot make the easy assumption of "moral acceptability" that is perfectly appropriate in an American discussion of forgoing life-sustaining treatment. Thus, in order to test our framing proposition—that some morally acceptable actions of killing should be legally prohibited and punished—we need first to suggest which actions are being hypothesized to be "morally acceptable." The type of conduct that is currently most debated is physician-administered or mediated euthanasia (or "aid-in-dying"). Although the American proposals to legalize this conduct are less rigorous, it seems appropriate to invoke the definition of the practice that is tolerated in the Netherlands, as that is the only one with which there is now widespread experience.

The guidelines for an act of euthanasia that will be free from prosecution in the Netherlands contain five major points:

1. that the patient's request be voluntary;
2. that the patient be undergoing intolerable suffering;
3. that all alternatives acceptable to the patient for relieving the suffering have been tried;
4. that the patient has full information;
5. that the physician has consulted with a second physician whose judgment can be expected to be independent.[2]

The Dutch also nominally require the physician to report each instance of euthanasia to the prosecutor, to permit an investigation to ensure that these criteria have been met, but this requirement seems to be violated in the overwhelming majority of cases, so it is not listed among the criteria here. Rather than debate whether any instance of medically administered killing is ethical, for purpose of this discussion, I will simply assume that a killing that meets these stipulations is morally acceptable and then ask whether good reasons exist for continuing to prohibit or punish such actions.

Prohibition. What are the major harms that might attach to allowing physicians to kill patients or directly assist patients in taking their own lives? Six bear special mention: (1) erosion of the trust that patients need to have that physicians will never use their tremendous powers (both technical powers and the authority they wield in the physician-patient relationship) to take their patients' lives; (2) abuse of patients for physicians' sake (such as to cover-up a medical failure or to relieve oneself of the on-going burden of caring for a "hopeless" case); (3) removing or diminishing the pressure on physicians to find the best means to ease pain while maintaining life and function; (4) the risk that patients' "voluntary" choice of euthanasia will be coerced by their family or others or at least result from their sense of not wishing to impose an unworthy burden on their family or others; (5) the risk that depression will distort some patients' evaluation of their own wishes and best interests; and (6) a general diminution of respect for human life. Some of these harmful consequences relate to the occurrence of involuntary deaths, others merely to increased apprehension among patients, and others to broad effects on society. Some relate to all patients, others to particular groups—the elderly, the mentally impaired, the poor (who depend on over-taxed public facilities and who lack a close, longstanding relationship with a particular physician).

All of the harmful effects just recited are, of course, speculative. There seems to me no sure way to prove that they will occur, any more than one can be certain that they won't. But to admit that they are speculative does not mean that they must be dismissed when framing social policy. Some of the objections are quite culturally bound: if physicians were sanctioned to perform euthanasia, patients might be as likely to distrust physicians who won't help "deliver" them from terminal illness as to worry about those who are willing to do so, provided they had some assurance of adequate oversight. Nonetheless, some of the predicted harms seem so likely—particularly that some patients' choices will be manipulated and that patients who have little entitlement to decent medical care today will be subject to circumstances that will make a swift and painless death seem an attractive alternative—that it seems to me that a policy that prohibited euthanasia could be justified by reference to them, provided that the harm done by outlawing the performance of euthanasia in the instances that truly met the moral standards set forth above did not outweigh the harm that would come from changing the policy.

The calculation of harm that would follow from continuing what is in effect a prohibition on physicians performing euthanasia (as part of the general prohibition on homicide and the widespread though not uniform prohibition on assisting in suicide) depends on the assumption that most physicians would obey the law. Yet even if that is true, the number of cases of morally justified euthanasia that would therefore not occur will be very small for two reasons. First, there are very few cases where pain cannot be treated successfully if only physicians use adequate ingenuity and involve the patient appropriately. Such efforts—along with other means of psychological and spiritual support—can eliminate most instances of suffering as well (recognizing that this concept encompasses more than solely physical pain). Second, in most of the remaining cases, an individual who is determined to take his or her own life can do so. Thus, the denial of the morally acceptable deaths in these few cases becomes the price of avoiding a large number of morally unacceptable deaths that would occur if the presumption were shifted from respecting life to allowing it to be taken.

Although several of the harms from changing the law that are recited are of the "erosion" variety, none is a "slippery slope" argument. There are, however, strong arguments for continuing to outlaw voluntary euthanasia of terminal patients to avoid slippery slopes. The slides are of two types. One is sociological: once physicians become used to dispensing mercy for voluntary, imminently dying patients with unrelievable suffering, they will move on to other cases: if killing is acceptable, why not exercise their discretion in cases that fall slightly outside the original perimeters of the law?

The second type of slope is logical and to me it seems steeper because it does not depend on predictions about human tendencies or analogies drawn to what happened to some German physicians during the Nazi period. The logical problem lies in the very justification for legalizing euthanasia in the first place. If this is rested on the principle of voluntary choice, then the requirements of unrelievable pain and incurable, terminal illness are not justified: euthanasia should be available to anyone who wants it. On the other hand, if it is rested on the relief of suffering, then surely voluntary choice is not morally relevant—a beneficent society (and beneficent physicians) would also give merciful release from the pain of life to any who suffer even if they are unable to request it. As Daniel Callahan observes, it might seem unfair to unlink these two criteria, if they have been put together as a safeguard against abuse; but, as he notes, their union is "jerry-rigged" since "each has its own logic, and each could be used to justify euthanasia," and the logic of each could not long remain suppressed "by the expedient of arbitary legal stipulations."[3]

Punishment. In discussing prohibitions, I suggested that they would be effective. Obviously, this will not always be the case. Sometimes a physician (or another person) would feel justified in violating the prohibition. Should that person be punished? My belief, as I stated at the outset, is that in such circumstances the answer should be "no," that the legal system should protect those persons. And my sense is that is exactly what has happened, through prosecutorial discretion and jury nullification. Indeed, there is to the best of my knowledge, no case of a physician being convicted for aiding a suicide in the circumstances that would meet our stipulated definition of a "morally acceptable" killing.

NOTES

1. Indeed, conduct may be "prohibited" even when the imposition of a penalty is nonexistent, at least by the state. Prohibitions on conduct by persons acting abroad, beyond the state's jurisdiction, fall in this category. Most other examples take one out of the realm of "legal prohibition" into the realm of moral rules; in fact, "moral wrong" is the term commonly used for prohibited conduct where there is no possibility of enforcement or punishment, beyond the disapproval of one's fellows or the judgment of a higher power.

2. This version of the Dutch requirements appeared in Battin, "Euthanasia: The Way We Do It, The Way They Do It," *Journal of Pain & Symptoms. Management* 6; July 1991: 298, 299.

3. Callahan, "'Aid-in-Dying': The Social Dimensions," *Commonweal* Aug. 9, 1991: 476, 479.

Intending or Permitting Death in Order to Conserve Resources

RAANAN GILLON

Imperial College, London, United Kingdom

When I limit my monthly donation to Oxfam to its current inadequate level, while I foresee that this limitation will be partly causal of more starving third world members dying than would have been the case if I increased my contribution, while I could prevent them so dying and do not, nonetheless I do not *intend* those deaths to occur, even though I *permit or allow* them to occur. Conversely, to be guided by Philippa Foot's example,[1] were I to send poisoned food to the appropriate villages in the third world with the aim of killing some of the villagers (perhaps to reduce their population, or perhaps to make a philosophical point) then clearly I should be *intending* to kill some people and the notion of permitting or allowing them to die would be either inapplicable—if they were not already dying for example—or *additionally* applicable if, for example, they were in any case already dying from causes that would kill them independently of my intention to kill them with poisoned food.

I believe I have said enough to justify henceforth assuming that there is indeed a conceptual distinction to be made between both allowing and intending a death and allowing or permitting a death that one nevertheless does not intend or aim at, such that all of us may, and indeed routinely do, allow or permit deaths without intending them, aiming at them or having them as our objective. Of course, we might both intend and allow a death, for example, if we were actively participating assistants in another's suicide, or if we allowed some other avoidable cause of death to kill someone whom we would otherwise have killed ourselves (the Rachels case[2]). In other cases of intending death it would be at least linguistically bizarre to say that we allowed or permitted the death, notably where we aimed at and successfully brought about someone's death who was not already dying from some other cause(s). For example, if an old fashioned executioner, having successfully chopped off the head of a condemned man, with the intention of killing him, then said that he had "allowed" or "permitted" the condemned man to die, most familiar users of English would assume that the executioner, however well he understood the art of decapitation, was either into heavy irony or else not much good at understanding or using the English language. Thus, I shall assume that within the class of all actions that in some sense cause death, whether by intervention or by omission to intervene, only a subclass of all those actions can be properly construed as intending death; that another subclass can properly be construed as allowing or permitting death, but not intending death; and that an intersecting class may be construed as both allowing and intending death.

My position, in summary, is the following:

1. that it is generally morally desirable to maintain the existing moral norm in medicine that prima facie rejects the intending of a patient's death, whether by commission or omission (though I leave to others to argue whether or not an exception should be permitted in the case of voluntary euthanasia);

2. that it would be morally undesirable to have a moral norm that required people to keep others alive as much as possible, or even a norm that required doctors to provide life-prolonging treatment (LPT) to all who could be kept alive;

3. that keeping people alive by life-prolonging treatment (LPT) is only morally desirable if it has an acceptable chance of fulfilling the medico-moral objective of producing net benefit over harm for the patient—otherwise, dying people should generally be allowed to die in the interests of avoiding excessive harm or mere lack of benefit and in the interests of avoiding waste of potentially beneficial resources;

4. that even when LPT can be anticipated to produce net benefit over harm for the patient, if the patient (or the patient's proper proxy) autonomously rejects the LPT, that rejection ought to be honored in the interests of respecting the patient's autonomy and in order to avoid the waste of resources for those who would both benefit and autonomously wish to benefit from those resources;

5. that even when the LPT can be expected to produce net benefit for the patient, and the patient or proper proxy desire the LPT, justice in the allocation of scarce resources may require rationing of the available LPTs and some patients may thus morally justifiably (though regrettably) be denied LPTs.

So far as (1) is concerned, I would argue that the existing norm that prohibits intending (aiming at) another's death, or indeed merely threatening it, is in the vast majority of cases morally highly desirable. Being deliberately killed by another generally over-rides one's autonomy, harms one, does not benefit one, and is unjust. Such actions and threats of such actions are thus easily seen to be morally reprehensible and their active prohibition easily justified. Doctors should be as much restricted by these prohibitions as any one else and indeed arguably should espouse such prohibitions even more positively and explicitly than others, given the vulnerability and mortal fear of many sick patients. (I leave it to others to argue about whether a special class of exceptions should be made in the case of voluntary euthanasia.)

So far as (2) is concerned, one has only to imagine a prima facie moral requirement that we must all make maximal efforts to keep every one alive—a moral obligation as strict as the existing prima facie moral obligation to make maximal efforts to avoid intentionally killing anyone—to realize (a) that it would be morally undesirable, and (b) that it would consume all our energies and resources if we tried seriously to fulfil it. (This contrasts markedly with the obligation to avoid intentionally killing others, which is in the overwhelming majority of cases morally desirable, easy to fulfil, and requires no resources.) Similar problems would arise, and be magnified, if such a moral requirement to make maximal efforts to keep all alive was restricted to doctors.

In relation to (3), the important point to be made is that a necessary moral condition for doctors seeking to prolong a person's life is that the LPT should stand an acceptable chance of fulfilling the basic Hippocratic moral objective of providing the patient with net benefit over harm, because the main moral purpose of both medicine and doctors is to benefit people. However, people are idiosyncratic in their views about what constitutes benefit and harm for them, so it is important for doctors not to rely entirely on their own assessments about whether administration of LPT would be regarded by the patient as likely to produce sufficient benefit and at an acceptable level of risk of harm. Hence, the moral importance of consulting patients (assuming they wish to be consulted and assuming such consultation is feasible) cr their proper proxies, which serves to improve the doctor's assessment of whether or not a proposed LPT is sufficiently likely to produce net benefit over harm for that particular patient in those particular circumstances.

This brings us to (4). If the patient or the patient's proper proxy autonomously rejects a proposed LPT, then the doctor has no right to impose the treatment, even if it is likely to benefit the patient. As with most of their treatments, doctors can properly only offer LPTs to their patients. They must not impose them. It is up to the patient to decide whether to accept the offer or not. (Special problems arise if there is doubt about whether the patient is adequately autonomous to make the decision to reject the proposed LPT. Or if the patient is unable to be consulted, there might be doubt about whether the patient's proxy who wishes to reject the LPT is acting according to the patient's prior expressed wishes or in the patient's best interests. Special problems also arise when a patient or proper proxy desires a LPT, and yet the doctor has reason to believe that provision of the LPT would be futile in being unable to produce, or being very unlikely to produce, the desired effect. Here I merely note such problems.)

In summary, life-prolonging treatment may be morally undesirable and withheld, foreseeing but not intending (aiming at) the patient's death, if the LPT is unlikely to provide net benefit for the patient. In addition, even potentially beneficial LPT may be properly withheld if the patient or the patient's proper proxy autonomously rejects it. In addition to avoidance of further harm to the patient and or respect for the patient's autonomy, such withholding of nonbeneficial and/or autonomously rejected LPT has the moral advantage that it releases scarce resources that would otherwise be denied them to others who would benefit and who do autonomously desire them, an advantage in distributive justice.

I shall now also argue that LPTs may be properly withheld in some circumstances even if both doctor and patient or proper proxy agree that the LPT would provide net benefit for the patient and even if patient or proper proxy autonomously desire the LPT. Again those circumstances essentially relate to justice in allocation of scarce resources, which brings us to (5).

As an example, I will take the case of persistent vegetative state (PVS) in which patients are reliably believed to be permanently unconscious (despite going through sleep wake cycles) but in which they may stay alive for many years provided they receive proper nutrition and hydration and are expertly nursed and treated medically, if they become infected or otherwise ill. In such cases it is important to establish whether the patient and or the patient's proper proxy believe that being kept alive, but permanently unconscious is beneficial to the patient. I presume that the large majority of people would regard such life preserving treatment as nonbeneficial and useless. Certainly, contemporary medical judgment is that PVS patients themselves are in permanent unconsciousness, without the possibility of having any sort of experiences, let alone any sort of the "Good Life," eudaimonia, or human flourishing.

Some, however, would claim that staying alive as long as possible is beneficial to the patient. They may be vitalists who believe in life for life's sake, rather than in life for the sake of some sort of a Good Life, a life the patient would consider worth having. Or they may reason that while there's life there's hope, and no matter how low the probability of that hope is of recovery to a life that the patient would consider worth having, they realized it is better than no hope at all, and therefore, such patients should be kept alive as long as possible.

To the first group, I would argue, by all means do raise funds from like minded people to enable you to keep people in persistent vegetative state alive as long as possible, but please do not expect the community more generally to devote part of its already very scarce medical resources to this purpose. The purpose of health services produced by the community for its sick members is to provide them with health care *benefits*, and, for the large majority of us, staying alive but permanently unconscious can not plausibly be regarded as a benefit. If such care cost little or nothing then respect for the autonomy of patient as previously expressed and of proper proxy as currently expressed, might justify its provision. When it requires expensive health-care skills and facilities and when health-care resources are already grossly overstretched, justice to others who could undoubtedly benefit but who otherwise would not, requires that a community health service withholds LPTs from those reliably diagnosed to be in PVS, even though they previously and their proxies currently believe that such LPTs should be provided.

To the second group, who argue that where there is life there is hope and there-fore PVS patients should be kept alive as long as possible, I would counterargue that the probability of such hope being realized is too low to justify allocating expensive and scarce health-care resources to preserving it. There are too many sick people dying for lack of indisputably beneficial LPTs, LPTs having a high probability of restoring those patients to a life that they would consider well worth living, to justi-fy spending those resources on the very low probability of obtaining the recovery of PVS patients, which in any case is at best likely to be highly impaired recovery.

What about the *needs* of PVS patients? It is widely agreed that need is one of the morally important criteria for the just allocation of health care resources and that people should be medically treated as equals if they have equal medical needs, and as unequals in proportion to their unequal medical needs. In decisions about withhold-ing or withdrawing LPTs, decisions must be made in relation to the medical needs of those concerned. Some would argue that since PVS patients are in obviously enor-mous need they should be given priority over those in lesser need, including all those whose illnesses are not life threatening.

My own tentative view, informed by Wiggins and Derman,[3] is that needs are those conditions without which one is harmed, and that medical needs are those con-ditions that, lacking them, one's health is harmed or risks being harmed. The greater the harm or threat of harm to one's health the greater one's medical need. Of course, if the harm to one's health is the risk of death then one will generally be in very much greater need than if the harm or risk to one's health is some nonfatal harm, such as pain or disability—though there are, I have no doubt, many nonfatal harms that are worse than death.

It follows from such a definition, admittedly rough, that one can be in great medical need even in the absence of any available medical treatment to meet that need. The needs-related objective of just health-care distribution would, however, be to give priority of such beneficial care, as was available to those in greatest medical need, even if their capacity to benefit was less than that of those in lesser need (i.e., those afflicted by lesser harm or risk of harm to their health).

For many dying people, no treatment is available that will meet their needs for averting the harms of their medical condition. No cure for their fatal condition is available and while life-prolonging treatments may do just that, the harms of the life-threatening condition are not averted, but merely extended by such treatment. LPTs, therefore, are not what these patients need, even though they are undoubtedly in des-perate need. However, among their needs that can be satisfied by way of beneficial health care are the needs for comfort, manifest concern, and relief of symptoms. Thus, according to this analysis, the provision of hospice type care to the dying, to meet their meetable needs would have a high priority, based on their high overall needs, meetable and unmeetable. On the other hand, given that dying people only need such life prolonging treatments as to avert the harms of their medical condition—beneficial LPTs—and given that no such beneficial LPTs are available, then they do not need the (nonbeneficial) LPTs that are available. This is why hospice care rarely provides LPTs, for they do not generally benefit the dying or avert the harms of their medical condition.

Patients in PVS are the paradigm of patients who have maximal needs, all of which are unmeetable—there is simply nothing that can be done to cure their medical condition or avert its harms, or provide them with benefits of any sort. Even the comfort, manifest concern, and relief of symptoms that can beneficially be provided to those who are conscious and dying are useless to the PVS patient, who therefore does not need them. (It is of course a separate matter how much they should be provided for the comfort of relatives, friends, and carers). Thus, while medical need is indeed an important criterion for just allocation of scarce resources, and the greater a person's needs the greater our prima facie obligation to meet that person's needs, it is vital to understand that it is only treatments that do meet needs—that do avert harms or provide benefits—that can be needed. LPTs that do not meet the needs of dying or PVS patients, can not be needed by those patients and I believe it is a conceptual as well as a moral mistake for health-care workers to provide such LPTs simply because they have no LPTs that really do meet their dying and PVS patients' needs.

Medical need, even meetable medical need, can not be the end of the matter of distributive justice in medicine, for it has nothing to say about just acquisition of the resources needed to finance the meeting of medical need. Part of the exercise of one's autonomy is to work for reward, to accumulate property as a result, to give and to accept gifts, and generally to hold or distribute one's property as one desires. The removal by taxation of part of one's property, whether for one's own benefit or for the benefit of others, is one of the functions of government. But, such taxation can only be *just* if it has the autonomous consent of those who are taxed—and democratic political systems can be interpreted as functioning in part as systems for obtaining the autonomous consent of citizens for the actions of their governments, including consent for their taxation policies (pace Robert Nozick[4]).

The importance of all this for just distribution of health-care resources is that any system for meeting health-care needs, if it is to be a just system, must be responsive to the will of the electorates who provide those resources through their taxes. Through their representative governments these electors will express varying views both about the amount to be taxed overall, and about how they want those taxes used and distributed. Such views roughly represent the autonomous views of those providing either gifts to others and or finance for use in their own interests, and thus should be highly influential in the organization of the system of health care financed by those taxes.

A similar sort of analysis would require the wishes of premium payers for health insurance organizations to be highly influential in the determination of how their premiums are spent—the important difference between the two systems being a lack of concern for the health care of others in insurance schemes. This is a fatal flaw for any insurance-based system of health-care distribution that also is concerned to distribute in proportion to need. Only those who pay get any medical care at all under a "pure" insurance system—though of course governments can use insurance schemes for universal provision of health care if they so choose.

The importance of this aspect of justice to the distribution of LPTs is that, however much those of us in health care may resent the fact, ultimately electors in a democratic system quite properly decide how much they are prepared to contribute to health care and how they want that contribution to be used and distributed—and they are beginning in the United States to do exactly that in the state of Oregon. We as health professionals can properly try to influence governments to give weight to the requirements of those in greatest health-care need; we can properly bring the attention of the public to the consequences of failing to meet their needs; we can properly and usefully participate not only as citizens but as expert citizens in public debate about health-care issues; some of us might even emulate Oregon senator Dr. John Kitzhaber and run for public office. But we must also recognize and accept that we have no right simply to ignore the decisions of the people who provide us with the public funds with which we provide health care, even if we disagree with those decisions. Those decisions may well override our desire to provide what we and our patients consider would be beneficial, life-prolonging treatments.

Thus, in an admittedly indirect way, respect for the autonomy of those who provide the resources for health care is another moral factor that may justifiably override the provision of beneficial LPTs for those who need them. (And those who still doubt such a conclusion should ask themselves how extensively people should be taxed against their will to provide beneficial LPTs, not only for their own nations and nationals, but for all those dying people who need them, whoever and wherever they are.)

As we have seen in the case of PVS, a further morally relevant factor in the just distribution of scarce resources is the quantity of benefit, along with its probability, produced by a unit of resource. All interested in benefiting people must be at least partially interested in the quantity of benefit we provide by our interventions, as well as its probability, and wish to provide as much as possible, with as high a probability as possible, for a given amount of effort and resources put in. This moral consideration too—the maximization of benefit for unit of resource needed to produce it—will require incorporation into any adequate theory of justice in allocation of scarce health-care resources.

Thus, one of the criteria that, as health-care workers we shall have to get used to is the notion that all our interventions need to be assessed for their efficacy, efficiency, and effectiveness and also for their costs and opportunity costs in producing benefit for patients and potential patients. Our best allies in achieving such assessments are the health economists. Their main professional interest in life—essentially assessing costs and benefits, with their notion of costs incorporating all costs involved in the production of any benefit including the opportunity costs—is entire-

ly consistent with our own. Even if we are only interested in providing medical benefits, provided we wish to produce as much medical benefit as we can per unit of
resource used (and how could we justify otherwise if we are interested in responding
as effectively as we can to the relief of medical need?) then they can help us achieve
our objective. Health economics should, I believe, be seen as a morally vital component of just distribution of health care, and as much in the area of health care involving LPTs as in any other. But health economists, like everyone else in the business,
need to be aware of the moral complexities involved.

I believe that in distributing scarce health-care resources for LPT, no less than
for any other sort of health-care treatment, the important thing is to recognize that a
variety of moral values are in conflict and that not all of them can be honored. Lack
of benefit, or of sufficient benefit, and or of sufficient probability of benefit; excessive harm and or probability of harm; respect for the autonomy of patients, or their
proper surrogates; all may conflict with and sometimes override the desire to prolong
life. So too, I have argued, may considerations of justice. Within any adequate theory of distributive justice for inadequate health-care resources, several potentially
competing moral concerns must be recognized—including provision of care in relation to extent of need, respect for the autonomy of those providing the resources to
meet that need, and a desire to maximize benefit per unit of resource used to obtain
it.

But even if all these moral concerns are acknowledged in a system for distributing inadequate life-prolonging treatments, I am under no illusion that the outcomes
will be satisfactory to all. Where moral claims are in conflict they can't all be satisfied, and where resources are scarce not all claims on them can be met, no matter how
just one's system is for adjudicating between them.

Calabresi and Bobbit vividly illustrate the moral problems of distributive justice in health care. They argue that the way societies attempt to reconcile competing
moral values in which not all can be met and in which failing to meet them all leads
to tragic choices is by mixing approaches, changing priorities, over time, so that
endangered values are reaffirmed even at the risk of endangering others—and when
these others are once again endangered societies change back again once more to
reaffirm the newly endangered value.[5]

Their metaphor is of a juggler with too many balls all of different and beautiful
colors and all of which he wants to keep in the air. He can't, so he drops one or two
for a while, and then picks them up, dropping others, and so on, endlessly failing to
keep all the colors up at once but over time juggling with them all. That seems a very
appropriate metaphor. The important thing is to recognize the variety of moral values
we want to keep up in the air when distributing scarce, lifesaving, medical resources,
the number and variety of moral balls we want—ought—to be juggling with. Then,
knowing that we will fail, we should try to keep them all up in the air for as much
time as we can. When we drop one, above all let us not deceive ourselves into believing it no longer exists, or content ourselves with keeping fewer balls in the air for
more of the time—for all the moral balls of justice have beautiful colors.

NOTES

1. Philippa Foot, "The Problem of Abortion and the Doctrine of Double Effect," *Oxford Review* 5; 1967: 5–15. (Widely reprinted.)
2. James Rachels, "Active and Passive Euthanasia," *New England Journal of Medicine* 292; 1975: 78–80. (Widely reprinted.)
3. David Wiggins and S. Derman, "Needs, Need, Needing," *Journal of Medical Ethics* 13; 1987: 62–68.
4. Robert Nozick, *Anarchy State and Utopia*. Oxford: Blackwell, 1974. On page 169 Nozik claims that taxation, even in a democracy, over and above what is needed to maintain the "minimal state" necessary to protect life and holdings, is "on a par with forced labour."
5. Guido Calabresi and Philip Bobbitt, *Tragic Choices*. New York: Norton, 1978.

On Permitting Death in Order to Conserve Resources

NORMAN DANIELS

Tufts University, Medford, Massachusetts

In this paper I will respond to Raanan Gillon's "Intending or Permitting Death in Order to Conserve Resources" and will sketch a largely deontological framework for thinking about permitting death for economic reasons.

There is much in Gillon's paper that I agree with, and some of my comments develop points that he makes. I largely agree with Gillon that we often may and many times must allow people to die because considerations of justice require that we use our limited resources to save some lives and not others. I am less confident that I understand, let alone agree with, what Gillon is claiming about the distinction between intending death and allowing it and the weight that should be put on it in determining what we may or ought to do.

Gillon's central claims include these: (1) Intentionally killing (innocent) people is generally proscribed by a strict duty. (2) In contrast, often we may and sometimes we ought to allow people to die (even when their deaths are foreseen and avoidable). (3) Our duty to save others is "complex" (compared to our duty not to kill) and must take into account their informed preferences, what we can effectively do, the costs to us of saving them, the relative needs of those competing for our assistance, the preferences of communities, and the rights of providers. Does Gillon think that the killing/letting die (or killing/permitting) distinction can be drawn in such a way that it maps exactly onto the distinction between proscribed and permitted (or required) deaths? I am assuming that this distinction would not be drawn by reference to intentions but rather by reference to causal sequences and appropriate counterfactual claims—and I think Gillon has this in mind as well, since he leaves room for intended allowings. He seems, for example, to leave the door open to permitting some intentional killings, such as active voluntary euthanasia (p. 205).

I am not sure that the killing/letting die distinction is either (1) clear enough to decide whether it can be mapped in this way, or (2) has the moral force the mapping implies. That is, it is not clear that this distinction provides the right- or wrong-making characteristic that can sustain such a basic difference as proscribed and permitted cases of foreseeable, avoidable deaths.

Gillon is more concerned with the intending/foreseeing distinction than the killing/letting die distinction. He claims that whether someone intends the death of another is an "empirical" matter; doing something that foreseeably leads to death is not logically sufficient for the death to be intended. For the death to be intended, a special mental event with a special content must be present—a specific intention (aim or objective) of the agent. We can find out if it is present either from the agent's description of what one intends (aims at) or by inferring from one's behavior what the intention (objective) must be (presumably an inference to the best explanation). Gillon appeals here to standard paradigmatic cases such as sending poison to villages in Africa and failing to increase one's donation to Oxfam. He asserts (too optimistically, I believe) that if paradigmatic cases can be made out, then the distinction is clear enough to use in the fashion required here.

Putting these points together, Gillon suggests that the intending/foreseeing and killing/allowing distinctions cut across each other; that is, sometimes we can both intend someone's death and allow it. Allowings can involve either intended deaths or not-intended deaths. Presumably, the man in James Rachels's example who intends to allow his 6-year-old cousin in a tub to drown from a fall (rather than drowning him) is an instance of someone who intends a death through an instance of allowing death. On the other hand, Gillon argues, as Bonnie Steinbock earlier did,[1] that a physician who prefers to treat a patient but who acquiesces to the patient's desire to terminate treatment does not thereby intend the patient's death.

The case of the cousin combined with that of the acquiescing physician might lead us to think that Gillon wants the intending/foreseeing distinction to map onto the distinction between proscribed deaths and deaths that are permitted or even required. Indeed, Gillon does claim, that it is generally desirable to maintain as a norm in medicine a restriction (albeit prima facie) against intending death. The escape clause here may imply that Gillon is uneasy about such a mapping. He should be; despite the paradigmatic cases, the distinction is (1) not clear enough to decide whether we can map it in this way, and (2) lacks the moral force the mapping requires. That is, the same problems apply here that apply in the case of the killing/letting die distinction.

The general point is brought out by a variant on the classic case of the fat spelunker blocking the escape route from the cave. Suppose we could snake a tube around to his mouth and give him water (we have plenty). We decide, however, to allow him to die of thirst. Once he is dead we can cut his body out of the way and escape. Our "aim" is to escape, not to kill him; indeed, we do nothing to him. We even hope that he miraculously deflates and wiggles out, but we allow him to die. Consider now someone who believes we operate under a strict (side-constrained) prohibition against killing an innocent person, even to save our own lives. Does the fact that we are letting the fat spelunker die of thirst really makes the example more acceptable than if we dynamite him? Does the fact that we only intend to save each other, and no one intends his death, make a relevant and decisive difference? Neither distinction should appease the advocate of a side-constrained right to life with correlative duties not to kill.

The same points can be brought out by medical cases. Consider the PVS patient occupying a bed in an ICU. If we bump the PVS patient from the unit, knowing he or she will then die more quickly, we can save the next two trauma patients (one is in the emergency room). It seems implausible that what matters here is that we do not "intend" the PVS patient's death, because we only intend to save the trauma patient. If there is any justification for giving priority to the trauma patients it must be because of (1) the consequences of doing so, or (2) their stronger moral claim on those resources, which may in turn have something to do with the consequences of giving people in their situation rather than PVS patients (or other patients we cannot save) ICU beds. For example, suppose we could agree that putting the trauma patients in the ICU takes priority on grounds of distributive justice. It then seems irrelevant whether we happen, in addition, to "intend" their deaths. Suppose an attending physician who moves the PVS patient also intends his or her death—for example, for the good of the patient and the family, or to save resources for other, more important purposes. Why should the additional intention mean that the act of moving the patient shifts from the category of permissible to that of prohibited deaths? (Remember, Gillon—correctly, I believe—says that there can be intended deaths in cases of allowing death.)

Gillon gives us another case that raises a similar point. Consider a physician who administers morphine to a patient who is terminally ill and in severe pain, with the patient's informed consent. Both know the morphine will hasten death. Gillon suggests the physician need not thereby intend death. Suppose that is true. But now suppose the physician does intend also the death as well as the easing of the pain. If the extra intention is present, will that shift the act from permissible to prohibited? If not, then what role should we assign to intentions in mapping acts onto permissions and prohibitions? We cannot just rely on the killing/letting die or intending/foreseeing distinctions to do the work for us.

Now I am not sure that anything I have said here in fact will worry Gillon. He may have paid the attention he did to the distinctions largely because of his title and topic. Like me, he may think these distinctions important for some purposes and in some contexts, but, since they lack clarity and decisive, right-making power, they are not adequate to the task of giving us a map of prohibited and permissible (or required) deaths. Thinking they had that power is part of one deontological strategy for keeping consequentialist considerations at bay—out of the domain in which they enter into our consideration of when taking life is permissible. In what follows I sketch a largely deontological framework for thinking about permitting death in order to conserve resources.

First, a terminological point. I will take the expression "conserve resources" in a broad sense to include both macro and micro allocation decisions. Thus, it includes cases in which we permit death in order not to spend more than our budget allows for health care. Health care is not the only good. Within our health-care budget, we must decide what kind of services to offer. Since including some services and not others means we benefit different groups of patients, we must decide which kinds of need should be given priority. Finally, conserving resources also includes "saving" a scarce resource, like an organ for the patient who has the strongest claim on it.

A central claim in Gillon's paper is that just distributions of resources sometimes require that we permit the death of some patients. He notes that not all needs for medical services are equally important, that we should give some priority to those who are more seriously ill, that we are only required to meet needs when the services we offer provide real benefit, and that resources are limited. I believe my "fair equality of opportunity" account of justice in health care,[2] supplemented by my "prudential lifespan account" of justice between age groups, offers a framework within which his points of needs are properly accommodated.[3]

The central idea of this account is that health care has as its primary function for purposes of distributive justice the maintenance or restoration of species-typical normal functioning. Impairments of normal functioning restrict the range of opportunities open to an individual. Specifically, an individual's fair share of the *normal opportunity range* for society is the array of life plans that individual, given his or her talents and skills, would have had available had disease or disability not interfered. We can rank the urgency of medical needs, at least in a crude way, by thinking of the impact of the disease or disability on the individuals share of the normal opportunity range. By relativizing the normal opportunity range to a stage of life, and by imagining that we must allocate a lifetime budget of claims on medical resources across all stages of our lives, we can accommodate concerns about fairness between age groups.

This account gives some priority to more serious health conditions, as Gillon urges. But we have no obligation to use measures that have little chance of restoring normal functioning; we do not want to pour resources ineffectively into the worst cases. Gillon also endorses this point. But just how we should view cases that produce very modest improvements at high cost for persons who are worst off is not clear. Like Gillon, I do not want to surrender the priority that should be given those whose opportunity range is most impaired to a principle telling us to allocate resources solely according to expected medical benefit or according to expected cost or benefit; but just what weight we should give to the worst off is not clear either. The account is therefore incomplete, and some would argue incompletable.[4]

I have also argued that the account need violate no basic liberties of providers (also a concern of Gillon). Just what restrictions on the autonomy of providers are necessary, however, will depend on many facts about the design of the health-care system, the scarcity of resources, and other facts about the society.[5] Another important issue concerning providers is the *strain of commitment* they feel in any system that imposes restrictions on the degree to which they may pursue the interests of their patients. To the extent that we want physicians to think of themselves as agents pursuing the best interests of their patients, we invite a strain of commitment when we impose further constraints on what services they can provide their patients. But considerations of fairness will impose some basic limits on pursuing the best interests of the physician's own patients. This suggests that the strain of commitment will be less if providers share the view that the distribution of resources in the system is fair overall. This fact means that rationing will be less stressful for providers in some systems than others. I have suggested it is particularly problematic in the U.S. system, where there is so little assurance that "conserving" resources leads to their use for patients who need them more.[6]

One other concern of justice noted by Gillon is more problematic than his brief remarks suggest. He notes that health-care budgets are the results of a democratic process that imposes a level of resource scarcity; this has implications for how much permitting death we must accept. The recent efforts in Oregon highlight the possible conflict between "community values," expressed as preferences about which services to offer, and some theoretical view about which health-care needs are more important to meet. In the Oregon ranking of Medicaid services, for example, hip replacement is given lower priority than vasectomy, which violates my concerns about impact on opportunity range. I am reluctant to surrender the ability to criticize such priorities on grounds of distributive justice even if they are the result of a fair democratic process.[7] In other cases, they might involve instances of permitting death in order to protect less important medical needs.

The account I have sketched, like Gillon's, means that sometimes we must allow people to die for reasons of distributive justice. The account gives us a way to rank the claims that people may make on the resources of others, and it establishes some priorities about which lives we are obligated to save and which deaths we allow. What the account proposes, for example, in its prudential lifespan version, gives us a way to include information about the consequences of treatment as part of a process for ranking claims within a deontological framework. The work is done entirely without making primary use of distinctions between intending and allowing or between killing and letting die.

I want to conclude with a remark about rationing. I mention it to raise a related, general issue for theories that depend on deontological principles. We tend to think of rationing as an exceptional practice responding to unusual scarcity, for example, the wartime use of coupons for gasoline, waiting lists for bodily organs, or battlefield triage. Philosophers have generally thought these practices peripheral to the central problems of distributive justice. In fact, however, rationing is a common and central practice. We ration whenever we design institutions and policies that embody our concerns about distributive justice under ordinary resource limitations. Viewed in this light, many examples of rationing come to mind: raising eligibility standards for welfare, job training programs, or Medicaid; funding public defenders or "reasonable accommodations" for the disabled; determining the ratio of learning disability specialists to "mainstream" teachers. We must often deny benefits to some who can plausibly claim they are owed them in principle. A general account of the ethical issues involved in rationing, broadly construed, is a "missing link" in ethical theory, as I shall explain.

Our beliefs about justice commonly tell us we must distribute important goods in accord with specific principles. For instance, we might think that health care or legal defense should be distributed according to need and not ability to pay. Nevertheless, resources are inadequate to meet all the claims individuals legitimately seem to have on these goods. We simply cannot afford to educate, treat medically, or protect legally people in all the ways their needs for these goods require or the distributive principles seem to demand. There is another level of decisionmaking that concerns who gets what when all can cite the principles on their behalf. Moreover, unlike money, the goods that we can provide in each domain are not sufficiently divisible to avoid unequal or "lumpy" distributions. For example, we cannot divide an organ; if one gets it, another does not. Or, if we introduce legal aid for criminal but not civil legal defense, some groups fare better than others.

Principles of distributive justice are thus too indeterminate to tell us just what range of policies or institutions properly satisfies them. How can highly indeterminate principles guide public policy and serve as a public basis for resolving conflicting claims on resources? Rawls suggests the problem is ultimately a legislative one. Adequately informed legislators, sensitive to conflicting claims, will design institutions that embody them and give them specific content. Are there, however, basic moral constraints on rationing that should inform or constrain how we and legislators interpret and apply the distributive principles? Or is this entirely a matter of political judgment free of moral constraints?

A theory of rationing would constitute a crucial bridge between different levels of reasoning about justice. We need such an account whether we believe in a general theory of distributive justice, or only in principles of distributive justice that are specific to particular "spheres." Several general questions should shape an inquiry into an account of rationing. When is it appropriate to rely on a fair process (a lottery, a publicly accountable democratic agency) to determine a fair rationing outcome, and when does fair rationing require some *pattern of outcomes*, perhaps reflecting the content of a particular distributive principle? For example, can we rely on a democratic commission to establish relevant priorities among health-care needs, as in the Oregon rationing plan, or is that commission constrained to choose among certain patterns of outcome, for example, giving priority to more serious conditions? When is it reasonable or fair to depart from giving people equal chances at a scarce good (e.g., an organ) in order to promote better outcomes from the use of that good? When, if ever, may we *aggregate the benefits* from a rationing scheme so that meeting a major educational or medical need of relatively few people may be outweighed by providing for the less important needs of a larger number of people? This question is sometimes cast as if it turned on a choice between utilitarian and more specific distributive principles, but the lumpiness of distribution raises the issue even within a domain governed by a nonutilitarian distributive principle.

Finally, by way of warning, philosophical techniques or models for thinking about rationing problems are both diverse and controversial. Can we rely on ordinary moral intuitions or considered judgments to answer questions about rationing? For example, Dan Brock and I have appealed to prudential reasoning from behind a veil of ignorance to suggest that it is reasonable to deny equal chances to persons in order to produce better outcomes. Others have argued against abandoning equal chances. Frances Kamm, for example, invokes the fact that fully informed individuals might reasonably regret discovering that they lost their only chance at an organ because someone else can use it longer. A theory of rationing must sort through many of these disputes, which also face other work in distributive justice.[8]

I believe that work on the theory of rationing is a prolegomenon to useful work in many areas of applied ethics, including when it is permissible to intend or permit death. Those responsible for public policy often complain that philosophical discussions of justice give them too little guidance about what to do. At the same time, work in this middle level of ethical theory has implications for more general theories of justice, as is clear from the relation between fair, democratic processes and the content of distributive principles.

NOTES

1. Bonnie Steinbock, "The Intentional Termination of Life," in Bonnie Steinbock, ed. *Killing and Letting Die*. Englewood Cliffs, NJ: Prentice Hall, 1980, pp. 71–72.

2. Norman Daniels, *Just Health Care*. Cambridge, MA: Cambridge University Press, 1985.

3. See my *Am I My Parents' Keeper? An Essay On Justice Between the Young and the Old*. New York: Oxford University Press, 1988, Chapters 3 and 4.

4. See my "Rationing Family: Programmatic Considerations," *Bioethics* 7; 1992: 224–233.

5. See my *Just Health Care*, Chapter 6.

6. See my "Why Saying No in the United States Is So Hard," *New England Journal of Medicine* 314; May 22, 1986: 1381–1383.

7. See my "Rationing Family," p. 231.

8. Francis Kamm, *Morality, Mortality*, vol. 1 of *Death and Whom to Save from It*. New York: Oxford University Press, 1993.

Suggested Supplementary Readings

ADMIRAAL, PIETER V. "Active voluntary euthanasia." In Downing, A.B.; Smoker, Barbara, eds. *Voluntary Euthanasia: Experts Debate the Right to Die.* London: Peter Owen, 1986: pp. 184–192.

ADMIRAAL, PIETER V. "Euthanasia in the Netherlands: Justifiable euthanasia." *Issues in Law & Medicine.* 1988 Spring; 3(4): 361–370; *The Euthanasia Review.* 1990 Fall-Winter; 3(2): 107–118.

ALVAREZ, A. *The Savage God.* New York: Random House, 1971.

American Geriatrics Society. Public Policy Committee. "Voluntary active euthanasia." *Journal of the American Geriatrics Society.* 1991 Aug; 39(8).

American Medical Association. Council on Ethical and Judicial Affairs. "Decisions near the end of life." *Reports of the Council,* No. 33. Chicago: American Medical Association. 1991 Jul: 49–63.

American Medical Association. Council on Ethical and Judicial Affairs. "Decisions near the end of life." *Journal of the American Medical Association.* 1992 Apr 22/29; 267(16): 2229–2233.

American Medical Association. Council on Ethical and Judicial Affairs. "Decisions to forgo life-sustaining treatment for incompetent patients." *Reports of the Council,* No. 34. Chicago: American Medical Association. 1991 Jul: 65–77.

American Medical Association. Council on Ethical and Judicial Affairs. "Physician participation in capital punishment." *Journal of the American Medical Association.* 1993 July 21; 270(3): 365–368.

American Medical Association. Council on Ethical and Judicial Affairs. "Treatment decisions for seriously ill newborns." *Reports of the Council,* No. 43. Chicago: American Medical Association. 1992 Jun: 66–75.

American Neurological Association. Committee on Ethical Affairs. "Persistent vegetative state: Report." *Annals of Neurology.* 1993 Apr; 33(4): 386–390.

American Thoracic Society. "Withholding and withdrawing life-sustaining therapy." *Annals of Internal Medicine.* 1991 Sep 15; 115(6): 478–485.

AMUNDSEN, DARREL W. "The physician's obligation to prolong life: A medical duty without classical roots." *Hastings Center Report.* Aug 1987; 8(4): 23–30.

ANNAS, GEORGE J. "Killing machines." *Hastings Center Report.* 1991 Mar–Apr; 21(2): 33–35.

ANNAS, GEORGE J.; GRODIN, MICHAEL. eds. *The Nazi Doctors and the Nuremberg Code.* New York: Oxford University Press, 1992.

ANSCOMBE, G.E.M. "Action, intention, and double effect." *Proceedings of the American*

Catholic Philosophical Association. 1982; 54: 12–25.

ANONYMOUS. "It's over, Debbie." *Journal of the American Medical Association.* 1988 Jan 8; 259(2): 258–272.

ARRAS, JOHN. "The right to die on the slippery slope." *Social Theory and Practice.* Fall 1982; 8(3): 285–328.

BARRY, ROBERT; MAHER, JAMES E. "Indirectly intended life-shortening analgesia: Clarifying the principles." *Issues in Law and Medicine.* 1990 Fall; 6(2): 117–151.

BATTIN, MARGARET PABST. *Ethical Issues in Suicide.* Englewood Cliffs, NJ: Prentice Hall, 1995.

BATTIN, MARGARET PABST. "Euthanasia." In VanDeVeer, Donald; Regan, Tom, eds. *Health Care Ethics: An Introduction.* Philadelphia: Temple University Press, 1987: pp. 58–97.

BATTIN, MARGARET PABST. "Euthanasia: The way we do it, the way they do it." *Journal of Pain and Symptom Management.* 1991 Jul; 6(5): 298–305.

BATTIN, MARGARET PABST. "The least worst death," *Hastings Center Report.* 1983 Apr; 13(2): 13–16.

BATTIN, MARGARET PABST. "Seven caveats concerning the discussion of euthanasia in Holland." *Perspectives in Biology and Medicine.* 1990 Autumn; 34(1): 73–77.

BATTIN, MARGARET PABST. "Voluntary euthanasia and the risk of abuse: Can we learn anything from the Netherlands?" *Law, Medicine and Health Care.* 1992 Spring-Summer; 20(1–2): 133–143.

BATTIN, MARGARET PABST; MAYO, D.J., eds. *Suicide: The Philosophical Issues.* New York: St. Martin's Press, 1980.

BEAUCHAMP, TOM L. "A reply to Rachels on active and passive euthanasia." In Beauchamp and Perlin, eds. *Ethical Issues in Death and Dying.* Englewood Cliffs, NJ: Prentice Hall, 1976.

BEAUCHAMP, TOM L. "Suicide." In Regan, Tom, ed. *Matters of Life and Death: New Introductory Essays in Moral Philosophy.* Third Edition. New York: Random House, 1993.

BEAUCHAMP, TOM L.; CHILDRESS, JAMES F. *Principles of Biomedical Ethics.* Fourth Edition. New York: Oxford University Press, 1994.

BEAUCHAMP, TOM L.; DAVIDSON, ARNOLD. "The definition of euthanasia." *Journal of Medicine and Philosophy.* 1979 Sept; 4(3): 294–312; and reprinted in S. Gorovitz, et al, eds., *Moral Problems in Medicine.* Second Edition. Englewood Cliffs, NJ: Prentice-Hall, 1983.

BEAUCHAMP, TOM L.; VEATCH, ROBERT, eds. *Ethical Issues in Death and Dying.* Second Edition. Englewood Cliffs, NJ: Prentice-Hall, 1996.

BENDER, LESLIE. "A feminist analysis of physician-assisted dying and voluntary active euthanasia." *Tennessee Law Review.* 1992 Spring; 59(3): 519–546.

BERGER, ARTHUR S.; BERGER, JOYCE, eds. *To Die or Not to Die? Cross-Disciplinary, Cultural, and Legal Perspectives on the Right to Choose Death.* New York: Praeger, 1990.

BERMAN, MARTIN B. "Whose rite is it anyway? The search for a constitutional permit to die." *Southwestern University Law Review.* 1992; 22(1): 105–158.

BLEICH, J.D. "Life as an intrinsic rather than instrumental good: The 'spiritual' case against euthanasia." *Issues in Law and Medicine.* 1993 Fall; 9(2): 139–49.

BLENDON, ROBERT J.; SZALAY, ULRIKE S., KNOX, RICHARD A. "Should physicians aid their patients in dying? The public perspective." *Journal of the American Medical Association.* 1992 May 20; 267(19): 2658–2662.

BOLE, THOMAS J. "Why almost any cost to others to preserve the life of the irreversibly comatose constitutes an extraordinary burden." In Wildes, Kevin, et al., eds. *Birth, Suffering, and Death: Catholic Perspectives at the Edges of Life.* Boston: Kluwer Academic, 1992: pp. 171–187.

BOYLE, JOSEPH. "Toward understanding the principle of double effect." *Ethics.* 1980; 90: 527–38.

BOYLE, JOSEPH. "Who is entitled to double effect?" *Journal of Medicine and Philosophy.* 1991 Oct; 16(5): 475–494.

BRAHAMS, DIANA. "Euthanasia in the Netherlands." *Lancet.* 1990 Mar 10; 335(8689): 591–592.

BRESCIA, FRANK J. "Killing the known dying: Notes of a death watcher." *Journal of Pain and Symptom Management.* 1991 Jul; 6(5): 337–339.

BROCK, DAN W. "Death and dying." In Veatch, Robert M., ed. *Medical Ethics.* Boston: Jones and Bartlett Publishers, 1989.

BROCK, DAN W. *Life and Death: Philosophical Essays in Biomedical Ethics.* New York: Cambridge University Press, 1993.

BROCK, DAN W. "Voluntary active euthanasia." *Hastings Center Report.* 1992 Mar–Apr; 22(2): 10–22.

BRODEUR, DENNIS. "Is a decision to forgo tube feeding for another a decision to kill?" *Issues in Law and Medicine.* 1991 Spring; 6(4): 395–406.

BRODY, BARUCH A. "Special ethical issues in the management of PVS patients." *Law, Medicine and Health Care.* 1992 Spring-Summer; 20(1–2): 104–115.

BRODY, BARUCH A. *Suicide and Euthanasia: Historical and Contemporary Themes.* Boston: Kluwer Academic, 1989.

BRODY, HOWARD. "Assisted death—a compassionate response to a medical failure." *New England Journal of Medicine.* 1992 Nov 5; 327(19): 1384–1388.

BRODY, HOWARD. "Causing, intending, and assisting death." *Journal of Clinical Ethics.* 1993 Summer; 4(2): 112–117.

BRODY, HOWARD. "Legislative ban on assisted suicide: Impact on Michigan's medical practice." *Michigan Medicine.* 1993 Feb; 92(2): 32–34.

BROWNE, ALISTER. "Assisted suicide and active voluntary euthanasia." *Canadian Journal of Law and Jurisprudence.* 1989 Jan; 2(1): 35–56.

BURGESS, J.A. "The great slippery-slope argument." *Journal of Medical Ethics.* 1993 Sep; 19(3): 169–174.

CAINE, ERIC D.; CONWELL, YEATES C. "Self-determined death, the physician, and medical priorities: Is there time to talk?" *Journal of the American Medical Association.* 1993 Aug 18; 270(7): 875–76.

CALLAHAN, DANIEL. "Aid-in-dying: The social dimensions." *Commonweal.* 1991 Aug 9; 118(14, Suppl.): 476–480.

CALLAHAN, DANIEL. "Pursuing a peaceful death." *Hastings Center Report.* 1993 Jul–Aug; 23(4): 32–38.

CALLAHAN, DANIEL. *The Troubled Dream of Life: Living with Mortality*. New York: Simon and Schuster, 1993.

CALLAHAN, DANIEL. "Vital distinctions, mortal questions: Debating euthanasia and health care costs." *Commonweal*. 1988 Jul 15; 115(3): 399–402.

CALLAHAN, DANIEL. "When self-determination runs amok." *Hastings Center Report*. 1992 Mar–Apr; 22(2): 52–55.

CALLAHAN, JOAN C. "Acts, omissions, and euthanasia." *Public Affairs Quarterly*. 1988 Apr; 2(2): 21–36.

CAMERON, NIGEL M. DE S., ed. *Death without Dignity: Euthanasia in Perspective*. Edinburgh: Rutherford House Books, 1990.

CAMPBELL, S.S. "Religious ethics and active euthanasia in a pluralistic society." *Kennedy Institute of Ethics Journal*. 1992 Sept; 2(3): 253–77.

CANTOR, NORMAN L. *Advance Directives and the Pursuit of Death with Dignity*. Bloomington: Indiana University Press, 1993.

CANTOR, NORMAN L. *Legal Frontiers of Death and Dying*. Bloomington: Indiana University Press, 1987.

CAPLAN, ARTHUR L. "The doctors' trial and analogies to the Holocaust in contemporary bioethical debates." In Annas, George J., Grodin, Michael A., eds. *The Nazi Doctors and the Nuremberg Code: Human Rights in Human Experimentation*. New York: Oxford University Press, 1992: pp. 258–275.

CAPLAN, ARTHUR L.; BLANK, ROBERT H., eds. *Compassion: Government Intervention in the Treatment of Critically Ill Newborns*. Totowa, NJ: Humana Press, 1992.

CAPRON, ALEXANDER MORGAN. "Euthanasia in the Netherlands: American observations." *Hastings Center Report*. 1992 Mar–Apr; 22(2): 30–33.

CASSEL, CHRISTINE K. "Physician-assisted suicide: Are we asking the right questions?" *Second Opinion*. 1992 Oct; 18(2): 95–98.

CASSEL, CHRISTINE K.; MEIER, DIANE E. "Morals and moralism in the debate over euthanasia and assisted suicide." *New England Journal of Medicine*. 1990 Sep 13; 323(11): 750–752.

CELOCRUZ, MARIA T. "Aid-in-dying: Should we decriminalize physician-assisted suicide and physician-committed euthanasia?" *American Journal of Law and Medicine*. 1992; 18(4): 369–394.

CHILDRESS, JAMES F. "Non-heart-beating donors: Are the distinctions between direct and indirect effects and between killing and letting die relevant and helpful?" *Kennedy Institute of Ethics Journal*. 1993 Jun; 3(2): 203–216.

CHILDRESS, JAMES F. "When is it morally justifiable to discontinue medical nutrition and hydration?" In Lynn, Joanne, ed. *By No Extraordinary Means: The Choice to Forgo Life-Sustaining Food and Water*. Bloomington: Indiana University Press, 1986: pp. 67–83.

CHURCHILL, LARRY R. "Examining the ethics of active euthanasia." *Medical Ethics for the Physician*. 1990 Apr; 5(2): 17–18.

CIESIELSKI-CARLUCCI, CHRIS. "Physician attitudes and experiences with assisted suicide: Results of a small opinion survey." *Cambridge Quarterly of Healthcare Ethics*. 1993 Winter; 2(1): 39–44.

CLEELAND, C.S., et al. "Pain and its treatment in outpatients with metastatic cancer." *New England Journal of Medicine*. 1994 Mar 3; 330(9): 592–596.

COHEN, CYNTHIA, Ed.. *Casebook on the Termination of Life-Sustaining Treatment and the Care of the Dying*. Bloomington: Indiana University Press, 1988.

CONNERY, JOHN R. "The ethical standards for withholding/withdrawing nutrition and hydration." *Issues in Law and Medicine*. 1986 Sep; 2(2): 87–97.

CONWELL, YEATES; CRAINE, ERIC D. "Rational suicide and the right to die." *New England Journal of Medicine*. 1991 Oct 10; 325(15): 1100–1102.

COYLE, N. "The euthanasia and physician-assisted suicide debate: Issues for nursing." *Oncology Nursing Forum*. 1992 Aug; 19(7): 41–46.

CRANFORD, RONALD E. "The contemporary euthanasia movement and the Nazi euthanasia program. Are there meaningful similarities?" In Caplan, Arthur L., ed. *When Medicine Went Mad: Bioethics and the Holocaust*. Totowa, NJ: Humana Press, 1992: pp. 201–210, 345–346.

CUNDIFF, DAVID. *Euthanasia Is Not the Answer: A Hospice Physician's View*. Totowa, NJ: Humana Press, 1992.

DAS, SOMEN. "Affirming voluntary and active euthanasia from a theological-ethical perspective." *Euthanasia Review*. 1987 Spring-Summer; 2(1,2): 96–106.

DAVIS, NANCY. "The doctrine of double effect: Problems of interpretation." *Pacific Philosophical Quarterly*. 1984; 65: 107–123.

DELANEY, JEFFREY J. "Specific intent, substituted judgment and best interests: A nationwide analysis of an individual's right to die." *Pace Law Review*. 1991 Summer; 11(3): 565–641.

DEVETTERE, RAYMOND J. "The imprecise language of euthanasia and causing death." *Journal of Clinical Ethics*. 1990 Winter; 1(4): 268–274.

DEVETTERE, RAYMOND J. "Sedation before ventilator withdrawal: Can it be justified by double effect and called allowing a patient to die?" *Journal of Clinical Ethics*. 1991 Summer; 2(2): 122–124.

DEVINE, PHILIP E. *The Ethics of Homicide*. Ithaca, NY: Cornell University Press, 1978.

DE WACHTER, MAURICE A.M. "Euthanasia in the Netherlands." *Hastings Center Report*. 1992 Mar–Apr; 22(2): 23–30.

DICKEY, NANCY W. "Euthanasia: A concept whose time has come?" *Issues in Law and Medicine*. 1993 Spring; 8(4): 521–532.

DOERFLINGER, RICHARD. "Assisted suicide: Pro-choice or anti-life?" *Hastings Center Report*. 1989 Jan–Feb; 19(1): S10–S12.

DONNELLY, JOHN, ed. *Suicide: Right or Wrong?* Buffalo, NY: Prometheus Books, 1990.

DORFF, ELLIOT N. "A Jewish approach to end-stage medical care." *Conservative Judaism*. 1991 Spring; 43(3): 3–51.

DORFF, ELLIOT N. "Rabbi, I want to die: Euthanasia and the Jewish tradition." In *Choosing Death in America*. Philadelphia: Westminster/John Knox, forthcoming.

DRESSER, REBECCA S., AND EUGENE V. BOISAUBIN, JR. "Ethics, law, and nutritional support." *Archives of Internal Medicine* 1985 January; 145: 122–124.

DUPUIS, HELEEN M. "Actively ending the life of a severely handicapped newborn: a Dutch ethicist's perspective." [Interview]. *Cambridge Quarterly of Healthcare Ethics*. 1993 Summer;

2(3): 275–280.

Dutch Paediatric Association. "To do or not to do? Boundaries of medical action in neonatology." In *Doen of laten? Grenzen van het Medisch Handelen in de Neonatologie.* Utrecht: The Association (P.O. Box 20059, NL-3502 LB Utrecht, The Netherlands), 1992: 11–15.

DWORKIN, RONALD. "Life is sacred—that's the easy part." *New York Times Magazine.* 1993 May 13: 36, 60.

DWORKIN, RONALD. *Life's Dominion: An Argument About Abortion, Euthanasia, and Individual Freedom.* New York: Knopf, 1993.

EDWARDS, BARBARA SPRINGER; UENO, WINSTON M. "Sedation before ventilator withdrawal." [Case presentation]. *Journal of Clinical Ethics.* 1991 Summer; 2(2): 118–122.

EMANUEL, EZEKIEL J. *The Ends of Human Life: Medical Ethics in a Liberal Polity.* Cambridge, MA: Harvard University Press, 1991.

EMANUEL, EZEKIEL J.; EMANUEL, LINDA L. "Proxy decision making for incompetent patients: An ethical and empirical analysis." *Journal of the American Medical Association.* 1992 Apr 15; 267(15): 2067–2071.

EMANUEL, LINDA L.; EMANUEL, EZEKIEL J. "Decisions at the end of life: Guided by communities of patients." *Hastings Center Report.* 1993 Sep–Oct; 23(5): 6–14.

ENGELHARDT, H. TRISTRAM JR. "Fashioning an ethics for life and death in a post-modern society." *Hastings Center Report.* 1989 Jan–Feb; 19(1): S7–S9.

ENGELHARDT, H. TRISTRAM JR. "Suicide and the cancer patient." *CA-A Cancer Journal for Clinicians.* 1986 Mar–Apr; 36(2): 105–109.

ENGELHARDT, H. TRISTRAM JR., AND MALLOY, MICHELLE. "Suicide and assisting suicide: A critique of legal sanctions." *Southwestern Law Journal.* 1982 Nov; 36(4): 1003–1037.

FEINBERG, JOEL. "Voluntary euthanasia and the inalienable right to life." *Philosophy and Public Affairs* 1978 Winter; 7: 93–123.

FEINBERG, JOHN S.; FEINBERG, PAUL D. "Euthanasia." *Ethics for a Brave New World.* Wheaton, IL: Crossway Books, 1993: 99–126, 419–426.

FENIGSEN, RICHARD. "A case against Dutch euthanasia." *Hastings Center Report.* 1989 Jan–Feb; 19(1): S22–S30.

FENIGSEN, RICHARD. "Euthanasia in the Netherlands." *Issues in Law and Medicine.* 1990 Winter; 6(3): 229–245.

FENIGSEN, RICHARD. "The report of the Dutch governmental committee on euthanasia." *Issues in Law and Medicine.* 1991 Winter; 7(3): 339–344.

FOLEY, K.M. "The relationship of pain and symptom management to patient requested for physician-assisted suicide." *Journal of Pain and Symptom Management.* 1991 Jul; 6(5): 289–97.

FOOT, PHILIPPA. "Euthanasia." *Philosophy & Public Affairs.* 1977 Winter; 6(2): 85–112.

FORDHAM, HELEN; BRODY, HOWARD; TOMLINSON, TOM; MCMURRAY, RICHARD J.; FAVERMAN, FRANCES, L. "Physician-assisted suicide: There are many difficult questions with no easy answers." *Michigan Medicine.* 1992 Jun; 91(6): 20–31.

FORTE, DAVID F. "The role of the clear and convincing standard of proof in right to die cases." *Issues in Law and Medicine.* 1992 Fall; 8(2): 183–203.

FREEDMAN, BENJAMIN. "The titration of death: A new sin." [Commentary on R. Devettere, "The imprecise language of euthanasia and causing death"]. *Journal of Clinical Ethics.* 1990 Winter; 1(4): 275–277.

FYE, W.B. "Active euthanasia: An historical survey of its conceptual origins and introduction into medical thought." *Bulletin of the History of Medicine.* 1978 Winter; 52(4): 492–502.

GALLAGHER, HUGH GREGORY. *By Trust Betrayed: Patients, Physicians, and the License to Kill in the Third Reich.* New York: H. Holt, 1990.

GAYLIN, WILLARD; KASS, LEON; PELLEGRINO, EDMUND; AND SIEGLER, MARK. "Doctors must not kill." *Journal of the American Medical Association* 1988 April 8; 259: 2139–2140.

GILLON, RAANAN. "Acts and omissions, killing and letting die." *British Medical Journal.* 1986 Jan 11; 292(6513): 126–127.

GILLON, RAANAN. "The principle of double effect and medical ethics." *British Medical Journal.* 1986 Jan 18; 292(6514): 193–194.

GLICK, HENRY R. *The Right to Die: Policy Innovation and Its Consequences.* New York: Columbia University Press, 1992.

GLOVER, JONATHAN. *Causing Death and Saving Life.* Harmondsworth, England: Penguin Books, 1977.

GODLEY, ELIZABETH. "Patients' right to die becoming major issue for MDs and MPs." *Canadian Medical Association Journal.* 1992 Feb 15; 146(4): 608–610.

GOLDBERG, RICHARD T. "The 'right' to die: The case for and against voluntary passive euthanasia." *Disabilty, Handicap and Society.* 1987; 2(1): 21–39.

GOMEZ, CARLOS F. "Euthanasia: Consider the Dutch." *Commonweal.* 1991 Aug 9; 118(14, Suppl.): 469–472.

GOMEZ, CARLOS F. *Regulating Death: Euthanasia and the Case of the Netherlands.* New York: Free Press, 1991.

GORBY, JOHN D. "Viewing the draft guidelines for state court decision making in authorizing or withdrawing life-sustaining medical treatment from the perspective of related areas of law and economics: A critique." *Issues in Law and Medicine.* 1992 Spring; 7(4): 477–510.

GOSTIN, LAWRENCE O. "Drawing a line between killing and letting die: The law, and law reform, on medically assisted dying." *Journal of Law, Medicine and Ethics.* 1993 Spring; 21(1): 94–101.

GRABER, GLENN; CHASSMAN, J. "Assisted suicide is not voluntary active euthanasia, but it's awfully close." *Journal of the American Geriatrics Society.* 1993 Jan; 41(1): 88–89.

GRANT, EDWARD R.; CLEAVER, CATHLEEN A. "A line less reasonable: *Cruzan* and the looming debate over active euthanasia." *Maryland Journal of Contemporary Legal Issues.* 1991 Summer; 2(2): 99–256.

GREEN, RONALD. "Good rules have good reasons: A response to Leon Kass." In Kogan, Barry S., ed. *A Time to Be Born and a Time to Die: The Ethics of Choice.* Hawthorne, NY: Aldine De Gruyter, 1991: pp. 147–155.

GUNDERSON, MARTIN; MAYO, DAVID J. "Altruism and physician assisted death." *Journal of Medicine and Philosophy.* 1993 Jun; 18(3): 281–295.

GUNNING, K.F. "Terminal patients in Holland." *Linacre Quarterly.* 1991 Feb; 58(1): 57–62.

HADDAD, MARK E. "*Cruzan* and the demands of due process." *Issues in Law and Medicine.* 1992 Fall; 8(2): 205–228.

HAMEL, RONALD P., ed. *Active Euthanasia, Religion, and the Public Debate.* Chicago: Park Ridge Center for the Study of Health, Faith, and Ethics, 1991.

Hastings Center. *Guidelines on the Termination of Life-Sustaining Treatment and the Care of the Dying.* Briarcliff Manor, NY: The Hastings Center, 1987.

HAVARD, J.D.J. "Aiding and abetting suicides, the right to die and euthanasia." In Brahams, Diana, ed. *Medicine and the Law.* London: Royal College of Physicians of London, 1990: pp. 33–41.

HEINER, AADRI. "Choosing death." *Health Quarterly.* 1993 March.

HELLEMA, HENK. "Life termination in the Netherlands." *British Medical Journal.* 1991 Apr 27; 302(6783): 984–985.

HELME, TIM. "The Voluntary Euthanasia (Legalisation) Bill (1936) Revisited." [England]. *Journal of Medical Ethics.* 1991 March; 17(1): 25–29.

HENDIN, H.; KLERMAN, GERALD. "Physician-assisted suicide: The dangers of legalization." *American Journal of Psychiatry.* 1993 Jan; 150(1): 143–145.

HERRERA, CHRISTOPHER. "Some ways that technology and terminology distort the euthanasia issue." *Journal of Medical Humanities.* 1993 Spring; 14(1): 23–31.

HOWE, EDMUND G. "On expanding the parameters of assisted suicide, directive counseling, and overriding patients' cultural beliefs." *Journal of Clinical Ethics.* (Summer 1993) 4: 107–11.

HUMBER, JAMES M.; ALMEDER, ROBERT F.; KASTING, G.A., eds. *Physician-Assisted Death.* Totowa, NJ: Humana Press, 1993.

HUMPHRY, DEREK. *Dying with Dignity: Understanding Euthanasia.* Secaucus, NJ: Carol Publishing Group, 1992.

HUMPHRY, DEREK. *Lawful Exit: The Limits of Freedom for Help in Dying.* Junction City, OR: Norris Lane Press, 1993.

HUMPHRY, DEREK; WICKETT, ANN. *The Right to Die: Understanding Euthanasia.* New York: Harper and Row, 1986.

Institute of Medical Ethics (Great Britain). Working Party on the Ethics of Prolonging Life and Assisting Death. "Withdrawal of life-support from patients in a persistent vegetative state." *Lancet.* 1991 Jan 12; 337(8733): 96–98.

JECKER, NANCY S.; SCHNEIDERMAN, LAWRENCE J. "Medical futility: The duty not to treat." *Cambridge Quarterly of Healthcare Ethics.* 1993 Spring; 2(2): 151–159.

JOCHEMSEN, HENK. "Life-prolonging and life-terminating treatment of severely handicapped newborn babies: A discussion of the report of the Royal Dutch Society of Medicine on Life-Terminating Actions with Incompetent Patients: Part I: Severely Handicapped Newborns." *Issues in Law and Medicine.* 1992 Fall; 8(2): 167–181.

JOHNSON, DAVID H. "Helga Wanglie revisited: medical futility and the limits of autonomy." *Cambridge Quarterly of Healthcare Ethics.* 1993 Spring; 2(2): 161–170.

Journal of Medicine and Philosophy. 1992; 17. Special issue on the Cruzan Case.

KADISH, SANFORD H. "Authorizing Death." In Coleman, Jules; Buchanan, Allen, eds. *Harm's Way.* Cambridge: Cambridge University Press, 1993.

KADISH, SANFORD H. "Letting patients die: Legal and moral reflections." *California Law Review*. 1992 Jul; 80(4): 857–888.

KAMISAR, YALE. "Are laws against assisted suicide unconstitutional?" *Hastings Center Report*. 1993 May–June; 23(3): 32–41.

KAMISAR, YALE. "When is there a constitutional right to die? When is there *no* constitutional right to live?" *Georgia Law Review*. 1991 Summer; 25(5): 1203–1242.

KAMISAR, YALE; ALEXANDER, LEO. *The Slide Toward "Mercy Killing."* [Booklet of two 1971 papers]. Oak Park, IL: National Commission on Human Life, Reproduction and Rhythm, 1987.

KASS, LEON R. "Death on the California ballot: Giving healers the sanction to kill." *American Enterprise*. 1992 Sep–Oct; 3(5): 44–51.

KASS, LEON R. "Death with dignity and the sanctity of life." In Kogan, Barry S., ed. *A Time to Be Born and a Time to Die: The Ethics of Choice*. Hawthorne, NY: Aldine De Gruyter, 1991: pp. 117–145.

KASS, LEON R. "Is there a right to die?" *Hastings Center Report*. 1993 Jan–Feb; 23(1): 34–43.

KASS, LEON R. "Neither for love nor money: Why doctors must not kill." *Public Interest*. 1989 Winter; (94): 25–46.

KASS, LEON R. "Suicide made easy: The evil of rational humaneness." *Commentary*. 1991 Dec; 92(6): 19–24.

KEOWN, JOHN. "On regulating death." [Book review essay]. *Hastings Center Report*. 1992 Mar–Apr; 22(2): 39–42.

KEVORKIAN, JACK. "The last fearsome taboo: Medical aspects of planned death." *Medicine and Law*. 1988 Jan; 7(1): 1–14.

KEVORKIAN, JACK. *Prescription Medicide: The Goodness of Planned Death*. Buffalo, NY: Prometheus Books, 1991.

KIMSMA, G.K. "Infanticide and the vulnerable newborn: The Dutch debate." *Cambridge Quarterly of Healthcare Ethics*. 1993 Summer; 2(3).

KIMSMA, G.K.; VAN LEEUWEN, E.; THOMASMA, DAVID C.; PUCA, ANTONIO. "Dutch euthanasia: Background, practice, and present justifications." *Cambridge Quarterly of Healthcare Ethics*. 1993 Winter; 2(1): 19–35.

KING, PATRICIA. "The authority of families to make medical decisions for incompetent patients after the *Cruzan* decision." *Law, Medicine and Health Care*. 1991 Spring-Summer; 19(1–2): 76–79.

KLUGE, EIKE-HENNER. "Doctors, death and Sue Rodriguez." *Canadian Medical Association Journal*. 1993 Mar; 148(6): 1015–1017.

KLUGE, EIKE-HENNER. "Euthanasia and related taboos." *Canadian Medical Association Journal*. 1991 Feb 1; 144(3): 359–360.

KOHL, MARVIN. "Euthanasia." In Becker, Lawrence C.; Becker, Charlotte B., eds. *Encyclopedia of Ethics*. Volume I. New York: Garland, 1992: pp. 335–339.

KOOP, C. EVERETT. "The challenge of definition." *Hastings Center Report*. 1989 Jan–Feb; 19(1): S2–S3.

KOOP, C. EVERETT. "Ethical and surgical considerations in the care of the newborn with congenital abnormalities." In Horan, D.J.; Delahoyde, M., eds. *Infanticide and the Handicapped*

Newborn. Provo, UT: Brigham Young University Press, 1982.

KOOP, C. EVERETT; GRANT, EDWARD R. "The 'small beginnings' of euthanasia: Examining the erosion in legal prohibitions against mercy-killing." *Notre Dame Journal of Law, Ethics and Public Policy.* 1986 Spring; 2(3): 585–634.

KOTTOW, M.H. "Euthanasia after the holocaust—is it possible?: A report from the Federal Republic of Germany." *Bioethics.* 1988 Jan; 2(1): 58–59.

KOWALSKI, SUSAN. "Assisted suicide: Where do nurses draw the line?" *Nursing and Health Care.* 1993 Feb; 14(2): 70–76.

KUHSE, HELGA. "Euthanasia." In Singer, Peter, ed. *A Companion to Ethics.* Cambridge, MA: Blackwell Reference, 1991: pp. 294–302.

KUHSE, HELGA. *The Sanctity-of-Life Doctrine in Medicine: A Critique.* Oxford: Clarendon Press, 1987.

KUHSE, HELGA; SINGER, PETER. "Euthanasia: A survey of nurses' attitudes and practices." *Australian Nurses' Journal.* 1992 Mar; 21(8): 21–22.

KUHSE, HELGA; SINGER, PETER. "Prolonging dying is the same as prolonging living—one more response to Long." *Journal of Medical Ethics.* 1991 Dec; 17(4): 205–206.

KURTZ, PAUL. "The case for euthanasia: A humanistic perspective." *Issues in Law and Medicine.* 1992 Winter; 8(3): 309–316.

LACHS, JOHN. "Active euthanasia." *Journal of Clinical Ethics.* 1990 Summer; 1(2): 113–115.

LATIMER, ELIZABETH J. "Ethical decision-making in the care of the dying and its applications to clinical practice." *Journal of Pain and Symptom Management.* 1991 Jul; 6(5): 329–336.

Law, Medicine and Health Care. 1989 Winter; 17(4). Special issue on the "Linares Case."

Law Reform Commission of Canada. *Euthanasia, Aiding Suicide and Cessation of Treatment.* Ottawa, Canada, 1982.

LECSO, PHILLIP A. "Euthanasia: A Buddhist perspective." *Journal of Religion and Health.* 1986 Spring; 25(1): 51–57.

LEENEN, H.J.J. "Euthanasia in the Netherlands." In Byrne, Peter, ed. *Medicine, Medical Ethics and the Value of Life.* New York: Wiley, 1990: pp. 1–14.

LEENEN, H.J.J.; CIESIELSKI-CARLUCCI, CHRIS. "*Force majeure* (legal necessity): Justification for active termination of life in the case of severely handicapped newborns after forgoing treatment." *Cambridge Quarterly of Healthcare Ethics.* 1993 Summer; 2(3): 271–274.

LIFTON, ROBERT J. *The Nazi Doctors: Medical Killing and the Psychology of Genocide.* New York: Basic Books, 1986.

LOEWY, ERICH H. "Healing and killing, harming and not harming: Physician participation in euthanasia and capital punishment." *Journal of Clinical Ethics.* 1992 Spring; 3(1): 29–34.

LONG, THOMAS A. "Two philosophers in search of a contradiction: A response to Singer and Kuhse." *Journal of Medical Ethics.* 1990 Jun; 16(2): 95–96.

LOUISELL, DAVID. "Euthanasia and biathanasia: On dying and killing." *Linacre Quarterly.* 1973 Nov; 40(4): 234–58.

LOWY, FREDERICK; SAWYER, DOUGLAS M.; WILLIAMS, JOHN R. "Canadian physicians and euthanasia: 4. Lessons from experience." *Canadian Medical Association Journal.* 1993 Jun 1; 148(11): 1895–1899.

LYNN, JOANNE. "The health care professional's role when active euthanasia is sought." *Journal of Palliative Care.* 1988 May; 4(1–2): 100–102.

LYNN, JOANNE, ed. *By No Extraordinary Means: The Choice to Forgo Life-Sustaining Food and Water.* Bloomington: Indiana University Press, 1986.

MACKLIN, RUTH. "Which way down the slippery slope? Nazi medical killing and euthanasia today." In Caplan, Arthur L., ed. *When Medicine Went Mad: Bioethics and the Holocaust.* Totowa, NJ: Humana Press, 1992: pp. 173–200, 343–345.

MAHER, JAMES C.; TENO, JOAN M.; LYNN, JOANNE; HOWELL, TIMOTHY; WATTS, DAVID T. "VAE versus assisted suicide." [Letters and response]. *Journal of the American Geriatrics Society.* 1993 May; 41(5): 583–585.

MANGAN, JOSEPH T., S.J. "An historical analysis of the principle of double effect." *Theological Studies.* 1949; 10: 41–61.

MARKER, RITA L.; STANTON, JOSEPH R.; RECZNIK, MARK E.; FOURNIER, KEITH A. "Euthanasia: A historical overview." *Maryland Journal of Contemporary Legal Issues.* 1991 Summer; 2(2): 257–298.

MARQUIS, DONALD B. "Four versions of double effect." *The Journal of Medicine and Philosophy.* 1991 Oct; 16(5): 515–544.

MATTHEWS, MARTHA ALYS. "Suicidal competence and the patient's right to refuse lifesaving treatment." *California Law Review.* 1987 Mar; 75(2): 707–758.

MAYNARD, FREDERICK M. "Responding to requests for ventilator removal from patients with quadriplegia." *Western Journal of Medicine.* 1991 May; 154(5): 617–619.

MAYO, DAVID J. "The concept of rational suicide." *The Journal of Medicine and Philosophy.* 1986 May; 11(2): 143–155.

MAYO, DAVID J.; GUNDERSON, MARTIN. "Physician assisted death and hard choices." *Journal of Medicine and Philosophy.* 1993 Jun; 18(3): 329–341.

MCCORMICK, RICHARD A. "Physician-assisted suicide: Flight from compassion." *Christian Century.* 1991 Dec 4; 108(35): 1132–1134.

MCCORMICK, RICHARD A.; AND HOOYMAN, NANCY. "Support for physician-assisted suicide must be quelled." *Health Progress* 1992 July–August; 73:51–52.

MCGOUGH, PETER M. "Washington State Initiative 119: The first public vote on legalizing physician-assisted death." *Cambridge Quarterly of Healthcare Ethics.* 1993 Winter; 2(1): 63–67.

MCMAHAN, JEFF. "Killing, letting die, and withdrawing aid." *Ethics.* 1993 Jan; 103(2): 250–279.

MCMILLAN, RICHARD C.; ENGELHARDT, H. TRISTRAM, JR.; SPICKER, STUART F., eds. *Euthanasia and the Newborn: Conflicts Regarding Saving Lives.* Dordrecht, The Netherlands: D. Reidel, 1987.

MEIER, DIANE E. "Physician-assisted dying: Theory and reality." *Journal of Clinical Ethics.* 1992 Spring; 3(1): 35–37.

MEILAENDER, GILBERT. "The distinction between killing and allowing to die." *Theological Studies.* 1976 Sept; 37(3): 467–70.

MEISEL, ALAN. "The legal consensus about forgoing life-sustaining treatment: Its status and its prospects." *Kennedy Institute of Ethics Journal.* 1992 Dec; 2(4): 309–345.

MEISEL, ALAN. *The Right to Die.* New York: John Wiley and Sons, 1989, with Cumulative Supplements published in 1992 and 1993. New York: Wiley.

MILLER, FRANKLIN G.; FLETCHER, JOHN C. "The case for legalized euthanasia." *Perspectives in Biology and Medicine.* 1993 Winter; 36(2): 159–176.

MILLER, FRANKLIN G.; QUILL, TIMOTHY; BRODY, HOWARD; FLETCHER, JOHN C.; GOSTIN, LAWRENCE O.; MEIER, DIANE E. "Regulating physician-assisted death." *The New England Journal of Medicine.* 1994; 331: 119–123.

MISBIN, ROBERT I. "Physicians' aid in dying." *New England Journal of Medicine.* 1991 Oct 31; 325(18): 1307–1311.

MISBIN, ROBERT I., ed. *Euthanasia: The Good of the Patient, the Good of Society.* Frederick, MD: University Publishing Group, 1992: pp. 43–51.

MITCHELL, KENNETH R.; KERRIDGE, IAN H.; LOVAT, TERENCE J. "Medical futility, treatment withdrawal and the persistent vegetative state." *Journal of Medical Ethics.* 1993 Jun; 19(2): 71–76.

MOMEYER, RICHARD W. *Confronting Death.* Bloomington: Indiana University Press, 1988.

National Center for the State Courts [and] Coordinating Council on Life-Sustaining Medical Treatment Decision Making by the Courts (Thomas Hafemeister, Project Director). *Guidelines for State Court Decision Making in Authorizing or Withholding Life-Sustaining Medical Treatment.* Williamsburg, VA: National Center for State Courts, 1991.

Netherlands. Central Bureau of Statistics. Department of Health Statistics. *The End of Life in Medical Practice: Findings of a Survey Sampled from Deaths Occurring.* July–November 1990. The Hague: SDU Publishers, 1992.

Netherlands. Ministry of Welfare, Health and Cultural Affairs. *Medical Practice with Regard to Euthanasia and Related Medical Decisions in the Netherlands: Results of an Inquiry and the Government View.* [Brochure]. Issued by the Ministerie van WVC, Postbus 5406, 2280 H.K. Rijswijk, Netherlands, 1992.

New York State Task Force on Life and the Law. *Life-Sustaining Treatment: Making Decisions and Appointing a Health Care Agent.* New York: New York State Task Force, 1987.

New York State Task Force on Life and the Law. *When Death is Sought: Assisted Suicide and Euthanasia in the Medical Context.* New York: New York State Task Force, 1994.

New York State Task Force on Life and the Law. *When Others Must Choose: Deciding for Patients Without Capacity.* New York: New York State Task Force, 1992.

NEWMAN, MARVIN E. "Active euthanasia in the Netherlands." In Berger, Arthur S.; Berger, Joyce, eds. *To Die or Not to Die?: Cross-Disciplinary, Cultural, and Legal Perspectives on the Right to Choose Death.* New York: Praeger, 1990: pp. 117–128.

NICHOLSON, RICHARD H. "A quick and painless death." *Hastings Center Report.* 1993 May–Jun; 23(3).

NOWELL-SMITH, PATRICK. "Euthanasia and the doctors—a rejection of the BMA's report." *Journal of Medical Ethics.* 1989 Sep; 15(3): 124–128.

ORENTLICHER, DAVID. "Physician-assisted dying: The conflict with fundamental principles of American law." In Blank, Robert H.; Bonnicksen, Andrea L., eds. *Medicine Unbound.* New York: Columbia University Press, 1994.

PARIS, JOHN J.; MURPHY, JAMES J. "Medical futility and physician refusal of requested treatment." *Clinical Ethics Report.* 1993; 7(2): 1–8.

PARKER, MALCOLM. "Moral intuition, good deaths and ordinary medical practitioners." *Journal of Medical Ethics.* 1990 Mar; 16(1): 28–34.

PEARLMAN, ROBERT A.; UHLMANN, RICHARD F.; JECKER, NANCY S. "Spousal understanding of patient quality of life: Implications for surrogate decisions." *Journal of Clinical Ethics.* 1992 Summer; 3(2): 114–121.

PELLEGRINO, EDMUND D. "Compassion needs reason too." *Journal of the American Medical Association.* 1993 Aug 18; 270(7): 874–875.

PELLEGRINO, EDMUND D. "Doctors must not kill." *The Journal of Clinical Ethics.* 1992 Summer; 3(2): 95–102.

PELLEGRINO, EDMUND D. "Ethics." *Journal of the American Medical Association.* 1991 Jun 19; 265(23): 3118–3119.

PENCE, GREGORY. *Classic Cases in Medical Ethics.* Second Edition. New York: McGraw-Hill Publishing Co., 1995.

Pennsylvania. Commonwealth Court. "Department of Public Welfare v. Kallinger." *Atlantic Reporter,* 2d Series. 1990 Aug 14 (date of decision); 580: 887–893.

PERSELS, JIM. "Forcing the issue of physician-assisted suicide: Impact of the Kevorkian case on the euthanasia debate." *Journal of Legal Medicine.* 1993 Mar; 14(1): 93–124.

PIJNENBORG, LOES; VAN DER MAAS, PAUL J.; VAN DELDEN, JOHANNES J.M.; LOOMAN, CASPAR W.N. "Life terminating acts without explicit request of patient." *Lancet.* 1993 May 8; 341(8854): 1196–1199.

POLLARD, BRIAN J. "Medical aspects of euthanasia." *Medical Journal of Australia.* 1991 May 6; 154(9): 613–616.

President's Commission for the Study of Ethical Problems in Medicine and Biomedical and Behavioral Research. *Deciding to Forego Life-Sustaining Treatment.* Washington: U.S. Government Printing Office, 1983.

QIU, REN-ZONG. "Chinese medical ethics and euthanasia." *Cambridge Quarterly of Healthcare Ethics.* 1993 Winter; 2(1): 69–76.

QUILL, TIMOTHY E. "The ambiguity of clinical intentions." *New England Journal of Medicine.* 1993 Sep 30; 329(14): 1039–1040.

QUILL, TIMOTHY E. "Death and dignity: A case of individualized decision making." *New England Journal of Medicine.* 1991 Mar 7; 324(10): 691–694.

QUILL, TIMOTHY E. *Death and Dignity: Making Choices and Taking Charge.* New York: W.W. Norton, 1993.

QUILL, TIMOTHY E. "Doctor, I want to die. Will you help me?" *Journal of the American Medical Association.* 1993 Aug 18; 270(7): 870–873.

QUILL, TIMOTHY E. "Incurable suffering." *Hastings Center Report.* 1994 Mar-Apr; 24(2): 45.

QUILL, TIMOTHY E.; CASSEL, CHRISTINE K.; MEIER, DIANE E. "Care of the hopelessly ill: Proposed clinical criteria for physician-assisted suicide." *New England Journal of Medicine.* 1992 Nov 5; 327(19): 1380–1384.

QUINN, WARREN S. "Actions, intentions, and consequences: The doctrine of double effect."

Philosophy and Public Affairs. 1989 Fall; 18(4): 334–351.

QUINN, WARREN S. "Reply to Boyle's 'Who is entitled to double-effect?'" *The Journal of Medicine and Philosophy.* 1991 Oct; 16(5): 511–514.

RACHELS, JAMES. "Active and passive euthanasia." *New England Journal of Medicine.* 1975 Jan 9; 292(2): 78–80.

RACHELS, JAMES. *The End of Life: Euthanasia and Morality.* Oxford: Oxford University Press, 1986.

RAMSEY, PAUL. *Ethics at the Edges of Life.* New Haven: Yale University Press, 1978.

RAMSEY, PAUL. *The Patient as Person.* New Haven: Yale University Press, 1970.

REICHENBACH, BRUCE R. "Euthanasia and the active-passive distinction." *Bioethics.* 1987 Jan; 1(1): 51–73.

REISNER, AVRAM ISRAEL. "A halakhic ethic of care for the terminally ill." *Conservative Judaism.* 1991 Spring; 43(3): 52–89.

RIGTER, H. "Euthanasia and the Netherlands: Distinguishing facts from fiction." *Hastings Center Report.* 1989 Jan–Feb; 19(1): S31–S32.

ROBERTSON, JOHN A. "Assessing quality of life: A response to Professor Kamisar." *Georgia Law Review.* 1991 Summer; 25(5): 1243–1252.

ROBERTSON, JOHN A. "Cruzan and the constitutional status of nontreatment decisions for incompetent patients." *Georgia Law Review.* 1991 Summer; 25(5): 1139–1202.

ROBINSON, JANE. "Euthanasia: The collision of theory and practice." *Law, Medicine and Health Care.* 1990 Spring-Summer; 18(1–2): 105–107.

ROSENBLUM, VICTOR G.; FORSYTHE, CLARKE D. "The right to assisted suicide: Protection of autonomy or an open door to social killing?" *Issues in Law and Medicine.* 1990 Summer; 6(1): 3–31.

ROUSE, FENELLA. "The role of state legislatures after Cruzan: What can—and should—state legislatures do?" *Law, Medicine and Health Care.* 1991 Spring-Summer; 19(1–2): 83–90.

Royal Dutch Medical Association. "Report of the Royal Dutch Society of Medicine on Life-Terminating Actions with Incompetent Patients, Part I: Severely Handicapped Newborns." [Translated summary]. *Issues in Law and Medicine.* 1991 Winter; 7(3): 365–367.

Sacred Congregation for the Doctrine of the Faith. "Declaration on euthanasia" (May 5, 1980). *Vatican Council II,* 1982; vol. 2: 510–516.

SAWYER, DOUGLAS M.; WILLIAMS, JOHN R.; LOWY, FREDERICK. "Canadian physicians and euthanasia: 2. Definitions and distinctions." *Canadian Medical Association Journal.* 1993 May 1; 148(9): 1463–1466.

SAWYER, DOUGLAS M.; WILLIAMS, JOHN R.; LOWY, FREDERICK. "Canadian physicians and euthanasia: 5. Policy options." *Canadian Medical Association Journal.* 1993 Jun 15; 148(12): 2129–2133.

SCHAFFNER, KENNETH F. "Recognizing the tragic choice: Food, water, and the right to assisted suicide." *Critical Care Medicine.* 1988 October; 16(10): 1063–68.

SCHNEIDERMAN, LAWRENCE J. "Is it morally justifiable *not* to sedate this patient before ventilator withdrawal?" *Journal of Clinical Ethics.* 1991 Summer; 2(2): 129–130.

SCHOTSMANS, PAUL. "When the dying person looks me in the face: An ethics of responsibility for dealing with the problem of the patient in a persistent vegetative state." In Wildes, Kevin Wm.; Abel, Francesc; Harvey, John C., eds. *Birth, Suffering, and Death: Catholic Perspectives at the Edges of Life*. Boston: Kluwer Academic, 1992: pp. 127–143.

SCOFIELD, G. R. "Privacy (or liberty) and assisted suicide." *Journal of Pain and Symptom Management*. 1991 July; 6(5): 280–288.

SHERLOCK, RICHARD. *Preserving Life: Public Policy and the Life Not Worth Living*. Chicago: Loyola University Press, 1987.

SHERMAN, JEFFREY C. "Mercy killing and the right to inherit." *University of Cincinnati Law Review*. 1993 Winter; 61(3): 803–876.

SHNEIDMAN, EDWIN S. "Rational suicide and psychiatric disorders." *New England Journal of Medicine*. 1992 Mar 26; 326(13): 889–891.

SHUMAN, CAROLYN R.; FOURNET, GLENN P.; ZELHART, PAUL F.; ROLAND, BILLY C.; ESTES, ROBERT E. "Attitudes of registered nurses toward euthanasia." *Death Studies*. 1992 Jan–Feb; 16(1): 1–15.

SIEGLER, MARK; WEISBARD, ALAN J. "Against the emerging stream: Should fluids and nutritional support be discontinued?" *Archives of Internal Medicine*. 1985 Jan; 145(1): 129–31.

SINGER, PETER A.; SIEGLER, MARK. "Euthanasia—a critique." *New England Journal of Medicine*. 1990 Jun 28; 322(26): 1881–1883.

SKENE, LOANE. "Legal issues in treating critically ill newborn infants." *Cambridge Quarterly of Healthcare Ethics*. 1993 Summer; 2(3): 295–308.

SLOMKA, JACQUELYN. "The negotiation of death: Clinical decision making at the end of life." *Social Science and Medicine*. 1992 Aug; 35(3): 251–259.

SMITH, ALEXANDER MCCALL. "Ending life." In Dyer, Clare, ed. *Doctors, Patients and the Law*. Oxford, Boston: Blackwell Scientific, 1992: pp. 106–119.

SMITH, CHERYL K. "What about legalized assisted suicide?" *Issues in Law and Medicine*. 1993 Spring; 8(4): 503–519.

SMITH, GEORGE P. "Recognizing personhood and the right to die with dignity." *Journal of Palliative Care*. 1990 Summer; 6(2): 24–32.

SMITH, R.S. "Ethical issues surrounding cancer pain." In Chapman, C.R.; Foley, K.M., eds. *Current and Emerging Issues in Cancer Pain: Research and Practice*. New York: Raven Press, 1993: pp. 385–392.

SMITH, WILLIAM B. "Is a decision to forgo tube feeding for another a decision to kill?" *Issues in Law and Medicine*. 1991 Spring; 6(4): 385–394.

Society for the Right to Die. *The Physician and the Hopelessly Ill Patient*. New York: Society for the Right to Die, 1985: 39–80; and *1988 Supplement:* 17–34.

Society for the Right to Die. *Refusal of Treatment Legislation, 1991: A State by State Compilation of Enacted and Model Statutes*. [Looseleaf binder]. New York: The Society, 1991 Mar. 1 v.

SOLOMON, MILDRED Z.; O'DONNELL, LYDIA; JENNINGS, BRUCE; GUILFOY, VIVIAN; WOLF, SUSAN M.; NOLAN, KATHLEEN; JACKSON, REBECCA; KOCH-WESER, DIETER; DONNELLEY, STRACHAN. "Decisions near the end of life: Professional views on life-sustaining treatments." *American Journal of Public Health*. 1993 Jan; 83(1): 14–23.

SOMERVILLE, MARGARET A. "The song of death: The lyrics of euthanasia." *Journal of Contemporary Health Law and Policy.* 1993 Spring/Nov Suppl; 9: 1–76.

SPREEUWENBERG, COR. "The story of Laurens." *Cambridge Quarterly of Healthcare Ethics.* 1993 Summer; 2(3): 261–263.

SPRUNG, CHARLES L. "Changing attitudes and practices in forgoing life-sustaining treatments." *Journal of the American Medical Association.* 1990 Apr 25; 263(16): 2211–2215.

STEINBOCK, BONNIE, ed. *Killing and Letting Die.* Englewood Cliffs: Prentice Hall, 1980.

SUHR, JOHN NICHOLAS. "Cruzan v. Director, Missouri Department of Health: A clear and convincing call for comprehensive legislation to protect incompetent patients' rights." *American University Law Review.* 1991 Summer; 40(4): 1477–1519.

TEN HAVE, HENK A.M.J.; WELIE, JOS V.M. "Euthanasia: Normal medical practice?" *Hastings Center Report.* 1992 Mar–Apr; 22(2): 34–38.

TENO, JOAN; LYNN, JOANNE. "Voluntary active euthanasia: The individual case and public policy." *Journal of the American Geriatrics Society.* 1991 Aug; 39(8): 827–830.

THOMASMA, DAVID C. "The range of euthanasia." *American College of Surgeons Bulletin.* 1988 Aug; 73(8): 4–13.

THOMASMA, DAVID C.; GRABER, GLENN C. *Euthanasia: Toward an Ethical Social Policy.* New York: Continuum Publishing Co., 1990.

THOMSON, JUDITH JARVIS. "Killing, letting die and the trolley problem." *The Monist* 1976 April 59: 204–217.

TOMS, STEVEN A. "Outcome predictors in the early withdrawal of life support: Issues of justice and allocation for the severely brain injured." *Journal of Clinical Ethics.* 1993 Fall; 4(3): 206–211.

TOOLEY, MICHAEL. *Abortion and Infanticide.* Oxford: Oxford University Press, 1983.

TRUOG, ROBERT D. "Allowing to die." *Critical Care Medicine.* 1990 Jul; 18(7): 790–791.

TRUOG, ROBERT D.; ARNOLD, JOHN H.; ROCKOFF, MARK A. "Sedation before ventilator withdrawal: Medical and ethical considerations." *Journal of Clinical Ethics.* 1991 Summer; 2(2): 127–129.

TRUOG, ROBERT D.; BERDE, CHARLES B. "Pain, euthanasia, and anesthesiologists." *Anesthesiology.* 1993 Feb; 78(2): 353–360.

TUOHEY, JOHN F. "Mercy: An insufficient motive for euthanasia." *Health Progress.* 1993 Oct; 74(8): 51–53.

UBEL, PETER A. "Assisted suicide and the case of Dr. Quill and Diane." *Issues in Law and Medicine.* 1993 Spring; 8(4): 487–502.

VAN DER MAAS, PAUL J., et al. *Euthanasia and Other Medical Decisions Concerning the End of Life: An Investigation Performed Upon Request of the Commission of Inquiry into the Medical Practice Concerning Euthanasia.* Amsterdam: Elsevier Science Publishers, 1992.

VAN DER MAAS, PAUL J., et al. "Euthanasia and other medical decisions concerning the end of life." *Lancet.* 1991 Sep 14; 338(8768): 669–674.

VAN DER WAL, GERRIT. "Unrequested termination of life: Is it permissible?" *Bioethics.* 1993 Jul; 7(4): 330–339.

VAN LEEUWEN, E.; KIMSMA, G.K. "Acting or letting go: Medical decision making in neonatology in the Netherlands." *Cambridge Quarterly of Healthcare Ethics.* 1993 Summer; 2(3): 265–269.

VAUX, KENNETH L. "Debbie's dying: Euthanasia reconsidered." *Christian Century.* 1988 Mar 16; 105(9): 269–271.

VAUX, KENNETH L. "Debbie's dying: Mercy killing and the good death." *Journal of the American Medical Association.* 1988 Apr 8; 259(14): 2140–2141.

VAUX, KENNETH L. "The theologic ethics of euthanasia." *Hastings Center Report.* 1989 Jan–Feb; 19(1): S19–S22.

VEATCH, ROBERT M. *Death, Dying, and the Biological Revolution: Our Last Quest for Responsibility.* Revised Edition. New Haven: Yale University Press, 1989.

VEATCH, ROBERT M. "Forgoing life-sustaining treatment: Limits to the consensus." *Kennedy Institute of Ethics Journal.* 1993 Mar; 3(1): 1–19.

VELASQUEZ, MANUEL G. "Defining suicide." *Issues in Law & Medicine.* 1987 Summer; 3(1): 37–51.

VELLEMAN, DAVID J. "Against the right to die." *Journal of Medicine and Philosophy.* 1992 Dec; 17(2): 665–81.

WALTON, DOUGLAS. *Slippery Slope Arguments.* Oxford: Clarendon Press, 1992.

WANZER, SIDNEY H. "Maintaining control in terminal illness: Assisted suicide and euthanasia." *Humane Medicine.* 1990 Summer; 6(3): 186–188.

WANZER, SIDNEY H.; FEDERMAN, DAN D.; EDELSTEIN, S.T., et al. "The physician's responsibility toward hopelessly ill patient: A second look." *New England Journal of Medicine.* 1989 Mar 30; 320(13): 844–849.

WATTS, DAVID T.; HOWELL, TIMOTHY. "Assisted suicide is not euthanasia." *Journal of the American Geriatrics Society.* 1992 Oct; 40(10): 1043–1046.

WATTS, DAVID T.; HOWELL, TIMOTHY; PRIEFER, BEVERLY A. "Geriatricians' attitudes toward assisting suicide of dementia patients." *Journal of the American Geriatrics Society.* 1992 Sep; 40(9): 878–885.

WEIR, ROBERT F. *Abating Treatment with Critically Ill Patients: Ethical and Legal Limits to the Medical Prolongation of Life.* New York: Oxford University Press, 1989.

WEIR, ROBERT F. *Ethical Issues in Death and Dying.* Second Edition. New York: Columbia University Press, 1986.

WEIR, ROBERT F. "Life-and-death decisions in the midst of uncertainty." In Caplan, Arthur L.; Blank, Robert H.; Merrick, Janna C., eds. *Compelled Compassion: Government Intervention in the Treatment of Critically Ill Newborns.* Totowa, NJ: Humana Press, 1992: pp. 1–33.

WEIR, ROBERT F. "The morality of physician-assisted suicide." *Law, Medicine and Health Care.* 1992 Spring-Summer; 20(1–2): 116–126.

WELIE, JOS V.M. "The medical exception: physicians, euthanasia and the Dutch criminal law." *Journal of Medicine and Philosophy.* 1992 Aug; 17(4): 419–437.

WESLEY, PATRICIA. "Physician assisted suicide: A physician's view." In Smith, Russell E., ed. *The Interaction of Catholic Bioethics and Secular Society: Proceedings of the Eleventh Bishops' Workshop.* Braintree, MA: Pope John Center, 1992: pp. 27–45.

WILDES, KEVIN WM. "Life as a good and our obligations to persistently vegetative patients." In

Wildes, et al, eds. *Birth, Suffering, and Death: Catholic Perspectives at the Edges of Life.* Boston: Kluwer Academic, 1992: pp. 145–154.

WILLIAMS, JOHN R. "When suffering is unbearable: Physicians, assisted suicide, and euthanasia." *Journal of Palliative Care.* 1991 Summer; 7(2): 47–49.

WILLIAMS, JOHN R.; LOWY, FREDERICK; SAWYER, DOUGLAS M. "Canadian physicians and euthanasia: 3. Arguments and beliefs." *Canadian Medical Association Journal.* 1993 May 15; 148(10): 1699–1702.

WOLF, SUSAN M. "Holding the line on euthanasia." *Hastings Center Report.* 1989 Jan–Feb; 19(1): S13–S15.

WREEN, MICHAEL. "The definition of euthanasia." *Philosophy and Phenomenological Research.* 1988 Jun; 48(4): 637–653.

WREEN, MICHAEL. "The definition of suicide." *Social Theory and Practice.* 1988 Spring; 14: 1–23.

YOUNG, ERNLE W.D. "The ethics of nontreatment of patients with cancers of the head and neck." *Archives of Otolaryngology—Head and Neck Surgery.* 1991 Jul; 117(7): 769–773.

ZUCKER, ARTHUR. "Euthanasia." *Death Studies.* 1991 Mar–Apr; 15(2): 231–236,

REFERENCE AND BIBLIOGRAPHICAL WORKS

BAILEY, DON V. *The Challenge of Euthanasia: An Annotated Bibliography on Euthanasia and Related Subjects.* Lanham, MD: University Press of America, 1990.

BECKER, LAWRENCE; BECKER, CHARLOTTE, eds. *Encyclopedia of Ethics.* New York: Garland Publishing Inc., 1992.

BUEHLER, DAVID A. "CQ sources: Suicide and euthanasia." [Bibliography]. *Cambridge Quarterly of Healthcare Ethics.* 1993 Winter; 2(1): 77–80.

FARBEROW, NORMAN L. *Bibliography on Suicide and Suicide Prevention, 1897–1957, 1958–1970.* DHEW Publication No. (HSM) 72-9080. Rockville, MD: National Institutes of Mental Health. Washington: U.S. Government Printing Office, 1972.

JOHNSON, GRETCHEN L. *Voluntary Euthanasia: A Comprehensive Bibliography.* Los Angeles: Hemlock Society, 1987.

LESTER, DAVID, et al. *Suicide: A Guide to Information Sources.* Detroit: Gale Research, 1980.

LINEBACK, RICHARD H., ed. *Philosopher's Index.* Vols. 1-. Bowling Green, OH: Philosophy Documentation Center, Bowling Green State University. Issued Quarterly. See under "Active Euthanasia," "Death," "Dignity," "Dying," "Euthanasia," "Killing," "Letting Die," "Life," "Sanctity of Life," and "Suicide."

McCARRICK, PATRICIA MILMOE. "Active Euthanasia and Assisted Suicide." *Kennedy Institute of Ethics Journal.* 1992 Mar; 2(1): 79–99.

REICH, WARREN ed. *Encyclopedia of Bioethics.* New York: Macmillan, 1995.

WALTERS, LEROY; KAHN, TAMAR JOY, eds. *Bibliography of Bioethics.* Vols. 1-. New York: Free Press. Issued annually. See under "Allowing to Die," "Euthanasia," "Killing," "Suicide," "Terminal Care," and "Treatment Refusal." (The information contained in the annual *Bibliography of Bioethics* can also be retrieved from BIOETHICSLINE, an on-line data base of the National Library of Medicine.)